An Introduction to Filipino
TAGALOG
FOR BEGINNERS

Joi Barrios

TUTTLE Publishing

Tokyo | Rutland, Vermont | Singapore

"Books to Span the East and West"

Tuttle Publishing was founded in 1832 in the small New England town of Rutland, Vermont [USA]. Our core values remain as strong today as they were then—to publish best-in-class books which bring people together one page at a time. In 1948, we established a publishing outpost in Japan—and Tuttle is now a leader in publishing English-language books about the arts, languages and cultures of Asia. The world has become a much smaller place today and Asia's economic and cultural influence has grown. Yet the need for meaningful dialogue and information about this diverse region has never been greater. Over the past seven decades, Tuttle has published thousands of books on subjects ranging from martial arts and paper crafts to language learning and literature—and our talented authors, illustrators, designers and photographers have won many prestigious awards. We welcome you to explore the wealth of information available on Asia at **www.tuttlepublishing.com**.

Paghahandog (Dedication)

To my husband Pierre and stepson Elia;
My aunt, Mila Barrios Rome, who taught me how to read,
and my cousin Peter Barrios, who always gives his unwavering support so that I can study and write.

Published by Tuttle Publishing, an imprint of Periplus Editions (HK) Ltd.

www.tuttlepublishing.com

Copyright © 2011 by Joi Barrios

Cover photo © Christopher Futcher | Dreamstime.com

Library of Congress Cataloging-in-Publication Data
Barrios, Joi.
  Tagalog for beginners : an introduction to Filipino, the national language of the Philippines / Joi Barrios. -- 1st ed.
  x, 374 p. : ill. ; 23 cm. + 1 MP3 audio disc (7 hr., 40 min. : digital ; 4 3/4 in.)
  Includes bibliographical references and index.
  ISBN 978-0-8048-4126-9 (pbk.)
1. Tagalog language--Textbooks for foreign speakers--English. 2. Tagalog language--Spoken Tagalog. 3. Tagalog language--Self-instruction. I. Title.
  PL6055.B38 2011
  499'.21182421--dc22
                2011006676

ISBN 978-0-8048-4126-9

Distributed by

North America, Latin America & Europe
Tuttle Publishing
364 Innovation Drive
North Clarendon, VT 05759-9436 U.S.A
Tel: 1 (802) 773 8930
Fax: 1 (802) 773 6993
info@tuttlepublishing.com
www.tuttlepublishing.com

Asia-Pacific
Berkeley Books Pte Ltd
3 Kallang Sector #04-01
Singapore 349278
Tel: (65) 6741-2178
Fax: (65) 6741-2179
inquiries@periplus.com.sg
www.tuttlepublishing.com

First edition
28 27 26 25 24   2312VP
16 15 14 13 12

Printed in Malaysia

TUTTLE PUBLISHING® is a registered trademark of Tuttle Publishing, a division of Periplus Editions (HK) Ltd.

Contents

SECTION 4: Pabiyahe-biyahe (Going Around)

To Download or Stream Audio Recordings:

1. You must have an internet connection.

2. Type the URL below into your web browser.

https://www.tuttlepublishing.com/tagalog-for-beginners-audio-pdfs

For support email us at info@tuttlepublishing.com.

Mga Tala Sa Kultura (Culture Notes)

Pagbabasa (Readings)

Pasasalamat (Acknowledgments)

To my teachers Nic Tiongson, Bien Lumbera, and Virgilio Almario, who taught me all I know about Philippine language and culture; and my poetry teacher, Fidel Rillo;

To Joey Baquiran, for his help in the grammar sections of this book; Roland Tolentino and Ilang-ilang Quijano, for contributing their pieces; my editors Nancy Goh and Sandra Korinchak; and the Tuttle illustrators, layout artists, editors, and marketing staff;

To fellow Filipino teachers: Teresita Ramos, Chat Aban, Karen Llagas, Masanao Oue, Elynia Mabanglo, Pia Arboleda, Ivy Dulay, Bing Magtoto, Irma Peña, Paz Naylor, Deling Weller, Letty Pagkalinawan, Leo Paz, Edith Borbon, Nenita Domingo, Atilio Alicio, Imelda Gasmen, Zenaida Fulgencio, Lester Hael, Rodney Jubilado, Tina Manueli, Noel Pangilinan, and SFUSD teachers;

To my colleagues at the University of the Philippines: chair Jimmuel Naval, my teachers Pamela Constantino and Lilia Antonio; and Vina Paz, Jovy Peregrino, Leo Zafra, Ligaya Rubin, Rose Yu, Tet Maceda, Althea Enriquez, Luna Sicat;

To the Dean's office of the College of Arts and Letters—Aurelia Carandang, Teresa Peralta, Evelyn Mariano, Socorro Villagracia, and Benjamin Posadas;

To my colleagues at UC Berkeley: Alexander von Rospatt, Jeff Hadler, Sylvia Tiwon, Penny Edwards, Raka Ray, Bac Hoai Tran, Ninik Lunde, Frank Smith, Susan Kepner, Supatra Chowchuvech, and Hanh Tran;

To my support system—Ralph Peña, Jorge Ortoll, Jina Umali, Marian Roque, Marivic Raquiza, Merce Planta, Francine Medina, Nerissa Balce; to CPWR—Pendong, Rob, Mau, Kat, Marconi, Tisay, Pj; and to Maria Kirk, for her beautiful house in Berkeley;

Pierre's family and friends—Guy Leblanc, Nicole Tanguay, Michel, Andre, Helene, Camille, Laurence, Francois and Veronique;

and to my family—siblings Yolanda and Amos; my cousin Lou Zambrano; "mother" Shayne, "sisters" Aya, Sining, Tala, Silay; the Contend family—Judy, Sarah, Tonchi, Roselle, Cora, Trina, Hasmin, Mykel, Bomen, Noni, Siao, Jonathan; and Peryante's Chyn, Chris, Malu, Bat, Nick, Bot, Marivik, Lina, Bong, Nikki, Lia, Bane, Ana, To, Paul, and Aureus.

Introduction

Are you a learner of Filipino descent who grew up in a home where your parents or other relatives spoke Filipino, the national language of the Philippines or Tagalog, the language on which it was based? Are you a second-language learner—a graduate student doing work on Southeast Asian studies, a researcher, business traveller, tourist, or someone whose significant other is Filipino? Are you a dedicated teacher exploring new ways of instruction for beginning students? Are you a classroom learner thinking of using this book as supplementary material? Are you an individual learner who would like to learn and use the language in a practical way?

This book is for you.

What's "a differentiated textbook"—and what does it mean to me?

You may have heard the term "differentiated instruction in the language classroom." This refers to a philosophy of learning where the teacher recognizes the diverse levels of the students and thus responds to their learning needs by using numerous strategies. In recent years, many teachers have been challenged in classrooms where some of the students were heritage language speakers and others were second-language learners. This book recognizes this and seeks to address the need for "differentiated instruction." Moreover, it also recognizes that some users are individual learners.

Thus, before using this book, it might be helpful to look into the ways by which it can best serve your own needs. Here are some good ways to begin.

1. **Look over what the book offers, and then start at the right place for you.**

   First, study the table of contents to understand what's here. For some of you, it would be best to start your learning by reading the *Appendixes*. These give you a history of the language and its orthography, explain common grammatical mistakes, acquaint you with the sounds of the Tagalog/Filipino language, and show you how you can use your increasing vocabulary in understanding Filipino culture.

   Also, you will find an *Index to Grammar Notes* at the end of the book. This will be helpful should you find yourself at a point in a lesson when you realize you've seemingly forgotten the rules taught in an earlier chapter. For example, let's say you need to remember how to conjugate the **mag** affix. Simply turn to the index and find the pages where you can read again about the **mag** affix.

   Should you encounter a word that was taught in a previous lesson but you cannot remember what it means, don't worry. There is a *Glossary* at the end of the book. In using the glossary, it is important to learn how to distinguish the "root word," something that this book will teach you in the first few chapters.

2. **Understand how to use the lessons to stack up "building blocks."**

   Each lesson starts with a dialogue. However, for most learners, it is better to study the vocabulary *first* before reading the dialogue.

   Also, remember to use each chapter's dialogue as simply a guide. Explore various other ways by which you can express yourself in a given situation—because that's the point of learning Filipino!

Think of a lesson in terms of building blocks. The lesson will start with words, then phrases, then sentences, then you can turn to (and understand!) an actual dialogue. For example, in Lesson 10 which is about shopping, you first learn some words and phrases for fruits and money, like:

mangga	*mango*	**sisenta pesos**	*sixty pesos*
mansanas	*apple*	**sitenta pesos**	*seventy pesos*
singkuwenta pesos	*fifty pesos*		

Knowing these words, you can now practice assembling them to build sentences:

Singkuwenta pesos ang isang kilo ng mangga.

A kilo of mangoes is fifty pesos.

Sisenta pesos ang isang kilo ng mansanas.

A kilo of apples is sixty pesos.

Now, you need to practice asking and answering questions. (This, by the way, will enable you to succeed in doing a role-play, which is found at the end of each lesson.) So, you learn to practice the question word **magkano** (*how much*):

Question : **Magkano ang isang kilo ng mangga?**

How much is a kilo of mangoes?

Answer : **Singkuwenta pesos ang isang kilo ng mangga.**

A kilo of mangoes is fifty pesos.

Knowing you need to practice the question word **magkano**, use words even if you are not sure of their translations in Filipino. For example:

Question : **Magkano ang *persimmons*?**

Answer : **Otsenta pesos ang isang kilo ng *persimmons*.**

Question : **Magkano ang mansanas?**

Answer : **Otsenta pesos ang isang *pound* ng *persimmons*.**

Note that the objective here is not to translate the word "persimmons" (which incidentally has no translation because it is not a fruit indigenous to the Philippines) and the word "pound." It is fine to say these words in English. What is more important is that you practice the structure "**Magkano ang X?**"

Similarly, in grammar, it is easier to start first with nouns, then learn some adjectives, and then learn some verbs. For example, in earlier lessons you learn nouns for objects you often use, such as those found in your bag. Among these are **libro** (*book*), **pitaka** (*wallet*), and **payong** (*umbrella*.) Then you learn adjectives, such as **maganda** (*beautiful*), **malaki** (*big*) and **maliit** (*small*).

Thus you can make several sentences:

Maganda ang pitaka.	*The wallet is beautiful.*
Maliit ang libro.	*The book is small.*
Malaki ang payong.	*The umbrella is big.*

Later, you learn the verb **bumibili** (*buy*), and thus can make more sentences:

Bumibili ako ng malaking pitaka.   *I am buying a big wallet.*
Bumibili ako ng maliit na libro.   *I am buying a small book.*

3. Get the most from the exercises.

By thinking of language learning in terms of building blocks, you will not be overwhelmed by the amount of information being introduced in each chapter. You will also understand the framework I used in creating the exercises.

These exercises were made using a practical approach. For example, in studying how to order at a restaurant, you will practice dialogues, such as this one which involves using a menu:

WAITER   : **Ano ho ang gusto ninyong orderin?**
What would you like to order?
CUSTOMER : **Lumpia na lang.**
Just lumpia [spring rolls].

By providing you with a menu, the book helps you practice with what is called an "authentic text." This means that it is an actual menu from a restaurant. This then simulates a more realistic environment, and moves you toward your goal: using the Filipino language in "the real world," in actual situations.

What "Authentic Texts" Can Do for You

Take a moment now to turn, in any lesson, to the reading and writing exercises, and look at them. These exercises are in each lesson for the following reasons:

1. to increase learner-need vocabulary;
2. to continually test comprehension skills;
3. to serve as a self-assessment summary of the lesson;
4. to provide additional insight into the culture of the Philippines.

Moreover, these reading exercises will hopefully encourage you to explore authentic materials such as Philippine newspapers, blogs written in Filipino, or even television programs or videos and films in Filipino which are available electronically. You may find yourself plodding through a text with a help of a dictionary. However, being able to understand 50 to 70% of "what is out there in the real world" is very rewarding.

Being a poet and a fictionist, I tried my best to keep the texts interesting and still be mindful of the words you know in each lesson. I also used natural language in writing, or the language I would use when writing my own literary work. For variety, I used several literary forms and writing styles: short essays, short short stories, legends, poetry, letters, short biographies of key figures in history, and news items.

In these texts, you may find that many foreign words (especially Spanish and English) have been integrated in the Filipino language. The Philippines has a long history of colonization (Spanish colonial period, 1564–1899; American colonial period, 1899–1945) which resulted in the introduction of a colonial culture, and with it, new words. Moreover, recent techological developments resulted in new words (computer, internet, solar power) which are either used in their original form or adapted using Tagalog affixes (for example, **nag-iinternet** for "using the internet").

Remember that language is dynamic, and through time, some words become more popular than most. Thus, in this textbook, you'll be introduced to the word **kalye** ("street"). You will then practice the word **kalye** in exercises to familiarize yourself with the word. However, some texts may contain phrases such as "Matalino Street" or "Roxas Boulevard." That is because street signs in the Philippines are written in English, and I wanted the reading piece to sound as natural as possible.

 ## About the Online Audio

The online audio files will help you learn and practice the language skills that are taught in each lesson. The audio material uses a conversational, natural style. Listen as you work through the book, and also while you're on the go!

Make This Book Your Own

If you are a classroom learner, go beyond the classroom. Challenge yourself. Write longer texts if you can.

If you are a heritage learner, practice with your family. Don't be bothered if they laugh at your pronunciation.

If you are an independent learner, take the time to write out dialogues and then say them aloud. All learners need to hear themselves. Use the audio disc to help you practice.

If you are a teacher, you know your students better than I do. Use this book as a guide and then design your lessons according to the needs of your students. Your heritage language students might already know many words, so it might be useful to ask them first if they know the meaning of the words in the vocabulary list (ask them to cover the English translations). You might also find that you need to change some exercises, or add more materials. You may even have suggestions for a revised edition of this textbook in the future. (You can write to me at mjbarrio2@mac.com.)

Finally, make the language your own. When practicing what you have learned, do not be afraid. So what if you forget some of the words and you end up saying something like "When **po kayo pupunta** to Manila?" (When are you going to Manila?) Yes, you may have forgotten the word **kailan** (*when*), and you actually did a lot of code-switching (mixing Filipino with English). However, chances are, the person you were talking to actually understood you. And you tried hard to be polite.

Recently, I asked a student, Laurie, what she was doing. She replied by saying: "**Nagfefacebook po ako.**" (I am "doing Facebook.") This learner has made the language her own.

Learning a language can be challenging, but if you stop thinking of the language police (people who stop you midway through a sentence to correct your grammar), it can be fun!

Pagpapakilala (Introductions)

  Diyalogo (Dialogue): Kumusta ka? (How are you?)

Read the dialogue below. After completing this chapter, practice this dialogue using your own information.

MARIA : **Ako si Maria.**
I am Maria.
PEDRO : **Ikinagagalak kong makilala ka, Maria. Pedro ang pangalan ko.**
Pleased to meet you. My name is Pedro.
MARIA : **Kumusta ka, Pedro?**
How are you, Pedro?
PEDRO : **Mabuti. Ikaw?**
Fine. And you?
MARIA : **Mabuti.**
Fine.

  Bokabolaryo (Vocabulary)

Study the following words and how they are used in sentences.

Ako	*I*
Ako si Maria.	*I am Maria.*
Ikaw	*You* (used at the beginning of a sentence)
Ikaw si Pedro.	*You are Pedro.*
Ka	*You* (used elsewhere in the sentence)
Si Pedro ka.	*You are Pedro.* (literally, Pedro you.)
Siya	*He/She*
Siya si Juan. Siya si Clara.	*He is Juan. She is Clara.*
Pangalan	*Name*
Maria ang pangalan ko.	*My name is Maria.*

Dagdag Na Bokabolaryo (Additional Vocabulary)

Study the following words that will enable you to talk about yourself and your gender, to use pronouns, to say "yes" or "no," and to ask questions.

Ano?	*What?*
Sino?	*Who?*
Babae	*Woman*
Lalaki	*Man*
Oo	*Yes*
Hindi	*No*
Ba	Word used for "yes" and "no" questions
Ko	*My* (singular pronoun, first person)
Mo	*Your* (singular pronoun, second person)
Niya	*His/Her* (singular peronoun, third person)
Nag-aaral	*Studying*
Nagtatrabaho	*Working*

Note: Learners who do not self-identify as **lalaki** (male/man) or **babae** (female/woman) can describe themselves as "transgender," as **bakla** (gay) or as **lesbiana** (lesbian).

Mga Ekspresyon (Expressions)

Study the following expressions that are useful when first meeting a person. If you are a heritage learner, try not to look at the English equivalents and try to guess the meaning of the words in Tagalog/Filipino.

Kumusta ka?/Kumusta?	*How are you?*
Ikinagagalak kong makilala ka.	*I am pleased to meet you.*
Mabuti.	*Fine/Good.*

Mga Pangungusap (Sentences)

Practice saying the below sentences aloud, to get a feel for how this chapter's vocabulary and grammar work in Filipino.

1.	**Ako si Maria.**	*I am Maria.*
2.	**Ikaw si Pedro.**	*You are Pedro.*
3.	**Siya si Clara.**	*She is Clara.*
4.	**Maria ang pangalan ko.**	*My name is Maria.*
5.	**Pedro ang pangalan mo.**	*Your name is Pedro.*

6. **Clara ang pangalan niya.**   *Her name is Clara.*
7. **Nag-aaral ako sa University of California.**   *I study at the University of California.*
8. **Physics ang major ko.**   *My major is Physics.*
9. **Nagtatrabaho ako sa Student Center.**   *I work at the Student Center.*
10. **Student assistant ako.**   *I am a student assistant.*
11. **Babae si Clara.**   *Clara is a woman.*
12. **Lalaki si Pedro.**   *Pedro is a man.*

Mga Gawain (Activities)

The following activities may be done in the classroom or by the independent learner.

Pagpapakilala sa sarili

Practice introducing yourself using the following format as a guide. What words can you use to introduce yourself?

Ako si Maria. Nag-aaral ako sa _____. _____ **ang major ko.**
I am Maria. I study at _____. *My major is* _____.

Ako si Pedro. Nagtatrabaho ako sa _____. _____ **ako.**
I am Pedro. I work at _____. *I am a* _____.

Ako si _____. _____. _____ **ako.**

Pagpapakilala sa Isa't Isa

Study the following words:

Estudyante	*Student*
Guro/Titser	*Teacher*
Doktor	*Doctor*
Pulis	*Police officer*
Kawani	*Employee*
Abugado	*Lawyer*
Manggagawa	*Worker*
Magsasaka	*Farmer*

Nars	Nurse
Tagapangasiwa ng opisina	Manager
Manunulat	Writer
Pintor	Painter
Mang-aawit	Singer
Mananayaw	Dancer
Negosyante	Businessperson

Each student draws a picture of himself or herself, then introduces himself/herself to a partner by saying:

Ako si _____. Nag-aaral/Nagtatrabaho ako sa _____. _____ ako.
I am _____. I study/work at _____. I am a _____.

Then, each student introduces his/her partner to the class using the third person pronoun "**siya**" or "**ito**":

Siya si _____. Nag-aaral/Nagtatrabaho siya sa _____. _____ siya.
He/she is _____. He/She studies/works at _____. He/she is a _____.

Ito si _____. Nag-aaral/Nagtatrabaho siya sa _____. _____ siya.
This is _____. He/She studies/works at _____. He/she is a _____.

 Awit (*Song*)

The following activity is for classroom learners. The teacher can use the melody of a popular song, such as "Jingle Bells," with the following lyrics. Each student should choose a partner. Then sing the song with actions, for example, shaking hands as you say "**Kumusta ka?**" or clapping when you say "**Pumalakpak.**" After singing, introduce yourselves to each other. Then move on to another partner.

Kumusta ka? Kumusta ka?	*How are you? How are you?*
Tayo'y magsaya.	*Let us have some fun.*
Pumalakpak, pumalakpak,	*Clap your hands, clap your hands,*
Ituro ang paa.	*And point to your foot.*

 ## Pagsasanay sa Pagtatanong at Pagsagot (Question and Answer Practice)

In Filipino, the word "**tanong**" means "question" and the word "**sagot**" means "answer." Both classroom students and independent learners should practice asking and answering questions. Make sure you practice these questions and answers by both speaking and writing.

Pagsasanay sa Pagsagot ng mga Tanong (Practice in Giving Answers to Questions)

Give the answers to the questions and provide the questions to the answers. In some instances, the answers are given to serve as a guide for the other numbers.

1. TANONG (Question) : **Kumusta ka?**
   SAGOT (Answer)   : _____.

2. TANONG : _____?
   SAGOT   : **Mabuti.**

3. TANONG : **Pedro ba ang pangalan mo?**
   SAGOT   : **Oo.**

4. TANONG : **Clara ba ang pangalan mo?**
   SAGOT   : **Hindi.**

5. TANONG : **Ano ang pangalan mo?**
   SAGOT   : _____ **ang pangalan ko.**

6. TANONG : **Babae ba si Pedro?**
   SAGOT   : _____.

7. TANONG : **Sino ang babae?**
   SAGOT   : **Babae si** _____.

8. TANONG : **Sino ang lalaki?**
   SAGOT   : _____.

9. TANONG : **Babae ka ba o lalaki?**
   SAGOT   : _____.

10. TANONG : **Nag-aaral ka ba sa New York University?**
    SAGOT   : **Hindi.**

11. TANONG : **Saan ka nag-aaral?**
    SAGOT   : _____.

12. TANONG : **Ethnic studies ba ang major mo?**
    SAGOT   : _____.

13. TANONG : **Ano ang major mo?**
    SAGOT   : _____.

14. TANONG : **Doktor ka ba?**
    SAGOT   : **Hindi**.

15. TANONG : **Ano ang trabaho mo?**
    SAGOT   : _____.

Pagsasanay sa Pagtatanong (Practice in Asking Questions)

Provide the questions to the given answers. This will enable you to practice the question words studied.

(Note that the question "**Sino ka?**" is not a good question to ask. It seems impolite. However, we can ask, "**Sino po kayo?**" using the plural form, "**kayo**." Or, alternatively, we can say, "**Ano ang pangalan mo?**" (*What is your name?*)

1. TANONG : _____?
   SAGOT   : **Lily ang pangalan ko.**

2. TANONG : _____?
   SAGOT   : **Oo, estudyante ako.**

3. TANONG : _____?
   SAGOT   : **Mabuti.**

4. TANONG : _____?
   SAGOT   : **Lalaki si Michel.**

5. TANONG : _____?
   SAGOT   : **Nag-aaral ako sa University of California Berkeley.**

6. TANONG : _____?
   SAGOT   : **Oo, nagtatrabaho ako.**

7. TANONG : _____?
   SAGOT   : **Nagtatrabaho ako sa Youth Center.**

8. TANONG : _____?
   SAGOT   : **Doktor ako.**

9. TANONG : _____?
   SAGOT   : **Sociology ang major ko.**

10. TANONG : _____?
    SAGOT   : **Angela ang pangalan niya.**

11. TANONG : _____?
    SAGOT   : **Alex ang pangalan niya.**

12. TANONG : _____?
    SAGOT   : **Nag-aaral siya sa Osaka University.**

13. TANONG : _____?
    SAGOT   : **Physics ang major niya.**

14. TANONG : _____?
    SAGOT   : **Abugado si Damien.**

15. TANONG : _____?
    SAGOT   : **Nagtatrabaho si Damien sa Gallini Law Firm.**

🔍 Gramatika (Grammar)

Study the information below to improve your Filipino grammar skills.

I. Markers
    Si and **ang** are markers.

    In the Filipino language, there is no direct equivalent of the articles "a," "an," and "the" in the English language. When the term "marker" is used, it refers to words that "mark," whether the next word, a noun, is the subject or the object of the sentence.
      Si is a "singular" marker used before a personal noun.
        EXAMPLE: **Ako *si* Maria.**   OR   ***Si* Maria ako.**
                  I am Maria.

    Note that both word orders are grammatically correct.

Ang is a "singular" marker used before a noun. "**Ang**" marks the subject of the sentence.

> EXAMPLE: **Maria ang pangalan ko.**
>
> *Maria is my name.* (Literally, Maria *marker* name my.)

II. Nominative Pronouns

Nagsasalita (First Person or Person Speaking): **Ako** — *I*
Kinakausap (Second Person or Person Addressed): **Ikaw, Ka** — *You*
Pinag-uusapan (Third Person): **Siya** — *He/She*

Use "**ka**" when the pronoun is not at the beginning of the sentence, or in this case, after the name of the person.

> EXAMPLE: **Si Pedro *ka*.**
>
> *You are Pedro.* (Literally, *Marker* Pedro you.)

Use "**Ikaw**" at the beginning of a sentence or before the name of the person.

> EXAMPLE: ***Ikaw* si Pedro.**
>
> *You are Pedro.* (Literally, You *marker* Pedro.)

Pronouns are not gendered in Filipino. Thus, "**siya**" is used to mean both "*he*" and "*she*."

> EXAMPLE: ***Siya* si Pedro. *Siya* si Maria.**
>
> *He is Pedro. She is Maria.*

III. Possessive Pronouns

Nagsasalita (First Person or Person Speaking): **Ko** — *My*
Kinakausap (Second Person or Person Addressed): **Mo** — *Your*
Pinag-uusapan (Third Person or Person Referred to): **Niya** (his/her) — *His/Her*

Use "**ko**" after the object, or in this case, the name.

> EXAMPLE: **Pedro ang pangalan *ko*.**
>
> *My name is Pedro.* (Literally, Pedro *marker* name my.)

Use "**mo**" also after the object, or in this case, the name.

> EXAMPLE: **Maria ang pangalan mo.**
>
> *Your name is Maria.* (Literally, Maria *marker* name your.)

IV. Prepositions

Sa is a preposition connoting place.

> EXAMPLE: **Nag-aaral ako *sa* Unibersidad ng California.**
>
> *I study at the University of California.*

V. Interrogatives

Ano and **Sino** are interrogative words.

"**Ano**" is an interrogative word meaning "*what*."

> EXAMPLE: **Ano ang pangalan mo?**
>
> *What is your name?* (Literally, What *marker* name you?)

Sino is an interrogative word meaning "*who*."

> EXAMPLE: **Sino siya?**
>
> *Who is she/he?* (Literally, Who she/he?)

Ba is used for yes or no questions.

> EXAMPLE: **Nag-aaral ka *ba* sa University of London?**
>
> *Do you study at the University of London?*
>
> (Literally, Study you **ba** at University of London?)

When used with personal names, **ba** precedes the name.

> EXAMPLE: **Nag-aaral *ba* si Maria sa University of California?**
>
> *Does Maria study at the University of California?*
>
> (Literally, Study **ba** *marker* Maria at University of California?)

When used with pronouns, **ba** goes before the pronoun. Look again at our first example:

> EXAMPLE: **Nag-aaral ka *ba* sa University of London?**
>
> *Do you study at the University of London?*
>
> (Study you **ba** at University of London?)

VI. The Particle "**Na**"

Particles are words that cannot be classified in any of the usual word classes such as nouns, pronouns, verbs, adjectives, and adverbs. They are "function words." For this lesson, we will focus on "**na**." The Tagalog/Filipino particle "**na**" is especially useful because it is used to connect words and phrases.

You may have already noticed the frequent use of the word "**na**." "**Na**" is a word used as a linker for adjectives and nouns, and phrases. It can be contracted, thus changing it to "**ng**" (pronounced as "**nang**"). Thus, "**ko na**" becomes "**kong**."

Let's study the sentence "**Ikinagagalak kong makilala ka.**" *Pleased to meet you.* (Literally, Pleased I *linker* meet you.)

The long form of this sentence is "**Ikinagagalak *ko na* makilala ka.**" However, in conversational Filipino, "**ko na**" is contracted into "**kong**," thus we say, "**Ikinagagalak *kong* makilala ka.**"

Diyalogo (Dialogue): How are you?
(pormal na sitwasyon or "formal situation")

Study the following dialogue between an older person and a younger person. Note the use of the honorific word "**po**" and the use of the plural form (in this case, "**kayo**") to indicate respect. At the end of this lesson, practice this dialogue using your own information.

Maria	:	**Ako po si Maria.**
		I am Maria.
Ginoong Santos	:	**Ikinagagalak kong makilala ka, Maria. Jose Santos ang pangalan ko.**
		Pleased to meet you. My name is Jose Santos.
Maria	:	**Kumusta po kayo, Mr. Santos?**
		How are you, Mr. Santos?
Ginoong Santos	:	**Mabuti. Ikaw?**
		Fine. (And) you?
Maria	:	**Mabuti po.**
		Fine.

Bokabolaryo (Vocabulary)

Po	Honorific word used to connote respect
Ginoong	A contraction of the word "**ginoo**" and the linker "**na**," here contracted as "**ng**"; Mr./Mister. In conversational Filipino, "Mister" is more commonly said, but **Ginoong** is sometimes used in formal occasions.
Kayo	Pronoun, second person, plural used in formal situations

Mga Gawain (Activities)

Study the new words below that can also be used to indicate respect. Give the answers to the questions and provide the questions to the answers. In some instances, the answers are given to serve as a guide for the other numbers.

Pagsasanay sa Pagtanong at Pagsagot (Question and Answer Practice)

Mga Bagong Salita (New Words)

Ninyo   *You* (second person plural; also used in formal situations)

1. TANONG (Question) : **Kumusta ka?** (older person addressing younger person)
   SAGOT (Answer)   : _____. (younger person addressing older person)

2. TANONG : _____ (younger person addressing older person)
   SAGOT   : **Mabuti.** (older person addressing younger person)

3. TANONG : **Ano ang pangalan mo?** (older person addressing younger person)
   SAGOT   : _____. (younger person addressing older person)

4. TANONG : **Ano po ang pangalan ninyo?** (younger person addressing older person)
   SAGOT   : **Juan Santos.** (older person addressing younger person)

5. TANONG : **Kumusta ka?** (teacher to student)
   SAGOT   : _____. (student to teacher)

6. TANONG : _____ (student to teacher)
   SAGOT   : **Mabuti.** (teacher to student)

7. TANONG : _____? (student to teacher)
   SAGOT   : **Guro ako.**

8. TANONG : _____? (student to teacher)
   SAGOT   : **Nagtuturo ako sa San Francisco Community College.**

9. TANONG : _____? (student to teacher)
   SAGOT   : **Dr. Domingo ang pangalan ko.**

10. TANONG : _____? (younger person to older person)
    SAGOT   : **Nagtatrabaho ako sa Manila Restaurant.**

Mga Tala Sa Kultura (Culture Notes)*

Politeness and respect are important values in Philippine culture. Several Philippine studies scholars attribute this to the interdependent nature of farming communities. Farmers depend on one another; they plant and harvest rice together, working on each other's farms in succession. Thus, they are careful to use polite language in addressing each other.

Polite language is characterized by the following:

1. First, the use of **"po"** and **"opo"** (*yes*) or **"ho"** and **"oho"** when addressing an older person or a stranger;
2. Second, by using plural pronouns such as **"kayo"** (plural form of **"ka"** or *"you"*) or **"ninyo"** (plural form of **"mo"** or *"your"*);
3. And third, by using the third person, such as **"sila"** (in this case, the third person plural is used as if it were a second person pronoun when addressing someone). For example, we say: **"Ano po ang pangalan ninyo** (second person, plural)?**" or **"Ano po ang pangalan nila** (third person, plural)?**"

What is the difference between **"po"** and **"ho"** and between **"opo"** and **"oho?"** Both are polite language, although the former is deemed to be more formal than the latter. For this book, we shall be using only **"po"** and **"opo"** for consistency, whenever formal language is required. Similarly, using the third person is deemed to be more formal than using the second person.

  Pagbabasa (Reading)

Read the following passage, and then answer the questions that follow.

Teksto (text): **Pagpapakilala sa Sarili** (Introducing Oneself)

Sarah : **Kumusta po kayo? Ako si Sarah. Estudyante ako. Nag-aaral ako sa UC Berkeley at nagtatrabaho ako sa cafeteria. Southeast Asian studies ang major ko. Ikinagagalak ko pong makilala kayo.**

Roland : **Ikinagagalak kong makilala ka, Sarah. Roland ang pangalan ko. Nagtatrabaho ako sa Unibersidad ng Pilipinas. Guro ako. Nagtuturo ako ng Physics.**

---

* In this lesson as well as in other lessons of this book, I shall explain how important it is to understand Filipino culture in learning the language. I am indebted to my teachers Nicanor Tiongson and Bienvenido Lumbera because in these Culture Notes, I draw from the notes I took in their classes more than two decades ago.

Estudyante/Mag-aaral	*Student*
Guro/Titser	*Teacher*
Trabaho	*Work* (noun)
Nagtuturo	*Teach*
Nag-aaral	*Study*
Nagtatrabaho	*Work* (verb)

Mga Tanong (Questions)

1. Saan nag-aaral si Sarah?

   _____.

2. Saan nagtatrabaho si Sarah?

   _____.

3. Saan nagtatrabaho si Roland?

   _____.

4. Ano ang major ni Sarah?

   _____.

5. Estudyante ba si Roland?

   _____.

6. Ano ang trabaho ni Roland?

   _____.

✏ Pagsusulat (Writing)

Using the vocabulary and grammar you have learned, try writing a short self-introduction in Filipino.

(Note: In this first lesson, it is not important to use the Filipino words for jobs or majors. These will be studied in later lessons. English words can be used at this point.)

Halimbawang Teksto (Sample Text)

Ako si Cora. Nag-aaral ako sa University of the Philippines (UP). **Linguistics ang major ko. Nagtatrabaho ako sa** UP Library. **Library assistant ako.**

Magsulat Tayo! (Let Us Write)

⚑ Paglalagom (Summing Up)

In **Aralin 1** (Lesson 1), you have learned:
1. How to talk about yourself,
2. Singular nominative and possessive pronouns,
3. Honorifics and polite language,
4. How to ask and answer yes and no questions,
5. The question words *what*, *who*, and *where*.

You should now be able to:
1. Introduce yourself.
2. Use honorifics for polite language.
3. Ask a yes or no question.
4. Use the question words *who*, *what*, and *where*.
5. Say where you study/work.
6. Say what your major is or what you do (even if the term used is in English, you should be able to construct the sentence).
7. Identify gender.

Pagbati (Greetings)

  Diyalogo (Dialogue): Ito Si Ginang Cruz (This is Mrs. Cruz)

Read the dialogue below. After completing this chapter, practice this dialogue on greetings and introductions using your own information.

PEDRO	:	**Magandang umaga po, Ginang Cruz.**
		Good morning, Mrs. Cruz.
GINANG CRUZ	:	**Magandang umaga naman, Pedro.**
		Good morning too, Pedro.
PEDRO	:	**Ginang Cruz, ito po si Maria. Kaklase ko siya.**
		Mrs. Cruz, this is Maria. She is my classmate.
GINANG CRUZ	:	**Ikinagagalak kong makilala ka, Maria.**
		Pleased to meet you, Maria.
PEDRO	:	**Maria, si Ginang Cruz. Guro ko siya.**
		Maria, this is Mrs. Cruz. She is my teacher.
MARIA	:	**Ikinagagalak ko rin pong makilala kayo.**
		Pleased to meet you too.

  Bokabolaryo (Vocabulary)

Study the following words and how they were used in the dialogue you just read.

Naman	an expression used here to mean *also* or *too*
Ito	*this*
Kaklase	*classmate*
Ginang (Gng.)	*Mrs.*
Rin/din	*too; also*

Mga Dagdag Na Bokabolaryo (Additional Vocabulary)

Study the following pronouns as well as additional words that can help you form new sentences.

Plural Pronouns:	
Kami	*We* (exclusive, not including the person/s being addressed)
Tayo	*We* (inclusive, including the person/s being addressed)
Kayo	*You* (plural)
Sila	*They*
Namin	*Ours* (exclusive, not including the person/s being addressed)
Natin	*Ours* (inclusive, including the person/s being addressed)
Nila	*Their*
Additional Words:	
Sina	Plural marker for personal names
Mga	Used for the plural form; equivalent to the letter "s" added to the word in English; always comes before the word
At	*And;* used as a linker
Binibini (Bb.)	*Miss*
Tao/Mga Tao	*Person/People*

Words You Can Use When Introducing Someone:
In the dialogue above, Pedro introduced Maria to Gng. Cruz as his **kaklase** or classmate. Here are some words that might be useful when you introduce someone you are with to another person. Use these words as you practice role-plays in the classroom or when you practice introducing someone to another person.

Kapatid	*Brother/Sister*
Kaibigan	*Friend*
Katrabaho	*Co-worker*
Kasambahay	*Person who lives in the same house*
Kapitbahay	*Neighbor*
Kababayan	*Of the same town; of the same country*

Mga Ekspresyon (Expressions)

Practice these expressions.

Magandang umaga!	*Good morning!*
Magandang tanghali!	*no exact equivalent; it literally means "Happy noontime!"*
Magandang hapon!	*Good afternoon!*
Magandang gabi!	*Good evening!*

Look at the following pictures. Give the appropriate expression or greeting.

Mga Pangungusap (Sentences)

Practice saying the below sentences aloud to get a feel for how this chapter's vocabulary and grammar work in Filipino.

1.	**Mga guro sina G. Santos at Gng. Cruz.**	*G. Santos and Gng. Cruz are teachers.*
2.	**Nagtuturo sila sa Unibersidad ng California.**	*They teach at the University of California.*
3.	**Mga estudyante po kami.**	*We are students.* (Situation: Students talking to a teacher)
4.	**Mga tao tayo.**	*We are people.* (Situation: Teachers talking to a student or students)
5.	**Pedro at Juan ang mga pangalan namin.**	*Our names are Pedro and Juan.*
6.	**Pedro at Juan ang mga pangalan ninyo.**	*Your names are Pedro and Juan.*
7.	**G. Santos at Gng. Cruz ang mga pangalan nila.**	*Their names are Mr. Santos and Mrs. Cruz.*

Mga Gawain (Activities)

I. **Mga Pagbati** (*Greetings*)

Study the situation given. Assume the identity of the person saying the dialogue. How would you greet the other person? Please use the honorific word "**po**" when necessary.

A. It is 9 A.M. You meet your teacher.

Student: _____!

B. It is 7 P.M. You meet a friend.

Titser: _____!

C. It is 4 P.M. You meet your friend's mother.

Student: _____!

II. **Pagbati sa Loob ng Silid-aralan (Greetings in the Classroom)**

For classroom learners, follow the instructions below to practice greetings.

The teacher shouts the time (in English). Students greet each other using "**Magandang umaga**" or "**Magandang hapon**" depending on the time; students can do this while going around the classroom. Students can also introduce themselves.

In the middle of the activity, try using the terms **Binibini**, **Ginang**, or **Ginoo**.

Pagsasanay sa Pagtatanong at Pagsagot (Question and Answer Practice)

Practice asking and answering questions. The questions below are in the plural form, so pretend that you are with a fictitious friend/classmate/colleague. Make sure you practice these questions and answers by both speaking and writing.

1. TANONG : **Ano ang mga pangalan ninyo?**

SAGOT : _____.

2. TANONG : **Mga estudyante ba kayo?**

SAGOT : _____.

3. TANONG : **Saan kayo nag-aaral?**

SAGOT : _____.

4. TANONG : _____?

SAGOT : **Gng. Domingo at Bb. Magtoto ang mga pangalan namin.**

5. TANONG : _____?

SAGOT : **Oo, mga guro kami.**

6. TANONG : _____?
   SAGOT : **Nagtuturo kami sa Tokyo University.**

7. TANONG : **Ano ang mga pangalan nila?**
           (referring to other people, not the one/s being addressed)
   SAGOT : _____.

8. TANONG : _____?
   SAGOT : **Nagtatrabaho sila sa Philippine Book Company.**

9. TANONG : **Mga doktor ba kayo?**
   SAGOT : _____.

10. TANONG : _____?
    SAGOT : **Mga nars kami.**

🔍 Gramatika (Grammar)

Study the following grammar notes. After looking at the examples, try to make your own sentence following the sentence structure given.

In this lesson, the plural pronouns are introduced. Although both the nominative and possessive pronouns are introduced, you may want to focus on the nominative pronouns. More exercises will be given on possessive pronouns in a later lesson.

I. Nominative Pronouns, Plural
   Many learners get confused because there are two Filipino plural first person pronouns, **kami** and **tayo**. Both these pronouns mean *"we."* However, **kami** refers only to the speakers, while **tayo** refers to both the speakers and those being addressed.

   A. First Person or Person/s Speaking, Plural, Exclusive
      Kami   *We*

      The first person exclusive plural, **kami**, can be used by one person speaking, referring to himself/herself and his/her companions; or by several people speaking together and talking only about themselves. The word "exclusive" means that when using this pronoun, the speaker/s are referring exclusively to himself/herself and his/her companions, and not to the person/people he/she is talking to. In the sentences below, for example, two students are talking to two teachers.

EXAMPLES:

Pedro and Clara (talking to G. Santos and Gng. Cruz):
Mga estudyante kami. *We are students.*

G. Santos and Gng. Cruz (talking to Pedro and Clara):
Mga guro kami. *We are teachers.*

Pedro and G. Santos (talking to Clara and Gng. Cruz):
Mga lalaki kami. *We are men.*

Gng. Cruz and Clara (talking to Pedro and G. Santos):
Mga babae _____. *We are women.*

B. First Person, Plural, Inclusive or Person/s Speaking and the Person/s Being Addressed

    Tayo   *We*

The first person inclusive plural **tayo** refers to the person/people speaking, as well as to the person/people he/she/they are talking to. The term "inclusive" calls for the pronoun **tayo** and "includes" the person/people addressed.

EXAMPLES:

Pedro (talking to Clara): **Mga estudyante tayo.** *We are students.*

G. Santos (talking to Gng. Cruz): **Mga guro tayo.** *We are teachers.*

Pedro and Clara (talking to two other students, Maria and Juan): **Mga estudyante tayo.** *We are students.*

Clara, Gng. Cruz, and Maria (talking to each other): **Mga babae** _____

_____.

Pedro, Juan and G. Santos (talking to each other): _____.

C. Second Person, Plural or Persons Being Addressed

    Kayo   *You (plural)*

The plural second person pronoun **kayo** refers to the people being addressed. It may be also used in formal situations or when the person being addressed is older.

EXAMPLES:

Gng. Cruz (talking to Pedro and Clara): **Mga estudyante kayo.** *You are students.*

Pedro and Clara (talking to G. Santos and Gng. Cruz): **Mga guro po kayo.** *You are teachers.*

D. Second Person, Plural or Persons Being Addressed
   Sila   *They*

The third person plural **sila** refers to people other than those speaking or being addressed. **Sila** is also considered to be the most formal way of addressing another person.

EXAMPLES:
> **Pedro and Clara** (talking to Maria and Juan about G. Santos and Gng Cruz): **Mga guro sila.** *They are teachers.*
> **G. Santos and Gng. Cruz** (talking to a parent about Pedro and Clara): **Mga estudyante sila.** *They are students.*

II. Possessive Pronouns, Plural
Similarly, plural possessive pronouns in the first person can also be challenging because the situation can be exclusive (referring only to the people speaking) or inclusive (both the person/people speaking and the person/people being addressed).

A. First Person, Plural, or Person/s Speaking, Exclusive
   Namin   *Our*

When the person speaking "excludes" the person/people he/she is talking to, **namin** is used.

EXAMPLE:
> **Pedro and Clara** (talking to Gng. Santos): **Pedro at Clara po ang mga pangalan namin.** *Our names are Pedro and Clara.*

B. First Person, Plural, Inclusive or Person/s Speaking and the Person/s Being Addressed
   Natin   *Our*

When the person speaking includes the person/people he/she is talking to, **natin** is used.

EXAMPLE:
> **Gng. Cruz: Gng. Cruz, G. Santos, Pedro, at Clara ang mga pangalan natin.** *Our names are Mrs. Cruz, Mr. Santos, Pedro, and Clara.*

C. Second Person, Plural or the Person/s Being Addressed
> **Ninyo**   *Your*

> When the speaker/s refer to more than one person, **ninyo** is used. **Ninyo** is also used when the person being addressed is older, or in formal situations.

> EXAMPLE:
> **Gng. Cruz** (talking to Pedro and Clara): **Pedro at Clara ang mga pangalan ninyo.** *Your names are Pedro and Clara.*

D. Third Person, Plural
> **Nila**   *Their*

> When the speaker/s refer to more than one person other than himself/herself/themselves, **nila** is used. **Nila** is also considered to be the most formal way by which one can address another.
> **Nila**   *Their*

> EXAMPLE:
> **Gng. Cruz** (talking to G. Santos about Pedro and Clara): **Pedro at Clara ang mga pangalan nila.** *Their names are Pedro and Clara.*

III. The Word "**Mga**" to Indicate Plurality
The word **mga** is used to make a word plural. Thus, the plural form of **pangalan** (name) is **mga pangalan** (names). When using English words that have been integrated into the Filipino language, for example, computer, say only **mga computer** instead of "**mga computers**."

IV. The Linker "**at**"
The linker **at** means "and." It can be used to link words and clauses. We can say, **Maria at Pedro ang mga pangalan nila**.

V. Particles
Din and **Rin** are enclictic particles. As we learned earlier, particles are "function words." **Din** and **rin** mean the same thing—"*too*" or "*also*."
Din is used when the preceding word ends with a consonant, and **rin** is used when the preceding word ends with a vowel. However, when the preceding word ends with a syllable that has the letter **r**, **din** is used.
> EXAMPLE: **Marie din ang pangalan ko.**
> *My name is also Marie.*

This is probably because in the indigenous script called **baybayin** (see also Appendix 3 on the history of the Filipino language), there is only one symbol for the letters **d** and **r**. The rules on **din** and **rin** were formulated with the standardization of the language by the Institute of Language.

VI. **Pagbuo ng Pangungusap** (Sentence construction)
Strictly speaking, there is no "verb *to be*" in Filipino. Let's study the sentence:
    EXAMPLE: **Kaklase ko siya.**
        She is my classmate. (Literally, Classmate my she.)

Thus, to form a sentence we only need the "relationship word" (in this case, "kaklase"), followed by the possessive pronoun **ko**, and then the nominative third person pronoun **siya**.

Diyalogo (Dialogue): Paalam (Goodbye)

Read the dialogue below. After completing this chapter, practice this dialogue on greetings and introductions using your own information.

GINANG CRUZ : **O, sige. May klase pa ako.**
                Okay. I (still) have a class.
PEDRO : **Sige po.**
                Okay/Goodbye.
MARIA : **Paalam po.**
                Goodbye.
GINANG CRUZ : **Paalam na sa inyo.**
                Goodbye to you.

Bokabolaryo (Vocabulary)

Sige	Okay; also used to say "goodbye."
Klase	*Class*
Paalam	*Goodbye*; considered to be an old-fashioned way of saying goodbye, but popular in many literary texts

Mga Tala Sa Kultura (Culture Notes)

In studying language, we can learn a lot about the culture of a people. The Filipino language, for example, has a complex system of affixes. One of its most interesting prefixes is **ka**. In this lesson, you learned the following words: **Kapatid** (*Brother/*

Sister); **Kaibigan** (*Friend*); **Katrabaho** (*Co-worker*); **Kasambahay** (*Person who lives in the same house*); **Kapitbahay** (*Neighbor*); and **Kababayan** (*Of the same town; of the same country*).

You may have noticed that all these words start with the prefix **ka**. **Ka**, in many cases, signals a relationship. The word **kapatid** is most interesting because the root word **patid** means "to cut," and the word **kapatid** literally means "cut from the same umbilical cord."

Many Filipinos take notice of another's last name. They will then try to "associate" with you or find a link. Should you say, for example, that your last name is Ledesma, they may ask, "**Kaano-ano mo ang mga Ledesma ng Bacolod?**" (*How are you related to the Ledesmas of Bacolod?*) Should you answer that they are your relatives, they will then ask you if you are related to someone they know, for example, "**Kilala mo ba si Connie?**" (*Do you know Connie?*) and then proceed to explain how they know this person. "**Kaklase ko siya sa** high school." (*She was my high school classmate.*)

This familiarity serves, in Filipino culture, to make the person more comfortable because you know someone he/she knows.

  Pagbabasa (Reading): Isang E-mail (An E-mail)

Study the list of new words introduced in the reading. Then read the short note of a college student to her father, and answer the questions that follow.

Tatay	*Father*
Klase	*Class*
Nagmamahal	*Love*

Kumusta Tatay,

Magandang umaga. Ito po ang mga kaibigan ko, sina Teresa at Barbara. Mga estudyante sila ng Ateneo University. **Mga kaklase ko po sila sa** Biology. **Si Bb. Pineda ang guro namin.**

Nagmamahal,
Melissa

Mga Tanong (Questions)

1. **Ano ang mga pangalan ng mga kaibigan ni Melissa?**

    _____ .

2. **Saan sila nag-aaral?**

    _____.

3. **Ano ang klase nila?**

    _____.

4. **Sino ang guro nila?**

    _____.

🖊 Pagsusulat (Writing)

Write a paragraph about your classmates or colleagues and friends. The objective of the exercise is to practice your use of the plural form of pronouns and nouns.

▥ Paglalagom (Summing Up)

In **Aralin 2** (Lesson 2), you have learned:

1. The plural form of nouns and pronouns,
2. Greetings,
3. Speaking about a "third" person,
4. The particles **din** and **rin**, and the linker **at**.

You should now be able to:

1. Introduce someone to another person.
2. Greet people (**Magandang umaga! Magandang hapon! Magandang gabi!**).
3. Use the linker **at**.
4. Speak/write about a third person.

Mga Bagay (Objects)

  Diyalogo: Ano Ito? (What is this?)

Read the dialogue below. After completing this chapter, practice this dialogue using objects you can find in the classroom. Try to identify as many objects as you can.

PEDRO : **Ballpen ba ito?**
Is this a ballpoint pen?

MARIA : **Hindi.**
No.

PEDRO : **Ano ito?**
What is this?

MARIA : **Lapis ito.**
This is a pen.

PEDRO : **Libro ba ito?**
Is this a book?

MARIA : **Oo. Libro ito.**
Yes. This is a book.

  Bokabolaryo (Vocabulary)

Study the following words and how they were used in the dialogue you just read.

Ballpen	*Ballpoint pen*
Lapis	*Pencil*
Hindi	*No*

Dagdag na Bokabolaryo (Additional Vocabulary)

Study the following words by practicing the question studied in the dialogue:

TANONG : **Ano ito?**

SAGOT : _____ **ito.**

Mga Bagay Sa Silid-Aralan (Things in the Classroom)

Papel	*Paper*
Aklat/Libro	*Book*
Kuwaderno	*Notebook*
Pisara	*Blackboard*
Tisa/chalk	*Chalk*
Bag	*Bag*
Pambura	*Eraser*
Mesa	*Table*
Silya	*Chair*

Mga Bagay Sa Loob Ng Iyong Bag (Things in Your Bag)

Telepono	*telephone*
Payong	*umbrella*
Susi	*keys*
Tubig	*water*
Panyo	*handkerchief*
Pamaypay	*fan*

Iba Pang Bagay Sa Silid-aralan At Iyong Bag (Other Things in the Classroom and Your Bag)

Look at other objects in the classroom or in your bag. With the help of your teacher or a dictionary, list "learner-need vocabulary"—that is, words (nouns) that you need to use.

Demonstrative Pronouns

Study the three demonstrative pronouns in Filipino. The demonstrative pronoun to be used is determined by the proximity of the object to the speaker.

Ito	*This* (object is near the speaker)
Iyan	*That* (object is far from the speaker)
Iyon	*That* (object is farther away from the speaker)

Mga Pangungusap (Sentences)

Study the following sentences.

1. **Telepono ito.** — *This is a telephone.*
2. **Hindi ito papel.** — *This is not paper.*
3. **Susi ito.** — *This is a key. (the key is near)*
4. **Silya iyan.** — *That is a chair. (the chair is far)*
5. **Pamaypay iyon.** — *That is a fan. (the fan is very far)*

 Pagsasanay (Practice)

Identify the objects in the following image. Mark your location in the picture. Then write sentences, following the structure of the sentences above.

1. _____

2. _____

3. _____

4. _____

5. _____

6. _____

7. _____

8. _____

9. _____

★ Gawain sa Silid-Aralan (Classroom Activity)

The following game can be played inside the classroom. For individual learners, try to convince a few friends to play the "This is a ..." game, even if you are the only person speaking Filipino in the game.

Laro (Game): Ito ay... (This is a ...)
- Students form a circle. The first student passes an object to the person on his/ her right, saying in Filipino, "This is a pen."
- The second student then asks, "What?"
- The first student answers, "A pen." He/she repeats the question and the answer.
- The second student then says, "Oh, a pen."

The game becomes more challenging when a student has to speak to two people on both sides.

📚 Dagdag-Aral (Additional Study)

Practice using the plural form for nouns and demonstrative pronouns, and using the linker "**at**."

1. **Maramihan** (Plural Form)
   To make nouns and demonstrative pronouns plural, add the word **mga**.

Mga lapis ito.	*These are pens.*
Mga libro ito.	*These are books.*

Tanong (Question)	:	**Ano ang mga ito?** *What are these?*
Sagot (Answer)	:	*These are pens.*

2. Using the linker or conjunction "**at**" (and)
   To link two nouns, use the linker **at**.

Lapis at papel ang mga ito.	*These are a pencil and paper.*
Ballpen at libro iyan.	*Those are a pen and a book.*
Silya at mesa ang mga iyon.	*Those are a chair and a table.*
	(farther away)

  ## Pagsasanay sa Pagtatanong at Pagsagot (Question and Answer Practice)

Both classroom students and independent learners should practice asking and answering questions. Make sure you practice these questions and answers by both speaking and writing.

1. Tanong : **Mga libro ba ito?**
              Are these books?
   Sagot : **Oo, mga libro ito.**
              Yes, these are books.

2. Tanong : **Mga libro ba ito?**
              Are these books?
   Sagot : **Hindi.**
              No.
   Tanong : **Ano ang mga ito?**
              What are these?
   Sagot : **Mga papel ito.**
              These are (pieces of) paper.

3. Tanong : **Ano ang mga ito?**
              What are these?
   Sagot : _____.

4. Tanong : **Ano ang mga ito?**
   Sagot : _____.

5. Tanong : **Ano ito?**
              What is this?
   Sagot : _____.

6. TANONG : **Ano ito?**
   SAGOT   : _____.

7. TANONG : **Ano ito?**
   SAGOT   : _____.

8. TANONG : _____?
   SAGOT   : _____.

🔍 Gramatika (Grammar)

Study the following summary of the grammar points we have learned.

I. Review of the Plural Form
    To make a noun plural, add the word **mga** before **ito**.
    EXAMPLE: **Mga libro ito.**
              These are books.

II. Demonstrative Pronouns (**Mga Pantukoy na salita**)
    Ito   *This*
    Iyan   *That (an object closer to the person being addressed than the speaker)*
    Iyon   *That (an object far from both the person speaking and the person being addressed)*

III. **Pagkaka-ayos ng mga Salita** (Word Order)
    In Filipino, the subject may come either before or after the predicate. For example, we can say both:
    Lapis ito.   *Literally, Pen this.*
    Ito ay lapis.   *Literally, This is pen.*

    In conversational Filipino, it is more natural for the predicate to precede the subject. However, in written Filipino, both are used.

IV. The particle "**ay**"
    The particle "**ay**" has several uses. In this lesson, it is used as "the verb *to be*"—for example, "**Ito ay libro.**" (*This is a book.*) However, bear in mind that in conversational Filipino, it is more common to say "**Libro ito.**" (literally, "*Book this.*")

Diyalogo (Dialogue): May Papel Ka Ba? (Do you have paper?)

Read the dialogue below. After completing this chapter, practice this dialogue using your own information.

MARIA : **May papel ka ba?**
Do you have paper?

PEDRO : **Oo.**
Yes.

MARIA : **Pakibigyan mo ako ng papel.**
Please give me paper.

PEDRO : **Aba, siyempre.**
Of course.

MARIA : **Salamat.**
Thank you.

PEDRO : **Walang anuman.**
Welcome.

  ## Bokabolaryo (Vocabulary)

Study the following words and how they were used in the dialogue you just read.

May	*Have*
Wala	*Don't have*
Pakibigyan	*Please give*

Mga Ekspresyon (Expressions)

Study the following expressions. These are useful in everyday conversations.

Salamat.	*Thank you.*
Walang anuman.	*Welcome.*
Aba, siyempre.	*Oh, of course.*

Mga Pangungusap (Sentences)

Practice saying the below sentences aloud. These sentences teach you how to talk about the things you have or don't have. Note that the words **may**, **mayroon**, and **meron** all mean "*have.*" Further explanations are given in the grammar section below.

1. **May payong ako.**   *I have an umbrella.*
2. **Mayroon akong libro./Meron akong libro.**   *I have a book.*
3. **Wala akong kuwaderno.**   *I don't have a notebook.*

Pagsasanay sa Pagtatanong at Pagsagot (Question and Answer Practice)

Both classroom students and independent learners should practice asking and answering questions. Make sure you practice these questions and answers by both speaking and writing. Follow the examples given.

1. TANONG : **May libro ka ba?**
             Do you have a book?
   SAGOT : **Oo, may libro ako.**
             Yes, I have a book.

2. TANONG : **May kuwaderno ka ba?**
             Do you have a notebook?
   SAGOT : **Wala, wala akong kuwaderno.**
             No, I don't have a notebook.

3. TANONG : **May lapis ka ba?**
             What are these?
   SAGOT : _____.

4. TANONG : **May susi ka ba?**
             Do you have a key?
   SAGOT : _____.

5. TANONG : _____?
   SAGOT : **Wala. Wala akong telepono.**

6. TANONG : **Mayroon ka bang papel?**
   SAGOT : **Wala akong papel.**

7. TANONG : **Mayroon ka bang payong?**
   SAGOT : **Oo, mayroon akong payong.**

8. TANONG : **Mayroon ka bang notebook?**
   SAGOT : _____.

9. TANONG　:　_____?
   SAGOT　　:　**Wala akong panyo.**

10. TANONG　:　**May silya ka ba?**
    SAGOT　　:　**Meron.** (variation of **mayroon**)

11. TANONG　:　**May mesa ka ba?**
    SAGOT　　:　_____.

12. TANONG　:　**May bag ka ba?**
    SAGOT　　:　_____.

🔍 Gramatika (Grammar)

Study the information below to improve your Filipino grammar skills. In this lesson, the focus of the grammar notes is to explain what may be confusing to you at this point. The notes are based on actual questions typically raised in Filipino-language learning classrooms.

I.　**May, Mayroon, Meron**
　　"When do we use **may**, **mayroon**, and **meron**?" This depends on the word order we prefer, and the situation where we need to use the words.
　　　We use **may** if we want the noun to follow **may**.
　　　　EXAMPLE:　**May libro ka ba?**
　　　　　　　　　　Do you have a book? (literally, Have book you **ba**?)

　　　We use **mayroon** if we want the pronoun to follow the word **mayroon**.
　　　　EXAMPLE:　**Mayroon ka bang libro?** (long form "**Mayroon ka ba na libro?**")
　　　　　　　　　　Do you have a book? (Have you **ba** *linker* book?)

We use **meron** in conversational Filipino. The only difference here is in the spelling where the word "**mayroon**" is spelled as it is spoken in everyday life. Thus, in many creative texts, especially plays and film or television scripts, **meron** is usually used. In formal written texts, such as critical essays, **may** or **mayroon** would be used.
　　May, **mayroon**, and **meron**, however, mean exactly the same thing. In this book, we will only be using **may** and **mayroon**, and not **meron**, to avoid confusion.

II.　Word Order in Questions (**Ba** and the pronoun when using **May** and **Mayroon**)
　　"How can I avoid being confused about the word order?" The word order changes in questions using **may** and **mayroon**.

First, remember that the sentence always begins with either **may** or **mayroon** (**meron**).

Second, the noun (the book, chair, pencil, etc.) follows the word **may**.

Third, when using **may**, the word **ba** (which, as explained earlier, is added when asking questions) the singular second person pronoun **ka**, and comes after all other pronouns which are found at the end of the sentence.

Example for **may** questions using the singular second person pronoun **ka**:

May libro ka ba?

Do you have a book? (literally, Have book you **ba**?)

Example for **may** questions using the plural second person pronoun **kayo** (also used in formal situations):

May libro ba kayo?

Do you have a book? (literally, Have book **ba** you?)

Example for **may** questions using the singular third person pronoun **siya**:

May libro ba siya?

Does he/she have a book? (literally, Have book **ba** he/she?)

Fourth, when using **mayroon**, **mayroon** is followed by the word **ba**, which is then followed by the pronoun (except for the singular second person pronoun **ka**), and then the noun.

Example for **mayroon** question using the singular second person pronoun **ka**:

Mayroon ka bang libro?

Do you have a book? (literally, Have you **ba** *linker* book?)

Example for **mayroon** question using plural second person pronoun **kayo**:

Mayroon ba kayong libro?

Do you have a book? (literally, Have **ba** you *linker* book?)

Example for **mayroon** question using singular third person pronoun **siya**:

Mayroon ba siyang libro?

Does he/she have a book? (literally, Have **ba** he/she book?)

III. The linker **na** contracted as "**ng**"

The linker **na** is used in **mayroon** questions but is not used in **may** questions.

It links either the word **ba** to the noun (when using the singular second pronoun **ka**) or the pronoun (when using all other pronouns) to the noun.

The linker **na** is contracted into "**ng**" and attached to either **ba** or the pronoun.

Not contracting results in outdated language we never find in contemporary life. You may notice that kind of language in old books.

Example of the (outdated) long form:

Mayroon ba sila na mga libro?

Do they have books? (Have **ba** they *linker* books?)

Example of the short form we should use:

Mayroon ba silang mga libro?

Do they have books? (Have **ba** they *linker* books?)

Mga Tala Sa Kultura (Culture Notes)

Why do some of the nouns studied above seem to be derived from Spanish or English?

The Philippines was a colony of Spain for around three hundred years (1562–1898), ending with the Philippine revolution of 1896 and the declaration of independence in 1898. The United States, at war with Spain, then sought to make the Philippines its own colony. Signed on December 10, 1898, the Treaty of Paris ended the war between the two nations, and Spain ceded the Philippines to the United States in exchange for twenty million dollars. Filipino revolutionaries resisted the new colonial power, resulting in the Philippine American War (1899–1902), also known as the Philippine War of Independence. The war ended with the surrender of the Filipino general Emilio Aguinaldo, and the Philippines then became a colony of the United States for forty years.

It is therefore not surprising that the Filipino language has many words derived from Spanish and English. Words such as "**mesa**" and "**silya**" were words introduced during the Spanish colonial period, at the same time that these furnishings were introduced in Filipino households. In precolonial times, Filipinos lived in the **bahay kubo** (literally, "cube house," but this term refers to houses made of bamboo) and did not have chairs or tables. Some households had very low tables (similar to other Asian cultures), which they called "**dulang**." Thus, the first words derived from Spanish came to be used because of the "imports" of the period.

Similarly, many words, especially those referring to technology, such as "**telepono**" or "**computer**," are derived from English. The spelling depends on the time period the word was introduced. Since the telephone became popular before the introduction of the letter **f** in the alphabet, we use "**telepono**" (influenced by *telefono* in Spanish). However, more people are inclined to just retain the spelling of "**computer**," because **c** has been in the alphabet since 1986, instead of "**kompyuter**."

Filipino has a complex system of affixes. To indicate politeness, the prefix "**paki-**" is used. **Paki** is equivalent to the English word "please." Thus, in this lesson we used the word "**pakibigyan**." This comes from the root word "**bigay**" and the imperative form of the verb "**bigyan**."

Diyalogo (Dialogue): Ilan Ang Lapis Mo? (How many pencils do you have?)

Read the dialogue below. After completing this chapter, practice this dialogue using your own information.

JUAN : **May lapis ka ba?**
Do you have a pencil?

MARIA : **Mayroon (Meron.)**
I do. (literally, Have.)

JUAN : **Ilan ang lapis mo?**
How many pencils do you have?

MARIA : **Dalawa ang lapis ko.**
I have two pencils.

 ## Bokabolaryo

Mga Numero (Vocabulary: Numbers)

There are two ways of counting in Filipino. In this lesson, study the indigenous and Spanish-derived ways of counting.

1 **Isa [uno]**	21 **Dalawampu't isa**	50 **Limampu**
2 **Dalawa [dos]**	**[beinte-uno]**	**[singkuwenta]**
3 **Tatlo [tres]**	22 **Dalawampu't dalawa**	60 **Animnapu [sisenta]**
4 **Apat [kuwatro]**	**[beinte-dos]**	70 **Pitumpu [sitenta]**
5 **Lima [singko]**	23 **Dalawampu't tatlo**	80 **Walumpu [otsenta]**
6 **Anim [sais]**	**[beinte-tres]**	90 **Siyamnapu [nobenta]**
7 **Pito [siyete]**	24 **Dalawampu't apat**	100 **Sandaan/Isang daan**
8 **Walo [otso]**	**[beinte-kuwatro]**	**[siyento]**
9 **Siyam [nuwebe]**	25 **Dalawampu't lima**	200 **Dalawang daan**
10 **Sampu [diyes]**	**[beinte-singko]**	**[dos siyentos]**
11 **Labing-isa [onse]**	26 **Dalawampu't anim**	1000 **Sanlibo/Isang libo [mil]**
12 **Labindalawa [dose]**	**[beinte-sais]**	10,000 **Sampung libo**
13 **Labintatlo [trese]**	27 **Dalawampu't pito**	**[diyes mil]**
14 **Labing-apat [katorse]**	**[beinte-siyete]**	100,000 **Isang daang libo**
15 **Labinlima [kinse]**	28 **Dalawampu't walo**	**[siyento mil]**
16 **Labing-anim [disisais]**	**[beinte-otso]**	1,000,000 **Isang milyon**
17 **Labimpito [disisiyete]**	29 **Dalawampu't siyam**	**[milyon]**
18 **Labingwalo [disiotso]**	**[beinte-nuwebe]**	1,000,000,000 **Isang bilyon**
19 **Labinsiyam [disinuwebe]**	30 **Tatlumpu [treinta]**	**[bilyon]**
20 **Dalawampu [beinte]**	40 **Apatnapu [kuwarenta]**	

*The Spanish-derived way of counting is given in brackets [ ].

📚 Dagdag na Bokabolaryo

Study the following additional words.

| **Ilan** | *How many* | | **lang** | *only* |

The word **lang** is commonly used when the answer to the question word **ilan** (*how many*) is "one." In conversational Filipino, we usually say "**Isa lang.**" or "*Only one.*"

Mga Pangungusap (Sentences)

Practice saying the below sentences aloud to get a feel for how this lesson's vocabulary and grammar work in Filipino.

1. **Sampu ang lapis ko.**   *I have ten pencils.*
2. **Binigyan ko siya ng lapis.**   *I gave him/her a pencil.*
3. **Binigyan niya ako ng papel.**   *He/she gave me paper.*
4. **Dalawapu't lima ang tao sa silid-aralan.**   *There are twenty-five people in the classroom.*

 ## Pagsasanay sa Pagtatanong at Pagsagot (Question and Answer Practice)

Both classroom students and independent learners should practice asking and answering questions. Make sure you practice these questions and answers by both speaking and writing.

1. TANONG : **Dalawa ba ang libro mo?**
   SAGOT : **Hindi.**

2. TANONG : **Lima ba ang libro mo?**
   SAGOT : **Hindi.**

3. TANONG : **Ilan ang libro mo?**
   SAGOT : **Tatlo ang libro ko.**

4. TANONG : **Ilan ang ballpen mo?**
   SAGOT : _____ **ang ballpen ko.**

5. TANONG : **Ilan ang kuwaderno mo?**
   SAGOT : _____ .

6. TANONG : **Ilan ang telepono mo?**
   SAGOT : _____.

7. TANONG : **Ilan ang bolpen mo?**
   SAGOT : _____.

8. TANONG : _____?
   SAGOT : **Dalawa ang pambura sa silid-aralan.**

9. TANONG : **Ilan ang tao sa silid-aralan?**
   SAGOT : _____.

10. TANONG : **Ilan ang babae at ilan ang lalaki sa silid-aralan?**
    SAGOT : _____.

11. TANONG : **Ilan ang estudyante sa University of California Berkeley?**
    SAGOT : _____.

12. TANONG : _____?
    SAGOT : **Dalawa ang bag ko.**

Pagsasanay sa Pagsulat ng Numero (Practice in Writing Numbers)

Write the following numbers:

36 _____

415 _____

6,894 _____

12, 486 _____

350,800 _____

1,500,000 _____

3,000,000,000 _____

⭐ Gawain (Activity)

Play the following game in the classroom.

Laro (*Game*) : Lumulubog na ang barko! (*The boat is sinking!*)
The students play this game while standing. The teacher shouts, in Filipino, "The boat is sinking. The lifeboat can fit <u>five</u>!" (Change the number each time.) The students group themselves into groups of five, or the appropriate number. Any "leftover" students with no group are eliminated.

Mga Tala Sa Kultura (Culture Notes)

As explained earlier, there are two ways of counting in Filipino. First, is the indigenous way, which we have studied in this lesson. Another system is derived from the Spanish language. This was introduced during the Spanish colonial period (1561–1898) in the Philippines. Although both systems can be used interchangeably, the Spanish-derived system is used more in telling the time, and will thus be introduced during that lesson.

  ## Pagbabasa (Reading)

Read the following short paragraph. Before reading, study the new word below. Then, after reading, answer the questions that follow.

Bulsa   *Pocket*

Ang Bag ni Cynthia

May bag si Cynthia. May lapis, ballpen, papel, notebook, at mga libro sa bag niya. Dalawa ang libro niya sa bag dahil estudyante siya. Mayroon din siyang telepono, lipstick, at mga susi sa bulsa ng bag. May party siya sa gabi.

1. **May bag ba si Cynthia?**
2. **Ano ang nasa bag ni Cynthia?**
3. **Ilan ang libro niya?**
4. **Ano ang nasa bulsa ng bag niya?**

✏ Pagsusulat (Writing)

Write a short paragraph based on the examples given.

Halimbawa 1 (Example 1)
May mga lapis si Maria. Lima ang lapis niya. Wala siyang ballpen.

Halimbawa 2
Mayroon akong mga libro. Tatlo ang libro ko. Wala akong notebook.

Sariling Halimbawa (Own Example)
Mayroon akong _____. _____ ang _____ ko. Wala akong
_____.

⚑ Paglalagom (Summing Up)

In **Aralin 3** (Lesson 3), you have learned:
1. Objects, possession (**may**, **mayroon**, **meron**), numbers and the indigenous way of counting,
2. The question word **ilan** (*how many?*),
3. The question "**Ano ito?**" (*What is this?*).

You should now be able to:
1. Count in Filipino.
2. Ask and answer the question: "What is this?"
3. Ask and answer the question: "**Mayroon ka bang...?**"
4. Know the difference between **may**, **mayroon**, and **meron**.

 Aralin
Lesson

4

Pagbisita sa Bahay ng Kaibigan (Visiting a Friend's House)

(Study Notes: From Lesson 4, only the dialogues will have translations. The learner is encouraged to study and understand the names of the lesson components, for example, **Bokabolaryo** (*vocabulary*) and **Gramatika** (*grammar*).

  Diyalogo: Tuloy Ka! (Welcome/come in!)

Read the dialogue below. After completing this chapter, practice this dialogue using your own information.

CLARA : **Tao po!**
(literally, A person is here!)
MARIA : **Sino iyan?**
(literally, Who is that?)
CLARA : **Si Clara ito.**
This is Clara.
MARIA : **Clara, ikaw pala! Tuloy ka!**
It's you, Clara! Welcome!
CLARA : **Kumusta ka?**
How are you?
MARIA : **Mabuti naman. Maupo ka.**
I am fine. Please sit down.
CLARA : **Salamat.**
Thank you.

 Bokabolaryo

Study the following words and how they were used in the dialogue you just read.

Umupo	*sit*
Maupo	*please sit*

Dagdag na Bokabolaryo

Study the following words and how they can be used in forming sentences based on the sentence structures you can derive from the dialogue.

Tumayo	*stand*
Nakatayo	*standing*
Naka-upo	*sitting*
Bahay	*house*
Bumibisita	*visits*

Mga Ekspresyon

Study the following expressions that are helpful in visiting someone's house.

Tao po! a traditional way of announcing one's arrival into another person's house (at a time before doorbells)

Ikaw pala! literally, "*It's you!*" An expression indicating surprise with the use of the word "**pala**"

Tuloy ka This literally means "*come in*" but can also mean "*Welcome!*"

Mga Pangungusap

Practice saying the below sentences aloud, to get a feel for how this lesson's vocabulary and grammar work in Filipino.

1. **Nakaupo ang mga estudyante.**	*The students are sitting.*
2. **Nakatayo ang mga guro.**	*The teachers are standing.*
3. **Pumunta si Clara sa bahay ni Maria.**	*Clara went to Maria's house.*
4. **Umupo si Clara.**	*Clara sat down.*

 ## Dagdag-Aral

Mga Pautos Na Pangungusap (Sentences that express a command)

Practice the following commands. Please note that it is more common to use numbers 3 and 4, because politeness is important in Filipino culture.

1. **Tumayo ka!**	*Stand!*
2. **Umupo ka!**	*Sit!*
3. **Maupo ka!/Maupo po kayo!**	*Please sit down.*
4. **Tumayo po kayo!**	*Please stand up.*

Gawain

Using the dialogue you read earlier as a guide, practice doing a role-play.

Sitwasyon (Situation) : **Bumisita sa bahay ng kaibigan.**
Visited a friend's house.

  **Diyalogo: Gusto Mo Ba ng Kape?
(Would you like some coffee?)**

Read the dialogue below. After completing this chapter, practice this dialogue using your own information.

MARIA : **Gusto mo ba ng kape?**
Would you like some coffee?

CLARA : **Huwag ka nang mag-abala.**
Please don't bother.

MARIA : **Sige na.**
Please.

CLARA : **Sige, salamat.**
Okay, thank you.

MARIA : **Heto. Eh, gatas? Asukal?**
Here. What about milk? Sugar?

CLARA : **Salamat.**
Thank you.

MARIA : **Puto?**
Rice cake?

CLARA : **Huwag na lang, salamat.**
No, thank you.

 Bokabolaryo

Study the following words and how they were used in the dialogue you just read.

Mga pangngalan (Nouns)	
Kape	*Coffee*
Gatas	*Milk*
Asukal	*Sugar*
Puto	*Rice cake*
Gusto	*want*

 **Dagdag na Bokabolaryo**

Study the following words and consider how they can be used later in making your own sentences following the structures studied in this lesson.

Ayaw	*Don't/doesn't want*
Tinapay	*Bread*
Sandwich	*Sandwich*
Tsaa	*Tea*
Juice	*Juice*
Tubig	*Water*
Kutsarita	*Teaspoon*
Tasa	*Cup*
Platito	*Saucer*

Mga Ekspresyon

Study the following expressions and how they can be used in everyday conversations. At this point in your learning, there will be no grammatical explanations given for these expressions. However, there will be some explanations in the culture notes of this chapter. Also, you may want to remember them because they are essential in everyday conversations.

Huwag na lang, salamat.	*No, thank you.* (Literally, Don't *linker* just, thanks.)
Huwag ka nang mag-abala	*Please don't bother.*
Sige na.	*Please.*
Sige.	*Okay/Sure.*

"**Sige**" and "**Sige na**" are contemporary popular expressions and are usually said one right after the other. "**Na**" in the expression "**Sige na**" should not be confused with the linker "**na**." Here, the meaning is closer to "already."

Eh does not mean anything per se. However, as an expression, followed by "**gatas**" (*milk*), it means, "*What about milk?*"

Mga Pangungusap

Practice saying these sentences aloud, to get a feel for how this chapter's vocabulary and grammar work in Filipino. In some cases, both the natural and literal translations are given in English. Try to analyze how sentence structures differ in Filipino.

1. **Gusto ni Clara ng kape.**   *Clara wants coffee.* (literally, wants *marker* Clara *linker* coffee.)

2. **Ayaw ni Clara ng puto.**   *Clara doesn't want rice cakes.*
                                       (literally, doesn't want marker Clara
                                       linker rice cakes.)

3. **Gusto niya ng tubig.**   *Clara likes water.*
4. **Ayaw niya ng tsaa.**   *Clara doesn't like tea.*
5. **Kumakain si Clara ng puto.**   *Clara is eating puto.*
6. **Umiinom si Clara ng kape.**   *Clara is drinking coffee.*

  Pagsasanay

Practice these questions and answers by both speaking and writing. Use the earlier pairs and the picture as a guide. In most instances, English words are used for things that are not indigenous to the culture, such as cake and sandwiches. Please use these words for more natural speech. The focus of this exercise is to practice sentence structures used in offering, accepting, and refusing something.

1. TANONG : **Gusto mo ba ng juice?**
   SAGOT : **Oo. Salamat.**

2. TANONG : **Gusto mo ba ng _____?**
   SAGOT : **Huwag na lang.**

3. TANONG : **Gusto mo ba ng _____?**
   SAGOT : _____.

4. TANONG : _____?
   SAGOT : **Huwag na lang.**

5. TANONG : **Gusto mo ba ng cake?**
   SAGOT : _____.

In these next exercises, try to imagine that you are speaking to an older person or that this is a formal situation. Practice the use of the honorifics **po** and **opo**. Use the first two pairs as examples.

6. TANONG : **Gusto po ba ninyo ng pie?**
   SAGOT : **Opo, salamat po.**

7. TANONG : **Gusto po ba ninyo ng asukal?**
   SAGOT : **Huwag na lang po.**

8. TANONG   :   _____?
   SAGOT   :   _____.

9. TANONG   :   **Ilang kutsaritang asukal ang gusto ninyo?**
                How many teaspoons of sugar would you like?
   SAGOT   :   **Dalawang kutsarita. Salamat.**

10. TANONG :   **Ilang kutsaritang asukal ang gusto mo?**
    SAGOT   :   _____.

🔍 Gramatika (Grammar)

Study the following new points about Filipino grammar.

I.   The words "**gusto**" and "**ayaw**" and the marker "**ni**"
     When using **gusto** and **ayaw**, the marker **ni** (used for proper nouns) is used indicating that it is Clara who likes coffee.
     Thus, we say, "**Gusto ni Clara ng kape.**"
     Do not use the marker **si**. The sentence, "**Gusto si Clara ng kape.**" means that "*Coffee likes Clara.*"

II. The words "**gusto**" and "**ayaw**" and pronouns
     The words **gusto** and **ayaw** are used with the possessive pronouns **ko, mo, niya, namin, natin, ninyo,** and **nila**.
     Thus we say, "**Gusto ko ng kape.**"
     Do not use the pronouns **ako, ikaw** or **ka, siya, kami, tayo, kayo,** and **sila**. The sentence "**Gusto ako ng kape.**" means that "*Coffee likes me.*"

III. The marker "**ng**" instead of the marker "**ang**"
     The use of **ng** instead of "**ang**" in the "coffee" dialogue can best be explained by equating it with English sentences:
     "**Gusto mo ba ng kape?**" *Would you like (some) coffee?*" In this sentence, by using the marker **ng**, "coffee" is marked as the object of the sentence.
     If we replace **ng** with the marker **ang**, then the meaning changes: "**Gusto mo ba ang kape?**" means "*Do you like the coffee?*"

IV. Studying the verbs **umiinom** *drinking*, **kumakain** *eating*, and **bumibisita** *visits*—subject focus using the prefix **um**
     In Filipino, verbs are inflected for aspect, rather than tense. Aspect shows if the action is completed, incomplete, or contemplated.

In this lesson, we have introduced three verbs, all incompleted: **umiinom**, **kumakain**, and **bumibisita**.

- To form the completed verb, we take the root word and add the prefix **um** before the first vowel.
- To form the incompleted verb, we take the first two syllables of the completed form and add the root word.
- To form the contemplated verb, we take the first syllable of the root word, and repeat it.

Root	Completed	Incompleted	Contemplated
inom	uminom	umiinom	iinom
kain	kumain	kumakain	kakain
bisita	bumisita	bumibisita	bibisita

EXAMPLES: **Uminom ako ng tubig.**
Umiinom ako ng tubig.
Iinom ako ng tubig.

In these sentences, we know that the focus is on the actor or the subject "**ako**" because the object "**tubig**" is marked by **ng**.

These sentences respond to *"who"* questions:

Sino ang uminom ng tubig? *Who drank the water?*
Ako ang uminom ng tubig. (literally, I *marker* drank *marker* water.)   OR
Uminom ako ng tubig. (literally, Drank I *marker* water.)

V. Studying the verbs "**umiinom** *drinking*," "**kumakain** *eating*," and "**bumibisita** *visits*"—object focus using the affix **in**

The most difficult part of grammar, however, is that the suffix changes depending on the focus. When the focus is on the object, we use the affix **in**.

To form the completed verb, put **in** before the first vowel of the root word.

To form the incompleted verb, use the first two syllables of the completed form and add the root word.

To form the contemplated verb, add the first syllable of the root word to the root word and then add **in**. If the last letter of the word is a vowel, add **h** before **in**.

Root	Completed	Incompleted	Contemplated
inom	ininom	iniinom	iinumin
kain	kinain	kinakain	kakainin
bisita	binisita	binibisita	bibisitahin

EXAMPLES: **Tubig ang ininom ko.**

Tubig ang iniinom ko.

Tubig ang iinumin ko.

In these sentences, we know that the focus is on the object because of the marker **ang**.

These sentences respond to *"what"* questions:

Ano ang ininom mo?

What did you drink?

Tubig ang ininom ko.

I drank water. (literally, Water *marker* drank I.)

★ Gawain

Expand your role-play options through dialogue variations and reviewing numbers.

Baryasyon Ng Diyalogo (Dialogue Variation):

Now that you have learned the basic dialogue above, increase your conversation skills by practicing other words and follow-up questions:

Paggamit ng iba pang salita—tsaa, limon, kalamansi, honey. (Use the following words: tea, lemon, calamansi or Philippine lemon, honey.)

Gusto mo ba ng isa pang tasa ng kape?

Would you like another cup of coffee?

Gusto mo ba ng isa pang puto?

Would you like another rice cake?

▤ Rebyu (Review)

Review numbers by integrating them in the dialogue. Use the first two pairs as a guide and then make up your own questions and answers to use in your role-play.

TANONG : **Ilang puto ang gusto mo?**

SAGOT : **Gusto ko ng dalawang puto.**

Tanong : **Ilang kutsaritang asukal ang gusto mo?**
Sagot : **Gusto ko ng _____ kutsaritang asukal.**

Mga Tala Sa Kultura

In earlier chapters, we have discussed how important it is to be polite in Philippine society, and this has influenced the language, resulting in the use of honorifics and the second person. This has also influenced everyday interaction, as shown in the friend's visit in this chapter.

In Philippine society, it is customary to refuse when one is first offered food or drink. Thus, we have the expressions "**Huwag ka nang mag-abala.**" (*Please don't bother.*) or "**Huwag na lang, salamat.**" (*No, thank you.*)

The host is then expected to repeat the offer by saying "**Sige na,**" an expression which means "*Please.*" It is only after the offer is repeated that the guest can then accept it, by saying "**Sige.**"

Thus, when receiving Filipinos in your house, it might be wise to offer them food or drink twice or thrice, should they refuse to accept your offers.

  Pagbabasa

Read the following passage, and then answer the questions that follow. As you answer, remember that there are several ways of answering a question. Although the person asking uses the object focus, you can answer with a sentence using the subject focus.

Bisita

Binisita ni Juan si Maria, ang kanyang kaibigan. Kaklase niya si Maria sa Ateneo University. Uminom siya ng tsaa at kumain ng cake. Ayaw niya ng kape.

---

1. **Kaano-ano ni Juan si Maria?** (*How is Juan related to Maria?*)

    _____.

2. **Gusto ba ni Juan ng kape?**

    _____.

3. **Sino ang bumisita kay Maria?**

    _____.

4. **Ano ang ininom ni Juan?**

_____.

5. Ano ang kinain ni Juan?

_____.

✏️ Pagsusulat (Writing)

Using the vocabulary and grammar you have learned, try writing a short paragraph about your visit to a friend's house or your friend's visit to your house.

🚩 Paglalagom (Summing Up)

In **Aralin 4**, you have learned:
1. Likes and dislikes,
2. Three verbs—**bisita**, **kain**, and **inom** (visit, eat, drink),
3. Subject/object focus.

You should now be able to:
1. Greet someone when visiting or being visited.
2. Conjugate three verbs.
3. Express likes and dislikes.

Ang Aking mga Gamit (My Things)

  ## Diyalogo: Aling Lapis? (Which pencil?)

Read the dialogue below. After completing this chapter, practice this dialogue using your own information.

PEDRO : **Paabot naman ng lapis.**
Please give me the pencil. (Literally, Please help me "reach" the pencil.)

MARIA : **Aling lapis?**
Which pencil?

PEDRO : **Iyong kulay asul.**
The blue pencil.

MARIA : **Heto.**
Here you are. (Literally, Here.)

PEDRO : **Salamat.**
Thank you.

MARIA : **Walang anuman.**
Welcome.

  ## Bokabolaryo (Vocabulary): Mga Kulay (Colors)

Study the following colors. In Filipino, some colors have indigenous names, others have both indigenous and Spanish names. In everyday conversations, most people use the words derived from Spanish or even use the English words (such as "pink.") However, it is useful to know both because you may encounter the indigenous words when reading, as they are popular among writers. The words **bughaw** and **luntian** are indigenous to the Tagalog language. The words **asul** and **berde** come from the Spanish language.

In a few instances, the words for colors are derived from nature, and are preceded by the word **kulay** meaning "color." For example, we say **kulay abo** (the color of ash) for "gray" and the **kulay kape** (or the color of coffee) for "brown."

Puti	*White*
Itim	*Black*
Bughaw o Asul	*Blue*
Pula	*Red*
Dilaw	*Yellow*
Luntian o Berde	*Green*
Kahel	*Orange*
Kulay abo	*Gray*
Kayumanggi o kulay kape	*Brown*
Lila	*Violet/Purple*
Kulay Rosas	*Pink*

Mga Pangungusap at Tanong

Practice saying these sentences aloud, to get a feel for how this chapter's vocabulary and grammar work in Filipino. As you will notice there are several ways of saying the same thing. Explore these options, so that you can learn how to speak naturally. Both the natural and literal translations are provided so you can study how sentence structures differ in Filipino.

Remember that the word **kulay** is optional here. For example, it is correct to say both "**Iyong kulay itim**," and "**Iyong itim**."

1. **Iyong kulay itim na bag ang bag ko.**
   The black bag is my bag. (literally, That color black *linker* bag *marker* bag my.)

2. **Bag ko ang kulay itim na bag.**
   My bag is the black bag. (literally, Bag my *marker* color black *linker* bag.)

3. **Iyong kulay itim.**
   The black one. (literally, That color black.)

4. **Kulay itim ang bag ko.**
   My bag is black. (literally, Color black *marker* bag my.)

5. **Kulay pula ang libro ni Juan.**
   Juan's book is red. (literally, Color red Juan's book.)

6. **Kaninong bag ito?**
   Whose bag is this? (literally, Whose bag this?)

7. **Kaninong payong ang dilaw na payong?**
   Whose umbrella is the yellow umbrella? (literally, Whose *marker* umbrella *marker* yellow *linker* umbrella.)

Pagsasanay

Practice these questions and answers by both speaking and writing. Use the earlier pairs as a guide. In this exercise, we are practicing two kinds of questions: **alin** (*which*) and **anong kulay** (*what color*).

1. TANONG : **Alin ang ballpen mo?**
   SAGOT : **Iyong kulay pula.**

2. TANONG : **Alin ang libro mo?**
   SAGOT : **Libro ko ang kulay itim na libro.**

3. TANONG : **Alin ang payong mo?**
   SAGOT : _____.

4. TANONG : **Ano ang kulay ng libro ng kaklase mo?**
   SAGOT : **Kulay itim ang libro ng kaklase ko.**

5. TANONG : **Ano ang kulay ng payong mo?**
   SAGOT : _____.

6. TANONG : _____ ?
   SAGOT : **Kulay rosas ang telepono ko.**

7. TANONG : **Alin ang telepono ng kaibigan mo?**
   SAGOT : _____.

8. TANONG : **Ano ang kulay ng notebook mo?**
   SAGOT : _____.

9. TANONG : _____ ?
   SAGOT : **Dilaw ang kulay ng notebook ng kaibigan ko.**

10. TANONG : _____ ?
    SAGOT : **Kulay puti ang silya ko.**

Gawain

Laro: Hawakan ang Kulay (Touch the Color)
In the classroom, the teacher can assign a student to start the game. The student, who plays the part of "it," calls out a color, and everyone else tries to touch an object of that color. The "it" person tries to tag someone before that other person can touch the color. The person tagged becomes "it," and is thus the next person to call out the colors.

If you are an independent learner, modify the game in this way: write the names of the colors in Filipino onto removable notes. Then, find objects around the room in that color and attach the notes to these objects. Make sure you are able to post all the notes. Practice naming the colors aloud as you go.

Gramatika (Grammar)

Study the information below to improve your Filipino grammar skills.

I.   The Question Word **Alin** (*which*)
The question word **alin** is easy to use when it is not followed by a linker.
> EXAMPLE: **Alin ang bag mo?**
> *Which is your bag?* (literally, Which *marker* bag your?)

It becomes confusing only when it is followed by the linker **na**, because the two words are contracted.
> EXAMPLE: **Aling bag ang bag mo?**
> *Which is your bag?* (literally, which *linker* bag *marker* bag your?)

In this sentence, the long form of "**aling bag**" is "**alin na bag**."
As you can see, both sentences mean the same thing; it's just two different ways of saying things.
However, some beginning learners tend to forget about the linker **na**, and incorrectly say "**Alin bag ang bag mo?**" This sentence is grammatically incorrect because there should always be a linker between the question word and the noun.

II. The Question Words **Anong Kulay** (*what color*)
The question words **anong kulay** travelled a different path. Earlier or more formal usage of this is: **Ano ang kulay...** (*What is the color...*) This, then, is contracted in everyday speech into, "**Ano'ng kulay...**"
> EXAMPLE: **Ano'ng kulay ng bag mo?**
> *What is the color of your bag?*

Because of the standardization of Filipino, recent spelling guidelines have deleted the apostrophe. Thus the spelling "**Anong**" is now acceptable.

> EXAMPLE: **Anong kulay ng bag mo?**
> *What is the color of your bag?* (literally, What *marker* color *marker* bag your?)

III. Linking Adjectives and Nouns

Adjectives—in this chapter, colors and nouns—are linked by **na**. The word order of adjectives and nouns is interchangeable. Thus, we can say **itim na bag** and **bag na itim**.

Many learners may get confused, however, because the linker **na** is contracted in conversational Filipino when it is preceded or followed by a word ending with a vowel. For example, **pula na telepono** becomes **pulang telepono**; and **telepono na pula** becomes **pulang telepono**.

As an example used in a sentence, we can say, **Kanino ang pulang telepono?** *Whose is the red phone?* (literally, Whose *marker* red *linker* phone?)

 ## Rebyu (Review)

Before proceeding to the next dialogue, it might be useful to review numbers and pronouns. Go back to the preceding chapter to review them.

1. **Mga Numero** (Numbers)
2. **Mga Panghalip** (Pronouns): **Ko**, **Mo**, **Niya**
3. **Mga Demonstratibong Panghalip** (Demonstrative Pronouns) **Ito**, **Iyan**, **Iyon**

🎧 💬 Diyalogo: Kaninong Bag Ito? (Whose bag is this?)

Read the dialogue below. After completing this chapter, practice this dialogue using your own information.

PEDRO : **Maria, bag mo ba ito?**
Maria, is this your bag?

MARIA : **Hindi akin iyan. Iyong nasa ibabaw ng mesa ang bag ko.**
That's not mine. The bag above the table is my bag.

PEDRO : **Kaninong bag ito?**
Whose bag is this?

MARIA : **Kay Clara iyan.**
That's Clara's bag.

 ## Bokabolaryo

Study the following words and how they are used in sentences.

Mga Salita hinggil sa Pag-aari (Words about Ownership)

Kay : Marker to indicate ownership. Used only for proper nouns.
Kay Clara iyan. *That is Clara's.* (literally, Of Clara that.)

Kina : Plural marker to indicate ownership. Used only for proper nouns.
Kina Maria at Clara ang mga iyan. *Those are Maria's and Clara's.*

Sa : Marker to indicate ownership. Used for nouns.
Sa kaibigan ko iyan. *That is my friend's.*

Kanya : *Hers*
Kanya iyan. *That is hers.*

Kanila : *Theirs*
Kanila iyan. *That is theirs.*

Akin : *Mine*
Akin iyan. *That is mine.*

Amin : *Ours* (plural exclusive pronoun)
Amin iyan. *That is ours.* (refers only to the person/s speaking)

Atin : *Ours* (inclusive pronoun)
Atin iyan. *That is ours.* (refers to both the person/s speaking and the person/s being addressed)

Mga Salita Hinggil sa Lugar ng isang Bagay (Words About the Location of an Object)

Look at the image below. As you read the sentences, try to locate the object/s in the image. This will help you understand the words below and how the words can be used in sentences. Note that when used in a sentence, these words need the preposition **nasa**, indicating location.

Ibabaw : *On*
Nasa ibabaw ng mesa ang libro.

Ilalim : *Under*
Nasa ilalim ng mesa ang payong.

Tabi : *Beside*
Nasa tabi ng lapis ang libro.

Loob : *In/Inside*
Nasa loob ng bag ang pamaypay.

Labas : *Out/Outside*
Nasa labas ng bag ang telepono.

Mga Pangungusap

Practice saying these sentences aloud, to get a feel for how this chapter's vocabulary and grammar work in Filipino. In some instances, two possible word orders are given. Study these two possibilities. Again, both the natural and literal translations are provided so that you can study Filipino sentence structures.

1. **Ito ay bag ni Clara.** *This is Clara's bag.* (literally, This is bag *possessive marker* Clara.)

2. **Bag ito ni Clara.** *This is Clara's bag.* (literally, Bag Bag this *possessive marker* Clara.) This sentence structure is more common in conversational Filipino.

3. **Pula ang bag ni Clara.** *Clara's bag is red.* (literally, Red *marker* bag *possessive marker* Clara.)

4. **Nasa ibabaw ng mesa ang bag ni Clara.** *Clara's bag is on the table.* (On top *marker* table *marker* bag *possessive marker* Clara.)

 Pagsasanay

Practice these questions and answers by both speaking and writing. Use some of the pairs as your guides in your own questions and answers. The focus of these exercises is to practice the question words **kanino** (*whose*) and **nasaan** (*where*). In some of the questions, you can assign any name to the characters in the picture.

1. TANONG : **Kaninong payong ito?**
   SAGOT : **Kay Christine iyan.**

2. TANONG : **Kaninong telepono ito?**
   SAGOT : **Kay _____ iyan.**

3. TANONG : **_____?**
   SAGOT : **Akin iyan.**

4. TANONG : **Kaninong payong ito?**
   SAGOT : **_____.**

5. TANONG : **Nasaan ang payong mo?**
   SAGOT : **Nasa ilalim ng silya ang payong ko.**

6. Tanong : **Nasaan ang susi mo?**
   Sagot   : **Nasa loob ng bag ang susi ko.**

7. Tanong : **Nasaan ang mga estudyante?**
   Sagot   : **Nasa loob ng klasrum (silid-aralan) ang mga estudyante.**

8. Tanong : **Nasaan ang _____?**
   Sagot   : **Nasa _____ ang _____.**

9. Tanong : **Nasaan ang mga susi mo?**
   Sagot   : _____.

10. Tanong : **Kaninong mga susi ito? (the key is owned by two people)**
    Sagot   : _____.

🔍 Gramatika (Grammar)

Study the information below to improve your Filipino grammar skills.

I. The Interrogative or Question Word **Kanino**
    The question word **kanino** means "*whose.*" When used in a sentence, it is usually followed by the marker **ang**, which precedes the noun. The noun is then followed by the linker **na** and an adjective or a demonstrative pronoun.

    EXAMPLES: **Kanino ang payong na pula?**
    Whose is the red umbrella? (literally, Whose *marker* umbrella *linker* red?)
    Kanino ang payong na ito?
    Whose is this umbrella? (literally, Whose *marker* umbrella *linker* this?)

    However, in conversational Filipino, **kanino** can also be followed by contracted linker **na**. The long form is "**Kanino na payong ito?**" With the contracted **na**, this becomes "**Kaninong payong ito?**" (*Whose umbrella is this?*) (literally, Whose *linker* umbrella this?) Note that in this sentence construction there is no linker between the noun **payong** and the demonstrative pronoun **ito**.
    Similarly, one can be more specific and use the noun after **kanino**.

    EXAMPLE: **Kaninong payong ang asul na payong?**
    Whose umbrella is the blue umbrella? (literally, Whose *linker* umbrella *marker* blue *linker* umbrella?)

Morever, it has been acceptable to drop the linker **na**. Thus, in conversational Filipino, we just say: **Kaninong payong ito?** (literally, Whose umbrella this?)

II. The Interrogative or Question Word **Nasaan** and the Preposition **Nasa**
The interrogative **nasaan** means *"where."* It is used when asking about location, and is followed by a noun (and the marker preceding the noun).

> EXAMPLE: **Nasaan ang libro?**
> *Where is the book?* (literally, Where *marker* book?)

To answer this question, the preposition **nasa** followed by the location is used. In conversational Filipino where the predicate usually precedes the subject, it is more common to start the sentence with **nasa**.

> EXAMPLE: **Nasa ibabaw ng mesa ang libro.**
> *The book is on the table.* (literally, On *marker* table *marker* book.)

In the example above, note that the Filipino **nasa ibabaw** is equivalent to the English preposition *"on."* Similarly, **nasa ilalim** is equivalent to *"under,"* and **nasa loob** means *"in."*

In written Filipino, some writers like to use the subject-predicate structure, and thus would use: **Ang libro ay nasa ibabaw ng mesa.** (*The book is on the table.*) (Literally, *Marker* book is on *marker* table.)

To sound more natural, you may want to use the predicate-subject structure.

III. The Ownership Markers **Kay/Kina** and **Sa**
In preceding chapters, you have studied the markers **si**, **ang**, and **ni**. The ownership markers **kay** and **kina** are used for proper nouns, the former for singular proper nouns and the latter for plural proper nouns. **Sa** is used for non-proper nouns.

Here are a few examples:

> EXAMPLE: **Kay Clara ang bag na iyan.** *That bag is Clara's.* (literally, Clara's *marker* bag *linker* that.)
> EXAMPLE: **Kina Clara at Juan ang mga librong iyan.** *Those bags are Clara's and Juan's.* (literally, Clara's and Juan's *marker* books those).
> EXAMPLE: **Sa kaibigan ko ang lapis na iyan.** *That is my friend's pencil.* (literally, Friend's my *marker* pencil *linker* that.)

Mga Tala Sa Kultura

In precolonial Philippines, life among many of the more than sixty ethnolinguistics groups was communal. People owned the land they could till and that they needed in order to survive, and they did not need documents to prove it was theirs.

The Banaue Rice Terraces in the Cordillera Mountains are an example of this. It is believed that the people of Banaue carved the mountains for hundreds of years to make rice terraces for their families and the community. A family planted rice for their needs, and when the children grew up and started their own families, they would make more rice paddies.

Today, the Banaue Rice Terraces are considered to be among the most amazing man-made "wonders" of the world, as the people of the Cordillera continue to struggle for their indigenous rights.

 Pagbabasa

Read the following passage, and then answer the questions that follow. Note how the linker **at** is used here to link clauses.

baul	*chest*	**ibinigay**	*was given*
nanay	*mother*		

Ang Baul ni Clara

Baul ito ni Clara. Ibinigay ito sa kanya ng nanay niya.

Kulay kayumanggi at itim ang baul niya. Nasa ibabaw ng baul ang isang libro at mga bulaklak. Walang notebook sa ibabaw ng baul. May carpet sa ilalim ng baul.

1. **Kanino ang baul?**
2. **Ano ang kulay ng baul?**
3. **Nasaan ang libro?**
4. **Ano ang nasa ilalim ng baul?**
5. **May notebook ba sa ibabaw ng baul?**

✏ Pagsusulat (Writing)

Using the vocabulary and grammar you have learned, try writing your own paragraph about your bag. Talk about where it is, and what is inside it. You can also expand the paragraph by talking about your other things or the things in the room where you are.

▶ Paglalagom (Summing Up)

In **Aralin 5**, you have learned:
1. Colors,
2. Words indicating ownership,
3. The interrogatives **Kanino** (*Whose*), **Alin** (*Which*), and **Nasaan** (*Where?*),
4. The preposition **nasa** indicating the location of an object.

You should now be able to:
1. Describe objects using color and location.
2. Talk about ownership.

Mga Bayan at Bansa at ang Aking Nasyonalidad (Cities and Towns; Countries and Citizenship)

  Diyalogo: Taga-Saan Ka? (Where are you from?)

Read the dialogue below. After completing this chapter, practice this dialogue using your own information.

MARIA : **Taga-Cebu City ka ba?**
Are you from Cebu City?

PEDRO : **Hindi ako taga-Cebu City.**
I am not from Cebu City.

MARIA : **Taga-saan ka?**
Where are you from?

PEDRO : **Taga-Ochando, New Washington ako.**
I am from Ochando, New Washington.

MARIA : **Nasaan ang Ochando, New Washington?**
Where is Ochando, New Washington?

PEDRO : **Nasa Aklan.**
In Aklan.

MARIA : **Saan ka na nakatira ngayon?**
Where do you live now?

PEDRO : **Nakatira ako sa Maynila.**
I live in Manila now.

Bokabolaryo (Vocabulary)

Study the following words and how they were used in the dialogue you just read.

Taga-saan	*From where*
Taga-Ilocos	*From Ilocos*
Nasa	*Preposition indicating location*
Nakatira	*Live*
Ngayon	*Now (also means today)*
Na	(in the sentence "**Saan ka na nakatira ngayon?**")
	Already (see explanation in Gramatika)

Mga Gabay Na Pangungusap (Sentence Guides)

Practice saying these sentences aloud, and study how they are constructed so that you can make your own sentences later.

1. **Ang Quezon City ay nasa Metro Manila.**   *Quezon City is in Metro Manila.*
   Nasa Metro Manila ang Quezon City.
2. **Ang Los Angeles ay nasa California.**   *Los Angeles is in California.*
   Nasa California ang Los Angeles.
3. **Ang Paete ay nasa Laguna.**   *Paete is in Laguna.*
   Nasa Laguna ang Paete.
4. **Taga-Boston ako.**   *I am from Boston.*
5. **Taga-Laguna si Marconi.**   *Marconi is from Laguna.*
6. **Taga-Aklan si Mauro.**   *Mauro is from Aklan.*
7. **Nakatira sina Chat at Pendong sa Daly City.**   *Chat and Pendong live in Daly City.*
8. **Nakatira si Nerissa sa Long Island.**   *Nerissa lives in Long Island.*

★ Gawain/Pagsasanay

Pag-aaral ng Mapa (Studying a Map)

Look at the map below. If you are an Independent learner, write at least five sentences about locations. Then, make a list of five friends who live in different cities. Write sentences about them. If you are studying in a classroom setting, ask and answer questions about location using the following questions and answers as a guide.

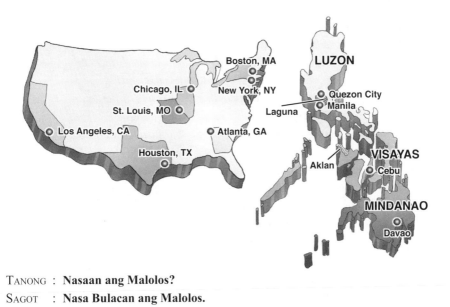

TANONG : **Nasaan ang Malolos?**
SAGOT   : **Nasa Bulacan ang Malolos.**
TANONG : **Nasaan ang San Francisco?**
SAGOT   : **Nasa** _____.
TANONG : **Nasaan ang** _____?
SAGOT   : **Nasa** _____.
TANONG : **Taga-saan si Jonathan?**
SAGOT   : **Taga-Pampanga si Jonathan.**
TANONG : **Taga-saan si** _____?
SAGOT   : **Taga-**_____ **si** _____.
TANONG : **Saan nakatira si Jonathan?**
SAGOT   : **Nakatira na si** _____ **sa** _____ **ngayon.**

🔍 Gramatika

Study the following explanation on Filipino grammar.

I. The affix **taga-**
   The affix **taga-** indicates where a person is from. A person may be living now in New York City but is originally from Roanoke, Virginia. Or one can be from Panabo, Davao del Norte but now living in Quezon City.

II. The word **na**
   "**Na**," previously introduced as a linker (or ligature), also means "already." If you are a heritage learner, you may have noticed that your parents or grandparents are fond of saying sentences in English using "already," for example, "I ate already." In their everyday speech Filipinos are fond of this usage of "**na**".

III. The prefix **naka-**

Naka- is a special Filipino prefix that indicates a state, condition, or appearance of a person or thing.

EXAMPLE:
nakatira	*live; reside*
Nakatira ako sa Berkeley.	*I live in Berkeley.*
naka-upo	*sitting*
Naka-upo si Lisa.	*Lisa is sitting.*

IV. The interrogative word **nasaan**; the preposition **nasa**

Nasaan is a question word that asks for the location of a person, an object or a place. It is answered by using the preposition **nasa**.

EXAMPLES:
Nasaan ang Stoneham?	*Where is Stoneham?*
Nasa Massachusetts ang Stoneham.	*Stoneham is in Massachusetts.*
Nasaan na si Raymond ngayon?	*Where is Raymond now?*
Nasa Pilipinas na si Raymond ngayon.	*He is in the Philippines [already] now.*

Bokabolaryo (Vocabulary)

Study the following words that enable you to talk about some countries and describe geographical divisions. Note that in most cases, you can also just use the English names of several countries (for example, Denmark, Thailand, Canada, and Malaysia), because these names have been incorporated into the Filipino language.

Pilipinas	*Philippines*
Espanya	*Spain*
Estados Unidos	*United States*
bansang Hapon	*Japan*
Pransiya	*France*
Tsina	*China*
Daigdig/Mundo	*world*
Kontinente	*continent*
Bansa	*country*
Isla	*island*
Probinsiya	*province*
Lungsod/Siyudad	*city*
Bayan	*town/country/people*
Baryo	*village*
Barangay	*smallest political unit in the Philippines*

★ **Gawain (Activity)**

Study how the words **bansa**, **probinsiya**, **lungsod**, **isla** and **baryo** are used in the following sentences. Note also how both the subject-predicate and predicate-subject word orders are used in the first several sentences.

If you are an independent learner, write at least five sentences talking about cities, provinces, states or prefectures that you know. You may also use the map above. If you are a classroom learner, practice asking and answering yes or no questions using the guides below.

1. **Ang Pilipinas ay isang bansa.**   *The Philippines is a country.*
   Isang bansa ang Pilipinas.
2. **Ang Samar ay isang probinsiya.**   *Samar is a province.*
   Isang probinsiya ang Samar.
3. **Ang Bacolod ay isang lungsod.**   *Bacolod is a city.*
   Isang lungsod ang Bacolod.
4. **Ang Capiz ay isang probinsiya.**   *Capiz is a province.*
   Isang probinsiya ang Capiz.
5. **Ang Baclayon ay isang bayan sa**   *Baclayon is a town in the province*
   probinsiya ng Bohol. Isang bayan sa   *of Bohol.*
   probinsiya ng Bohol ang Baclayon.
6. **Ang Libertad ay isang barangay sa**   *Libertad is a village in the town of*
   bayan ng Baclayon sa probinsiya ng   *Baclayon in the province of*
   Bohol. Isang barangay sa bayan ng   *Bohol.*
   Baclayon sa probinsiya ng Bohol
   ang Libertad.
7. **Ang Antique ay nasa isla ng Panay.**   *Antique is on the island of Panay.*
   Nasa isla ng Panay ang Antique.
8. **Nasa silangan ang Leyte.**   *Leyte is in the east.*
9. **Nasa kanluran ang Negros Occidental.**   *Negros Occidental is in the west.*

Mga Tala Sa Kultura

According to historian Damon Woods, contrary to Western concepts of space that are more specific and inflexible, Tagalog words such as **bayan** can have a variety of meanings. It can refer to a country, the people of a country or a town. Thus, we can say **"sa aming bayan ng Malolos** (*in our town of Malolos*), **"bayang Pilipinas"** (*the country Philippines*), or **"bayang Pilipino"** (*the Filipino people*).

Dagdag na Bokabolaryo

> **Mga Pang-uri Na Naglalarawan Sa Lugar**
> **(Additional Vocabulary: Adjectives That Describe a Place)**

Study the following adjectives and how they are used in sentences. These adjectives are being introduced first because they can be used to describe places.

Maganda	*Beautiful*
Maganda ang Laguna.	*Laguna is beautiful.*
Malaki	*Big/Huge*
Malaki ang California.	*California is big.*
Maliit	*Small*
Maliit ang Ochando.	*Ochando is small.*
Malinis	*Clean*
Malinis na bansa ang bansang Hapon.	*Japan is a clean country.*
Madumi/Marumi	*Dirty*
Madumi ang lungsod na ito.	*This city is dirty.*

Tulong sa Pag-Aaral ng Wika (Language Learning Tip):
In this chapter, it is helpful to study opposite adjectives as you try to increase your vocabulary in Filipino. For example, think of the following words that we have just introduced. Try to write your own sentences using these adjectives.

Maganda	–	*Pangit*
Malaki	–	*Maliit*
Malinis	–	*Madumi*

  ## Dagdag-Aral

Study the following addtional adjectives and how comparatives and superlatives are formed in Filipino. For comparatives, add the word **mas** before the adjective, and then use the word **kaysa**. For superlatives, attach the prefix **pinaka-**. Some of these adjectives refer to places and some to people.

Malaki *Big*	EXAMPLE: **Malaki ang lungsod ng Makati.**
Mas Malaki *Bigger*	EXAMPLE: **Mas malaki ang lungsod ng Quezon kaysa sa lungsod ng Makati.**
Pinakamalaki *Biggest*	EXAMPLE: **Pinakamalaki ang lungsod ng Davao.**

Maliit *Small*	EXAMPLE: **Maliit ang Pilipinas.**
Mas Maliit *Smaller*	EXAMPLE: **Mas maliit ang Netherlands sa Pilipinas.**
Pinakamaliit *Smallest*	EXAMPLE: **Pinakamaliit ang Singapore.**

Mahaba *Long*	EXAMPLE: **Mahaba ang lapis.**
Mas Mahaba *Longer*	EXAMPLE: **Mas mahaba ang ballpen sa lapis.**
Pinakamahaba *Longest*	EXAMPLE: **Pinakamahaba ang payong.**

Using the sentences above as a guide, make your own sentences for the following comparatives and superlatives.

Maiksi *Short*	
Mas Maiksi *Shorter*	
Pinakamaiksi (not used for people) *Shortest*	

Mataas *Tall*	
Mas Mataas *Taller*	
Pinakamataas (not usually used for people) *Tallest*	

Matangkad *Tall*	
Mas Matangkad *Taller*	
Pinakamatangkad (used for people) *Tallest*	

Pandak *Short*	
Mas Pandak *Shorter*	
Pinakapandak (used for people) *Shortest*	

Cultural Note: It is not polite, however, to say that a person is "**pandak**." Short people would rather be called "**maliit**" because **pandak** is deemed derogatory.

  Pagsasanay (Practice)

Practice the question words **ano**, **alin**, and **sino** and the adjectives you have just studied. Ask and/or answer the following. You may also make your own questions.

1. TANONG : **Aling bansa ang mas malaki, Tsina o Estados Unidos?**
   SAGOT : _____.

2. TANONG : **Aling kontinente ang pinakamaliit?**
   SAGOT : _____.

3. TANONG : _____?
   SAGOT : **Mas maliit ang Singapore kaysa sa Pilipinas.**

4. TANONG : _____?
   SAGOT : _____.

5. TANONG : _____?
   SAGOT : _____.

6. TANONG : **Sino ang mas matangkad, si _____ o si _____?**
   SAGOT : **Mas matangkad si _____ kaysa kay _____.**

7. TANONG : **Sino ang pinakamaliit?**
   SAGOT : _____.

8. TANONG : _____?
   SAGOT : _____.

9. Tanong : _____?
   Sagot : _____.

10. Tanong : **Aling lapis ang pinakamahaba?**
    Sagot : _____.

11. Tanong : _____?
    Sagot : **Mas mahaba ang _____ lapis kaysa sa _____**
             na lapis.

12. Tanong : _____?
    Sagot : _____.

13. Tanong : _____?
    Sagot : _____.

★ Gawain (Activity)

Laro: "Form a Line"

This game can be played in the classroom. The students are asked to form several lines. Then they should arrange themselves in the line according to the instructions of the teacher. For example, the teacher may call out "**Humanay tayo!** (*Form a line!*) **Mula sa Pinakapandak Hanggang sa Pinkamatangkad...** (*From the smallest to the tallest...*).

Dagdag-aral Tungkol sa Nasyonalidad at Etnisidad (Additional Lesson About Nationality and Ethnicity)

Study the following words that depict one's nationality or ethnicity. Note that in some cases, the words are gendered. For men, the word ends with the vowel **o**; for women, the vowel **a**.

Filipino/a ako.	*I am Filipino.*
Amerikano/a ako.	*I am American.*
Filipino-American ako.	*I am Filipino-American.*
Kastila ako.	*I am a Spaniard.*
Hapon ako.	*I am Japanese.*
Koreano/a ako.	*I am Korean.*
Tsino ako.	*I am Chinese.*

Pagbabasa (Reading)

Read the following passages, and then answer the questions that follow. Study the new word **pero** (*but*) as it will help you form complex sentences.

Ako at ang Aking mga Kaibigan (My Friends and I)

Pilipino ako. Taga-Bontoc ako. Nasa Mountain Province ang Bontoc at nasa Cordillera Administrative Region ang Mountain Province. Nasa hilaga ng isla ng Luzon ang Cordillera Administrative Region. Nakatira na ako ngayon sa Maynila.

Amerikano si Robert. Taga-Connecticut siya pero nakatira siya sa San Francisco. Ang lungsod ng San Francisco ay nasa California. Maganda ang San Francisco.

Hapon si Ginoong Oue. Taga-Hiroshima siya pero nakatira siya sa lungsod ng Minoo. Nasa Osaka sa bansang Hapon ang Minoo-shi. Malinis ang Minoo-shi.

---

1. Taga-saan si Robert?
2. Saan nakatira si Ginoong Oue?
3. Aling lungsod ang malinis?
4. Taga-Hiroshima ba si Robert?
5. Sino ang taga-Hiroshima?

Pagsusulat (Writing)

Using the vocabulary and grammar you have learned, try writing one or two paragraphs in Filipino.

Paglalagom (Summing Up)

In **Aralin 6**, you have learned:
1. Geographical locations,
2. Adjectives that describe places and people,
3. The interrogatives **saan** and **nasaan**,
4. Comparatives and superlatives.

You should now be able to:
1. Talk about your hometown, where you live now, and your citizenship.
2. Describe and compare objects, places and people.

Ang Aking Pamilya (My Family)

 ## Diyalogo: Tiya Mo Ba Siya? (Is she your aunt?)

Read the dialogue below. After completing this chapter, practice this dialogue using your own information.

PEDRO : **Kumusta? Ako si Pedro Santos.**
How are you? I am Pedro Santos.

CLARA : **Ako naman si Clara Dimagiba.**
I am Clara Dimagiba.

PEDRO : **Kaano-ano mo si Binibining Perpetua Dimagiba?**
How are you related to Miss Perpetua Dimagiba?

CLARA : **Tiya ko siya.**
She is my aunt.

PEDRO : **Talaga? Kapitbahay ko siya.**
Really? She is my neighbor.
(Ituturo ni Clara ang tiya niya.)
(Clara points to her aunt.)

CLARA : **Kapatid siya ng tatay ko. Hayun ang tatay ko. Siya ang lalaking naka-suot ng puting polo-shirt at itim na pantalon.**
She is the sister of my father. That's my father. He is the man wearing a white shirt and black pants.

Bokabolaryo

Study the following words that you can use when talking about family. Also, review the words you studied in chapter 1 that refer to relationships. Then, study Additional Vocabulary below, to learn additional words that also refer to relationships.

Mga Miyembro ng Pamilya (Family Members)

Asawa	*Husband/Wife*
Magulang	*Parent*
Anak	*Son/Daughter*
Nanay	*Mother*
Tatay	*Father*
Kapatid	*Brother/Sister*
Kuya	*Elder Brother*
Ate	*Elder Sister*
Tiya/Tita	*Aunt*
Tiyo/Tito	*Uncle*
Pinsan	*Cousin*
Lolo	*Grandfather*
Lola	*Grandmother*
Apo	*Grandchild*
Pamangkin	*Niece/Nephew*
Alagang aso	*Pet dog*
Alagang pusa	*Pet cat*

Mga Relasyon (Relationships)

Kamag-anak	*Relative*
Ka-opisina	*Of the same office*
Kasama	*Companion/comrade*
Kasama sa trabaho	*Coworker*
Kababata	*Childhood friend*
Matalik na kaibigan	*Close friend*
Kakilala	*Acquaintance*

Ekspresyon

Study the following expression that is useful for more natural speech.

Talaga?	*Really?*

★ Gawain (Activity)

Draw a picture of your family. Using the following example as a guide, write at least five sentences. For classroom learners, introduce the members of your family to your classmates.

Study some new words that may be useful:

Yumao	*Passed away*
Alagang ibon	*Pet bird*
Alagang isda	*Pet fish*

Halimbawa 1 (Example 1):
Ito ang nanay ko. Ang pangalan niya ay Mila. Ito ang tatay ko. Ang pangalan niya ay Carlos. Dalawa ang kapatid ko. Mario ang pangalan ng kuya ko. Maria ang pangalan ng ate ko. Mayroon kaming alagang pusa.

Halimbawa 2 (Example 2):
Ito ang tatay ko. Virgilio ang pangalan niya. Wala akong kapatid. May alaga kaming aso. Yumao (passed away) **na ang nanay ko.**

Sariling Halimbawa (Own Example):
Ito ang _____ ko. _____ ang pangalan niya. Meron akong _____ kapatid. Meron akong alagang _____.

Balik-Aral

Review the words for colors that you have previously studied. These words will be useful when you describe clothes.

Dagdag na Bokabolaryo

Study the following words so that you can describe clothing.

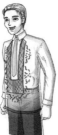

Mga Kasuotan/Damit (Clothes)

Blusa	*Blouse*
Palda	*Skirt*
Bestida/Damit	*Dress*
Pantalon	*Pants*
Polo	*Shirt*
Barong Tagalog	*Filipino national costume for men (embroidered shirt made of native fabrics and worn outside)*
Baro't Saya	*Traditional blouse and skirt worn by women*
Kurbata	*Tie*
Amerikana	*Suit*
Uniporme	*Uniform*
Sumbrero	*Hat*
Sapatos	*Shoes*
Sandalyas	*Sandals*

Mga Pangungusap

Practice saying these sentences aloud, to get a feel for how this chapter's vocabulary and grammar work in Filipino.

1. **Ang tatay ko ang lalaking nakasuot ng Barong Tagalog.**
   My father is the man wearing a Barong Tagalog.
2. **Nakasuot ng mga puting bestida ang mga pinsan ko.**
   My cousins are wearing white dresses.
3. **Puting blusa at asul na palda ang uniporme ng mga estudyante.**
   The students' uniform is a white blouse and a blue skirt.

  Pagsasanay

Practice these questions and answers by both speaking and writing them. Use the photos and the earlier pairs as a guide. Classroom learners can then ask each other what they or their classmates are wearing.

1. TANONG : **Ano ang suot ni Pedro?**
   SAGOT : **Nakasuot siya ng itim na pantalon.**

2. TANONG : **Ano ang suot ni Silay?**
   SAGOT : **Nakasuot siya ng pulang damit.**

3. TANONG : **Ano ang suot ni _____?**

   SAGOT : **Nakasuot siya ng _____.**

4. TANONG : **Ano ang suot mo?**

   SAGOT : **Nakasuot ako ng _____.**

5. TANONG : **_____?**

   SAGOT : **_____.**

6. TANONG : **Sino ang babaeng nakasuot ng pulang bestida?**

   SAGOT : **Si Silay ang babaeng nakasuot ng pulang bestida.**

7. TANONG : **Sino ang nakasuot ng asul na polo?**

   SAGOT : **_____.**

8. TANONG : **_____?**

   SAGOT : **Si _____ ang _____ nakasuot ng _____.**

9. TANONG : **_____?**

   SAGOT : **_____.**

10. TANONG : **_____?**

    SAGOT : **_____.**

⭐ Gawain (Activity)

Go back to your drawing. Describe what each member of the family is wearing.

🔍 Gramatika (Grammar)

I. **Na** as relative pronoun

    Na, previously introduced as a linker between adjectives and nouns, and as a word meaning "already," can also be used as a relative pronoun. Many native speakers tend to be confused with the variety of pronouns in English—"who, that, which, where…." In Filipino, simply use **na**.

    Similar to the way it is used as a linker, contract **na** when it comes before a word that ends with a vowel. Thus, "**lalaki na**" becomes "**lalaking**."

    EXAMPLE: **Ang lalaking nakasuot ng puting polo ang kapatid ko.**

    The man wearing a white shirt is my brother. (literally, *Marker man relative pronoun wearing white shirt marker brother my.*)

II. Conjunctions

Earlier, you studied the conjunctions **at** (*and*) and **pero** (*but*). Three other useful conjunctions which will help you make more complex sentences are **dahil** (*because*) and **habang** and **samantalang** (*while*).

> EXAMPLES: **Nakasuot ako ng baro't saya dahil Philippine Independence Day ngayon.**
> *I am wearing a baro't saya because it is Philippine Independence Day today.* (literally, Wearing I *marker* **baro't saya** because Philippine Independence Day today.)
>
> **Nakasuot si Lourdes ng kulay rosas na bestida samantalang nakasuot naman ng kulay pulang bestida si Teresa.**
> *Lourdes is wearing a pink dress while Teresa is wearing a red dress.* (Literally, Lourdes *marker* wearing *marker* color pink *linker* dress while wearing **naman** *marker* color red dress *marker* Teresa.)

III. Conjugating the root word "**suot**"

You have learned the use of the prefix **naka-** with the verb **suot**. As explained earlier, **naka-** is a special prefix that expresses a person or an object's state, condition or appearance. In this chapter we used **naka-** for the word **nakasuot** (wearing).

Let us now study how we can use other suffixes to express different aspects of the verb **suot**. The first set are the verbs used in sentences where the focus is on the subject while in the second set, the focus is on the object.

Here are the formulas:

Mag affix:
- Completed—**nag** + root word;
- Incompleted—first two syllables of completed form + root word;
- Contemplated—change **n** to **m** of the incompleted form

In affix:
- Completed—insert **in** before the first vowel of the root word and then add **i** before the word;
- Incompleted—first syllables of the completed form + root word;
- Contemplated—**i** + first syllable of root word + root word

Affix	Completed	Incompleted	Contemplated
nag	nagsuot	nagsusuot	magsusuot
in	isinuot	isinusuot	isusuot

Here are some examples of sentences:

1. **Nagsuot ako ng asul na bestida sa birthday party.**
   I wore a blue dress at the birthday party. (literally, wore I *marker* blue dress at birthday party.)

2. **Asul na bestida ang isinuot ko sa birthday party.**
   A blue dress is what I wore at the birthday party. (Blue dress *marker* wore I at birthday party.)

3. **Nagsusuot ang mga kawani ng uniporme sa opisina.**
   Office workers wear uniforms at the office. (literally, Wear I *marker* uniforms at office.)

4. **Uniporme ang isinusuot ng mga kawani sa opisina.**
   Uniforms is what office workers wear at the office. (literally, Uniforms *marker* wear I at office.)

5. **Magsusuot si Lily ng baro't saya.**
   Lily will wear a baro't saya. (literally, Wear *marker* Lily *marker* **baro't saya**.)

6. **Baro't saya ang isusuot ni Lily.**
   Baro't saya is what Lily will wear. (literally, **Baro't saya** *marker* will wear *marker* Lily.)

Pagsasanay

Practice the grammar points you have just learned by asking and answering questions. Remember that there are several ways by which a question can be answered. Independent learners should write at least three questions and answers. Classroom learners should form pairs and ask each other questions.

1. Tanong : **Ano ang isinuot mo sa party?**
   Sagot : **Nagsuot ako ng itim na bestida sa party.**
   Itim na bestida ang isinuot ko sa party.

2. Tanong : **Ano ang isinusuot ng mga estudyante?**
   Sagot : _____.

3. Tanong : _____?
   Sagot : **Magsusuot ako ng Barong Tagalog.**

4. Tanong : _____?
   Sagot : _____.

5. Tanong : _____?
   Sagot : _____.

6. TANONG : _____?
   SAGOT   : _____.

 ## Dagdag na Bokabolaryo

Mga Pang-uri na Naglalarawan sa Tao (Adjectives that Describe a Person)

Review the adjectives referring to people that you learned earlier. Then, study the additional adjectives below. Remember that it is usually easier to remember adjectives if you pair contrasting ones. Write at least five sentences using these adjectives. Use the sentences for the first adjective as an example. Remember to use the markers **si** (for proper nouns) and **ang** (for nouns).

Maganda	*Beautiful*
Maganda si Maxine.	
Maganda ang kapatid ko.	
Pangit/Hindi Maganda	*Ugly*
Payat	*Thin*
Mataba	*Fat*
Matalino	*Intelligent*
Mabait	*Kind/Nice*
Masipag	*Industrious*
Masungit	*Grouchy*
Madaldal	*Talkative*
Masayahin	*Always happy*
Malungkutin	*Always sad*
Masakitin	*Sickly*

  ## Dagdag-Aral

Paggamit ng mga Numero Para sa Paglalarawan ng Pamilya (Using Numbers to Talk about the Family)

Review your numbers to ask and answer questions about your family. Use the first questions and answers as a guide. Individual learners should write down at least three questions and answers. Classroom learners should ask each other questions. Note that more than one answer is possible.

(Note the use of the linker **na** as relative pronoun. This has been discussed earlier.)

1. Tanong : **Ilan ang pinsan mo?**
   Sagot : **Labinlima ang pinsan ko. / Meron akong labinlimang pinsan.**

2. Tanong : **Ilan ang tiya mo na nasa Amerika?**
   Sagot : **Tatlo ang tiya ko na nasa Amerika./Meron akong tatlong tiya na nasa Amerika.**

3. Tanong : **Ilan ang pinsan mong lalaki?**
   Sagot : _____.

4. Tanong : _____?
   Sagot : **Dalawa ang pinsan kong babae.**

5. Tanong : _____?
   Sagot : _____.

6. Tanong : _____?
   Sagot : _____.

7. Tanong : _____?
   Sagot : _____.

Mga Tala Sa Kultura

You may have heard of Corazon Aquino (1933–2009), former President of the Philippines. Aquino was installed as the 11th President of the Philippines, following the 1986 EDSA People Power Revolt that ended the authoritarian rule of Ferdinand Marcos. It is believed that she was a popular candidate and President because she was called "**Tita** Cory" (Aunt Cory), indicating familiarity.

In the Philippines, even non-relatives are called **Tita/Tito/Tiya/Tiyo** (*aunt/uncle*), **Ate/Kuya** (*elder brother/sister*), or even the Ilocano/Visayan **Manang/Manong** (*elder sister/elder brother*). This establishes a bond between the speaker and the person being addressed. It brings close family friends even closer; promotes a casual atmosphere in the workplace; enables the shopper to get a better bargain at the wet market; and even diffuses sexual tension among scholars conducting field research.

This also brings to mind communities in the rural areas where it is not uncommon to attach the words **'Nay** (*mother*) and **'Tay** (*father*) to the names of the older members of the community. This connotes not only respect and familiarity, but also emphasizes an interdependent way of living, where the community seems to be an extended family.

Pagbabasa

Read the following passage, and then answer the questions that follow. Before reading, study the new vocabulary that will enable you to understand the paragraphs better and write more complex sentences for your short paragraph. The new vocabulary words are marked in bold.

New Words

Iba	*Different*
Kasal	*Wedding*
Yumao	*Passed on; died*

Ang Aking Pamilya

Ito ang pamilya ko sa araw ng kasal ko. Nakasuot ako ng mahabang puting bestida at nakasuot ang asawa kong si Pierre ng Barong Tagalog. Kasama namin sa larawan ang nanay kong si Shayne, ang tatay kong si Bien, at ang mga kapatid kong sina Silay at Sining. Nasa larawan din ang anak ni Sining na si Maxine at ang asawa ni Silay na si Vencer. Nakasuot din si Bien ng Barong Tagalog at nakasuot naman si Shayne ng baro't saya. Sina Silay at Sining ay nakasuot ng asul at kahel na mga bestida at si Vencer ay nakasuot ng puting polo.

Wala sa larawan ang anak namin ni Pierre na si Elia. Iba ang nanay ni Elia pero anak ko na rin siya ngayon. Labindalawang taon na si Elia.

Wala rin sa larawan ang tunay kong mga magulang dahil yumao na sila. Pero may pamilya ako at nasa larawan sila.

---

1. Ano ang suot ng nanay ko?
2. Sino ang mga nakasuot ng Barong Tagalog?
3. Ano ang kulay ng mga bestida nina Silay at Sining?
4. Ano ang pangalan ng asawa ni Silay?
5. Ilang taon na si Elia?

✏ Pagsusulat (Writing)

Using the vocabulary and grammar you have learned, try writing a paragraph about your family in Filipino.

⚑ Paglalagom (Summing Up)

In **Aralin 7**, you have learned:
1. Words about the family and clothing,
2. How to conjugate the verb **suot**,
3. **Na** used as a relative pronoun,
4. Adjectives that can be used to describe people,
5. The conjunctions **dahil**, **habang**, and **samantalang**.

You should now be able to:
1. Talk about your family.
2. Construct complex sentences.
3. Talk about what people are wearing.
4. Make more sentences using the subject and object focus with more ease.

Ang Aming Bahay (Our House)

  Diyalogo: Sa Telepono (On the phone)

Read the dialogue below. After completing this chapter, practice this dialogue using your own information.

(Tutunog ang telepono.) (*Phone rings*.)

GINANG SANTOS	:	**Hello. Magandang umaga.**
		Hello. Good morning.
MARIA	:	**Hello. Magandang umaga naman.**
		Hello. Good morning too.
GINANG SANTOS	:	**Nandiyan po ba si Ginang de la Cruz?**
		Is Mrs. de la Cruz there?
MARIA	:	**Nasa kuwarto po siya. Sino po sila?**
		She is in the bedroom. Who is this please?
GINANG SANTOS	:	**Si Ginang Santos ito. Puwede ko ba siyang makausap?**
		This is Mrs. Santos. Can I speak to her?
MARIA	:	**Sandali lang po.**
		One moment please.

  Bokabolaryo

Study the following words. Some of these words were used in the dialogue while some of them are words that are useful in talking about houses and the things we find in houses. In most cases, appliances and electronic devices are called by their

English names (such as refrigerator, oven, microwave, computer) because there are no indigenous words for them in Filipino.

Mga Salita Tungkol sa Bahay (Words About Houses)

Practice saying these sentences aloud, and study how they are constructed so that you can make your own sentences later.

Kuwarto/Silid-Tulugan	*Bedroom*
Kusina	*Kitchen*
Sala	*Living room*
Silid-kainan/Komedor	*Dining Room*
Banyo	*Bathroom*
Kubeta	*Toilet*
Hardin	*Garden*
Bakuran	*Yard/Area surrounding the house*
	(usually that which is enclosed by a fence)
Garahe	*Garage*
Palapag	*Floors/Stories*
Sahig	*Floor*
Bubong	*Ceiling*
Dingding	*Walls*
Pintuan	*Door*
Tarangkahan	*Gate*
Balkonahe	*Balcony*

Mga Gamit o Bagay sa Loob at Labas ng Bahay (Words About Things Inside and Outside the House)

Mesa	*Table*
Silya/upuan	*Chairs*
Sofa	*Sofa*
Hapag-kainan	*Dining table*
Tokador	*Dresser*
Kalan	*Stove*
Telebisyon	*Television*
Kotse	*Car*

Additional Words on Location

Use **nandito/narito**, **nandiyan/nariyan** and **nandoon/naroon** to answer **nasaan** questions. Use **dito/rito**, **diyan/riyan**, and **doon/roon** to answer **saan** questions.

Nandito/Narito/Dito/Rito	*Here*
Nandiyan/Nariyan/Diyan/Riyan	*There*
Nandoon/Naroon/Doon/Roon	*Over there*

Mga Pangungusap

Practice saying these sentences aloud, to get a feel for how this chapter's vocabulary and grammar work in Filipino.

1. **Nasa kuwarto ni Maria ang computer niya.**	*Maria's computer is in her room.*
2. **Nasa kusina ang kalan.**	*The stove is in the kitchen.*
3. **Nasa hardin ang aso.**	*The dog is in the garden.*
4. **Nandito ang lola ko.**	*My grandmother is here*
5. **Wala rito ang kapatid kong lalaki.**	*My brother is not here.*
6. **May tatlong kuwarto ang bahay namin.**	*There are three bedrooms in our house*
7. **May dalawang kotse sa garahe nina Teresita at Victor.**	*There are two cars in Teresita and Victor's garage.*

  Pagsasanay

Both classroom students and independent learners should practice asking and answering questions. Make sure you practice these questions and answers by both speaking and writing. Independent learners should write at least three questions and answers. Classroom learners should form pairs and ask each other questions.

1. TANONG : **Nasaan ang telebisyon ninyo?**
   SAGOT : **Nasa sala ang telebisyon namin.**

2. TANONG : **Nasaan ang tatay mo?**
   SAGOT : **Nasa kusina ang tatay ko.**

3. TANONG : **Nasaan ang _____?**
   SAGOT : **Nasa _____ ang _____.**

4. TANONG : **Nandiyan ba ang lolo mo?**
   SAGOT : _____.

5. TANONG : _____?
   SAGOT : **Wala rito ang mga pinsan ko.**

6. TANONG : **Ilan ang computer sa bahay mo?**
   SAGOT : _____ .

7. TANONG : _____ ?
   SAGOT : **Dalawa ang kalan sa bahay namin.**

8. TANONG : _____ ?
   SAGOT : _____ .

9. TANONG : _____ ?
   SAGOT : _____ .

10. TANONG : _____ ?
    SAGOT : _____ .

Balik-Aral & Dagdag Aral (Review & Additional Study)

Review the adjectives you have studied in earlier chapters. Then, study the additional adjectives below. You can use these adjectives in describing objects. Remember that it is easier to remember adjectives if you study contrasting words together.

- **Mga Pang-uri na Naglalarawan sa Tao** (Adjectives that Describe a Person)
- **Mga Pang-uri na Naglalarawan sa Bagay** (Adjectives that Describe an Object)
- **Bago – Luma**   *New – Old*
- **Mahal – Mura**   *Expensive – Cheap*
- **Malaki – Maliit**   *Big – Small*
- **Yari/Gawa sa ...**   *Made of ...*
- **...(kahoy, metal, salamin, bato)**   *... (wood, metal, glass, stone)*

Dagdag-Aral sa Mga Pangungusap (Additional Study of Sentences)

1. **Ang maliit na mesa ang nasa kuwarto.**   *It is the small table that is in the room.*
2. **Ang bagong telebisyon ay nasa sala.**   *The big television is in the living room.*
3. **Nasa komedor ang mesa na yari sa kahoy.**   *The table made of wood is in the dining room.*

🔍 Gramatika

Study the information below to improve your Filipino grammar skills.

I. **Gamit ng "ay" at "ang"**

Many learners ask: "What is the difference between using **ay** and **ang** in sentences? When do we know what to use?" Consider the following sentences:

> **Ang itim na pusa ay nasa bakuran.** *The black cat is in the yard.*

This sentence answers the question "**Nasaan ang itim na pusa?**" (*Where is the black cat?*)

> **Ang itim na pusa ang nasa bakuran.** (*It is the black cat that is in the yard.*)

(This answers the question "**Aling pusa ang nasa bakuran?**" *Which cat is in the yard?*)

Thus, when deciding whether to use **ay** or **ang**, think of the following:

A. What question is being asked?

B. What would you like to emphasize?

If you want to emphasize that it is the black cat (not the white cat or the yellow cat) that is in the yard, use **ang**.

If not, using **ay** is fine. Also, you can reverse the word order and say: **Nasa bakuran ang itim na pusa**.

II. Words that Express Location

In the vocabulary list, you studied the following words:

Nandito/Narito/Dito/Rito	*Here*
Nandiyan/Nariyan/Diyan/Riyan	*There*
Nandoon/Naroon/Doon/Roon	*Over There*

There are no differences in meaning between the choices **nandito** and **narito**, **nandiyan** and **nariyan**, **nandoon** and **naroon**, as well as **dito** and **rito**, **diyan** and **riyan**, **doon** and **roon**.

As explained earlier, use **nandito/narito**, **nandiyan/nariyan** and **nandoon/ naroon** to answer **nasaan** questions. Use **dito/rito**, **diyan/riyan**, and **doon/roon** for **saan** questions.

> EXAMPLES: **Nandito ang nanay ko.**
> *My mother is here.* (literally, Here *marker* mother my.)
> **Nakatira ako dito.**
> *I live here.*

But when do we use **d**, and when do we use **r**? Use **d** when the preceding word ends with a consonant and use **r** when the preceding word ends with a vowel.

It is also helpful to know that **d** and **r** (as explained in Appendix 3) used to have only one symbol in the ancient Tagalog script. This indicates that sometimes these would be used interchangeably, and then when reading the script, the Tagalog people just knew by instinct which letter the word referred to.

> EXAMPLE: **Nakasuot ako ng baro't saya dahil Philippine Independence Day ngayon.**
>
> *I am wearing a **baro't saya** because it is Philippine Independence.*

III. Gawa/Yari sa/ng

The words **gawa** and **yari** have the same meaning: "made." With the preposition **sa**, it can mean either "made of" or "made in." With the preposition **ng**, you can refer to the maker of the product. With this use, it is more common to use **gawa** rather than **yari**.

> EXAMPLES: **Yari sa salamin ang mesa.**
>
> *The table is made of glass.*
>
> **Yari sa Piipinas ang mga mesa.**
>
> *The tables are made in the Philippines.*
>
> **Gawa ng Philippine Computer company ang computer ko.**
>
> *My computer is made by the Philippine Computer company.*

  Pagsasanay

Practice these questions and answers by both speaking and writing. Use the given pairs as a guide.

1. TANONG : **Aling pusa ang nasa sala?**
   SAGOT : **Ang puting pusa ang nasa sala.**

2. TANONG : **Aling telebisyon ang nasa kusina?**
   SAGOT : **Ang maliit na telebisyon ang nasa kusina.**

3. TANONG : **Aling _____ ang nasa _____ ?**
   SAGOT : **Ang _____ na _____ ang nasa _____ .**

4. TANONG : **Nandito ba ang nanay mo?**
   SAGOT : _____ .

5. TANONG : **Ano ang yari ng sahig ng bahay mo?**
   SAGOT : **Yari sa kahoy ang sahig ng bahay ko.**

6. TANONG : **Saan yari ang computer mo?**
   SAGOT : **Yari ang computer ko sa** _____ .

7. TANONG : **Sino ang may gawa ng** _____ **mo?**

   SAGOT : **Gawa ng** _____ **ang** _____ **ko.**

8. TANONG : _____?

   SAGOT : _____.

9. TANONG : _____?

   SAGOT : _____.

10. TANONG : _____?

    SAGOT : _____.

Mga Tala Sa Kultura

One can learn a lot about Filipino geography and history by studying Filipino houses. Let us consider two houses: the **bahay kubo** (literally, cube house) and the **bahay na bato** (stone house.)

The **bahay kubo** is made of bamboo and nipa, which are abundant in the Philippines. It is raised so that animals cannot easily come into the house, and so that the family can use the area below the house for storage. It has a sloping roof and large windows to better cope with the tropical heat. Thus, it is a house that takes into consideration the geographical characteristics of the Philippines.

The **bahay na bato** became popular during the Spanish colonial period (1565– 1898). It is a two-story house made of stone and wood, but the living quarters are mainly in the upper floor. The living room/dining room is an open space usually surrounded by the bedrooms. Like the **bahay kubo**, it has large windows but the popular material for these windows are wood and capiz shells. The **bahay na bato** became a symbol of affluence during the Spanish colonial period, thus emphasizing the economic gap between the land-owning Spaniards and few wealthy Filipinos and the indios, the latter term referring to native Filipinos.

Pagbabasa/Pag-Awit

Read or sing the following folk song. The meanings of the new words, many of which refer to vegetables, come after the song.

Folk Song: Bahay Kubo

Bahay kubo, kahit munti
Ang halaman doon, ay sari-sari
Singkamas at talong, sigarilyas at mani
Sitaw, bataw, patani.
Kundol, patola, upo't kalabasa
At saka mayroon pa, labanos, mustasa
Sibuyas, kamatis, bawang, at luya,
Sa paligid-ligid, ay puno ng linga.

Munti	*small*
Halaman	*plants*
Sari-sari	*various*
Singkamas	*turnip*
Talong	*eggplant*
Sigarilyas	*winged bean*
Mani	*peanut*
Sitaw	*string bean*
Bataw	*hyacinth bean*
Patani	*lima bean*
Kundol	*wax goard*
Patola	*luffa*
Upo	*white squash*
Kalabasa	*pumpkin*
Labanos	*radish*
Mustasa	*mustard*
Sibuyas	*onion*
Kamatis	*tomato*
Bawang	*garlic*
Luya	*ginger*
Paligid-ligid	*around*
Puno	*full*
Linga	*sesame seed*

Pagbabasa

Read the following passage, and then answer the questions that follow.

Ang Bago Kong Apartment

Nakatira ako sa bahay ng kapatid ko. Kasama niya sa bahay ang asawa niya, ang dalawa niyang anak, at ang tatlo nilang pusa. May apat na kuwarto sa kanilang bahay at dalawang banyo. Sa kuwarto ko, mayroon akong tokador, telebisyon, at computer.

Sa susunod na linggo, lilipat ako sa isang apartment. Maliit lang ang apartment ko pero may dalawang palapag at dalawang kuwarto. Ilalagay ko sa isang kuwarto ang kama at tokador ko, at sa isang kuwarto, ang computer ko at mga libro. At sa kusina, ilalagay ko ang bago kong microwave.

1. Saan ako nakatira?
2. Sino ang kasama sa bahay ng kapatid ko?
3. Ilan ang kuwarto sa bahay ng kapatid ko?
4. Ano ang alagang hayop ng kapatid ko?
5. Ilan ang banyo sa bahay ng kapatid ko?
6. Ano ang ilalagay ko sa mga kuwarto ko?
7. Ano ang ilalagay ko sa kusina?

Pagsusulat

Using the vocabulary and grammar you have learned, try writing one or two paragraphs in Filipino about the house or apartment you live in.

Paglalagom (Summing Up)

In **Aralin 8**, you have learned:
1. Words about houses and things inside houses,
2. Adjectives that can be used to describe houses and things inside houses,
3. Words that refer to places,
4. Words and phrases that can be used in answering the phone.

You should now be able to:
1. Talk/write about your own home and the things inside it.
2. Answer the telephone.

Sa Kalye, sa Lungsod at sa Nayon
(On the Street, in the City and in Our Village)

  Diyalogo: Nasaan Ang Tindahan ng Prutas?
(Where is the fruit stand?)

Read the dialogue below. After completing this chapter, practice this dialogue using your own information.

MARIA : **Mawalang-galang na ho, nasaan ho ang tindahan ng prutas?**
Excuse me, where is the fruit store?
PULIS : **Ang tindahan ho ng prutas ay nasa tapat ng Treehouse Restaurant.**
The fruit store is across from Treehouse Restaurant.
MARIA : **Malapit ba rito ang tindahan ng prutas?**
Is the fruit store near here?
PULIS : **Oho. Malapit lang dito.**
Yes. It is near here.
MARIA : **Salamat ho.**
Thank you.
PULIS : **Wala hong anuman.**
You're welcome.

  Bokabolaryo

Study the following words. Some of them were used in the dialogue you just read and some of them will be useful when you make your own sentences for your dialogues.

Mga Lugar

Tindahan	*Store*
Tindahan ng Prutas	*Fruit store*
Tindahan ng Bulaklak	*Flower shop*

Tindahan ng Laruan	*Toy store*
Groseri	*Grocery*
Bangko	*Bank*
Ospital	*Hospital*
Restawran	*Restaurant*
Panaderya	*Bakery*
Sinehan	*Movie theater*
Estasyon ng Pulis	*Police station*
Botika	*Drugstore*
Paradahan	*Parking lot*
Bus Stop	*Bus stop*
Eskuwelahan	*School*
Simbahan	*Church*
Aklatan	*Library*
Post Office	*Post office*

Mga Salitang Tumutukoy sa Kinaroroonan at Kinalalagyan ng mga Bagay o Lugar (Words That Describe the Location of a Place or an Object)

Kanan	*Right*
Kaliwa	*Left*
Harap	*Front*
Likod	*Back*
Tapat	*Across*

Mga Pang-uring Tumatalakay sa Lokasyon (Adjectives that Describe a Location)

Malapit	*Near*
Malayo	*Far*

Mga Pangungusap

Practice saying these sentences aloud, to get a feel for how this chapter's vocabulary and grammar work in Filipino.

1. **Nasa tapat ng restawran ang tindahan ng prutas.** *The fruit store is across from the restaurant.*
2. **Nasa harap ng bangko ang bus stop.** *The bus stop is in front of the bank.*
3. **Nasa kanan ng bangko ang restawran.** *The restaurant is on the right of the bank.*

4. **Malapit ang tindahan ng prutas sa simbahan.**   *The fruit store is near the church.*

 ## Pagsasanay

Draw your own street. Make sure you draw blocks or squares to signify a bank, a hospital, a restaurant or other places. Practice these questions and answers by both speaking and writing. Use the earlier pairs as a guide. Independent learners should write at least four questions and answers. Classroom learners should work as pairs and ask each other questions.

1. TANONG : **Nasaan ang panaderya?**
   SAGOT : **Nasa kaliwa ng tindahan ng prutas ang panaderya.**

2. TANONG : **Nasaan ang sinehan?**
   SAGOT : **Nasa kanan ng restawran ang sinehan.**

3. TANONG : **Nasaan ang _____?**
   SAGOT : **Nasa _____ ang _____.**

4. TANONG : **Ano ang nasa tapat ng ospital?**
   SAGOT : _____ ang nasa tapat ng ospital.

5. TANONG : _____ ang nasa _____ ng _____?
   SAGOT : _____ ang nasa _____ ng _____.

6. TANONG : _____?
   SAGOT : _____.

7. TANONG : _____?
   SAGOT : _____.

8. TANONG : **Malapit ba ang bangko sa estasyon ng pulis?**
   SAGOT : _____.

9. TANONG : _____?
   SAGOT : _____.

10. TANONG : _____?
    SAGOT : _____.

11. TANONG : **Ano ang malapit sa eskuwelahan?**
    SAGOT   : **Malapit ang** _____ **sa eskuwelahan.**

12. TANONG : _____ **?**
    SAGOT   : _____ .

13. TANONG : _____ **?**
    SAGOT   : _____ .

  ## Awit

In the classroom, read/sing the following children's song. After singing the four lines of the song, the teacher/leader shouts instruction 1. Everyone follows. Then the song is sung again. After the song, the leader shouts both instructions 1 and 2. This goes on and on until everyone is singing, with arms raised, feet stomping and hips sashaying.

Ang Giyera ni Lapu-Lapu

Ang giyera ni Lapu-lapu	*The war of Lapu-lapu*
Isang mahabang giyera	*Is a long long war.*
Hindi matapos-tapos	*It is never done.*
Ating itutuloy.	*We will continue.*

Leader:
1. **Itaas ang kanang kamay!**   *Raise your right hand!*
2. **Itaas ang kaliwang kamay!**   *Raise your left hand!*
3. **Ipadyak ang kanang paa!**   *Stomp your right foot!*
4. **Ipadyak ang kaliwang paa!**   *Stomp your left foot!*
5. **Kumendeng kendeng!**   *Sashay your hips!*

 ## Gawain

Pagdodrowing (Drawing)
Study the following additional words:

Puno	*Tree*
Ilog	*River*
Palayan	*Ricefield*
Bundok/Kabundukan	*Mountain/s*
Dalampasigan	*Seashore*
Dagat/Karagatan	*Ocean*

Gubat/Kagubatan	*Forest*
Araw	*Sun*
Buwan	*Moon*
Bituin/Tala	*Star*
Ibon	*Bird*
Isda	*Fish*
Hayop	*Animal*
Ibabaw	*Above*
Itaas	*On top*
Gitna	*Center*
Pagitan	*Between*

Draw a house. Include tree/s, a river, a ricefield, a mountain, a dog, a cat, birds and other things near the house.

For independent learners, write a paragraph on the picture that you just drew. Use the new words above, as well as the words expressing location (**harap, tapat, tabi, kanan, kaliwa, ilalim, loob, labas, at ibabaw**). It might be useful to review earlier lessons where you learned about location.

For classroom learners, work in pairs. Give instructions to your partner so that he/she can imagine your drawing. Use words such as "Compare the two drawings."

Use the following questions as your guide in making your drawing, writing sentences, or asking questions.

1. **Nasaan ang mga bundok?**
2. **Ilan ang ibon?**
3. **Nasaan ang mga isda?**
4. **Ano ang nasa kanan ng bahay?**
5. **Nasaan ang pusa?**
6. **Aling hayop ang nasa tabi ng puno?**
7. **Aling hayop ang nasa loob ng bahay**
8. **Ano ang nasa gitna ng drowing mo?**
9. **Ano ang nasa ibabaw ng palayan?**
10. **Ilan ang bituin?**

🔍 Gramatika

Study the information below to improve your Filipino grammar skills.

I. Words with the suffix **-an**

By now, you may have realized that affixes can provide clues about the meaning of a word. For example, as discussed earlier, words that start with **ka-** (such as

kapatid, kaibigan, kapitbahay) signal relationships. Similarly, words that start with **ma-** are usually adjectives (**mabait, maganda, masungit**).

In this chapter, we studied words such as **palayan, kabundukan, tindahan, eskuwelahan**, and **simbahan**. Note that these words end with the suffix **-an**. Thus, we can deduce that these words probably indicate a place.

By being aware of these affixes, it might be easier for you to deduce the meaning of words when reading passages. For example, you now know that the word **simbahan** means church. Later, should you encounter a sentence such as "**Nagsisimba ako**," you can ask yourself, "*What could **nagsisimba** mean?*" Recognizing the prefix **nag-**, you could conclude that **nagsisimba** is probably a verb meaning "to go to church."

Similarly, in this chapter, you studied the word **isda** (*fish*). Ask yourself: what could **palaisdaan** mean? If you answered fishpond, you are correct.

II.   Nasa/Nasa Ibabaw/Nasa Itaas

In an earlier chapter, you studied the words **nasa ibabaw**: for instance, "**Nasa ibabaw ng mesa ang libro**." (*The book is on the table* or *The book is on top of the table*) (literally, On top *marker* table *marker* book).

In Tagalog/Filipino, the sentence means *on, on top of,* and *above*. Isn't this confusing? It is, but only for non-native speakers. As I explain at length in Appendix 3 on the history of Tagalog/Filipino orthography, one characteristic of the Tagalog/Filipino language is its "ambivalence." Two letters are signified by one character. Similarly, people say "No, thank you" when offered some food even when they mean "Please ask me again."

In this chapter, we use **nasa ibabaw** to mean *above*. Thus, the birds can be flying **sa ibabaw ng puno** (above, not on top of, a tree).

This is further complicated by the practical question: How then do we say that a cat, for example, is on top of the tree? The answer would be "**nasa itaas**." This means that the object "is high up something."

Should you be confused, it might be better to simply use **nasa** when referring to things that are on top of something, to use **nasa itaas** to refer to things that are high up, and to use **nasa ibabaw** to refer to things that are above.

EXAMPLES: **Nasa mesa ang aso.**   *The dog is on the table.*
Nasa itaas ng puno ang pusa.   *The cat is high up the tree.*
Nasa ibabaw ng puno ang ibon.   *The bird is above the tree.*

Mga Tala Sa Kultura

During the Spanish colonial period in the Philippines (1565–1898), plazas or town centers were created. At the center of the town was a rectangular piece of land used as a park and a place where people would gather for festivities. Around it were the church, the largest, most imposing structure; government buildings such as the office of the **gobernadorcillio** ("little" governor heading the town) and the police station; schools or hospitals; and houses of privileged families. One's economic status was determined by the proximity of one's house to the plaza. In Tagalog/Filipino, the term **nasa ilalim ng kampana ng simbahan**, "under the bells of the church," meant that these people were Christians, and thus recognized the authority of the church. The term implicated the "non-Christians" and considered them as **pagano** (pagans), a derogatory term used for indigenous peoples who did not convert to Christianity and thus retreated into the mountains.

According to cultural historian Bienvenido Lumbera in *Philippine Literature: A History and Anthology,* 1997, this dichotomy between the Christian and the non-Christian, the urbanized and the non-urbanized, created a wedge among the Filipinos. This also resulted in a different culture for the **taga-bayan** (from the town or urban center) and the **taga-bukid** (from the rural village). The former tried to imitate the colonizer's culture in everything from the **bahay na bato** (stone houses) with its European furnishings to food, with Spanish dishes such as **paella, mechado,** and **afritada**, while looking down at the ways of the indigenous people.

This tension is portrayed in the nineteenth-century Tagalog **sainete** or short comic play *La India elegante y el Negrito amante* (The Elegant India and the Negrito Lover), n.d., by Francisco Baltazar. In this **sainete**, Capitan Toming is an Aeta, also known as the Negrito, one of the Philippines' approximately sixty ethnolinguistic groups. Characterized by their dark skin, short height, and kinky hair, and portrayed disparagingly in early nineteenth-century photographs, the Aetas have long struggled with discrimination in Philippine society. In Baltazar's play, Capitan Toming tries to impress the Tagala (from the Tagalog region) Menangue by discarding his indigenous loincloth, wearing the tagabayan's **barong Tagalog** (the shirt of the Tagalog) and speaking in Spanish, the language of the colonizer and the educated class. However, toward the end of the play, she recognizes that it is the **kalooban** or one's heart that is more important.

The play is thus an indictment of Filipinos who discarded their indigenous culture to embrace that of the colonizers.

 Pagbabasa

Read the following passage, and then answer the questions that follow. Study the following new words so that you can understand the passage better.

Taong 1967	*Year 1967*
nanonood	*watch*
Pasko	*Christmas*
sine	*movie*
bumibili	*buy*

manok	*chicken*
naaalala	*remember*

Cubao

Taong 1967, at nag-aaral ako ng kindergarten sa Stella Maris College. Nasa Cubao ang eskuwelahan ko. Malaki ang eskuwelahan ko, at maganda at malinis ang Cubao. Nakasuot kaming mga estudyante ng puting blusa na may "sailor collar" at asul na palda. May maliit na simbahan sa loob ng eskuwelahan namin.

Malapit sa eskuwelahan namin ang maraming tindahan at restawran. Bumibili kami ng school supplies sa Vasquez at ng sapatos sa Gregg's, kumakain ng siopao at mami sa restawrang Ma Mon Luk at ng manok sa Kobe chicken; at nanonood ng sine sa sinehang New Frontier. Sa Pasko, nanonood kami ng Christmas display sa C.O.D. Department store at ng "Holiday on Ice" sa Araneta Coliseum. Madumi at maingay na ngayon ang Cubao, pero ito ang Cubao na naaalala ko.

---

1. Saan ako nag-aaral ng kindergarten?
2. Nasaan ang eskuwelahan ko?
3. Ano ang suot ng mga estudyante?
4. Ano ang binibili namin sa Vasquez?
5. Saan kami kumakain ng mami at siopao?
6. Nasaan ang simbahan?

🖉 Pagsusulat (Writing)

Using the vocabulary and grammar you have learned, try writing one or two paragraphs in Filipino.

🚩 Paglalagom (Summing Up)

In **Aralin 9**, you have learned:
1. Words about places in your neigborhood,
2. Asking and answering questions about location.

You should now be able to:
1. Talk and write about your community.
2. Talk and write about location.

Pamimili (Shopping)

  Diyalogo: Pagbili ng Prutas (Buying fruits)

Read the dialogue below. After completing this chapter, practice this dialogue using your own information.

Juan	:	**Pabili nga ho ng mangga.**
		Please let me buy some mangoes.
Tindera	:	**Aling mangga?**
		Which mangoes?
Juan	:	**Iyon hong hinog na mangga. Magkano ho?**
		The ripe mangoes. How much?
Tindera	:	**Sitenta pesos isang kilo. Matamis 'yan!**
		Seventy pesos a kilo. That's sweet!
Juan	:	**Meron ho bang tawad?**
		Is there a discount?
Tindera	:	**May tawad. Sisenta pesos na lang.**
		There is a discount. [You can pay] just sixty pesos.
Juan	:	**Heto ho ang isang daang piso.**
		Here is a hundred pesos.
Tindera	:	**Heto ho ang sukli niyo.**
		Here is your change.
Juan	:	**Salamat ho.**
		Thank you.

Diyalogo Variation

After practicing the dialogue above, do it again with the variation below.

JUAN : **Mawalang galang na ho, kulang ho yata ang sukli niyo.**
Excuse me, perhaps the change is not enough.
TINDERA : **Pasensiya na kayo. Heto ho ang tamang sukli.**
Sorry. Here is the correct change.

  Bokabolaryo

Study the following words. Some of them were used in the dialogue you just read and some of them will be useful when you make your own sentences for your dialogues.

Mga Prutas sa Pilipinas

Study the Tagalog/Filipino names of these Philippine fruits. Some of them do not have English names.

Mangga	*Mango*
Saging	*Banana*
Lansones	*Lanzones*
Chico	*Chico*
Atis	*Sugar apple*
Rambutan	*Rambutan (fruit of an evergreen bushy tree)*
Langka	*Jackfruit*
Durian	*Durian*
Star apple	*Star apple*
Pinya	*Pineapple*
Bayabas	*Guavas*
Buko	*Young coconut*
Niyog	*Old coconut*

Iba pang Prutas (Other Fruits)

Note that except for apples, most fruits from temperate countries retain their English names.

Mansanas	*Apple*
Orange	*Orange*
Cherries	*Cherries*

Mga Pang-uri na Naglalarawan sa Prutas
(Adjectives That Describe Fruits)

Hilaw	*Unripe*
Hinog	*Ripe*
Manibalang	*Between unripe and ripe*
Matamis	*Sweet*
Maasim	*Sour*
Mapakla	*Acrid*
Lasa	*Taste*

Mga Pandiwa (Verbs)

Bumibili	*Buying*
Nagtitinda	*Selling*

Mga Salita sa Pamimili (Words Used in Shopping)

Bayad	*Payment*
Sukli	*Change*
Tawad	*Discount*
Kulang	*Lacking*

Mga Halimbawang Salita na tumutukoy sa Pera
(Words That Describe Money)

Piso	**Peso** (use when using indigenous system of counting)
Pesos	**Peso** (use when using the Spanish-derived system of counting)
Sentimo	**Centavos** (use when using the indigenous system of counting)
Sentimos	**Centavos** (use when using the Spanish-derived system of counting)

Iba Pang Salita (Other Words)

Yata	*Perhaps*

Mga Halimbawang Pangungusap

Practice saying these sentences aloud, to get a feel for how this chapter's vocabulary and grammar work in Filipino.

1. **Bumibili si Juan ng mga mangga.**
   Juan is buying mangoes.
   (literally, Buying Juan *marker* mango.)

2. **Mga mangga ang binibili ni Juan.**
   Juan is buying mangoes.
   (literally, Mangoes *marker* buying *marker* Juan.)

3. **Nagtitinda ang tindera ng mga prutas.**
   The saleswoman is selling fruits.
   (literally, Selling *marker* saleswoman *marker* fruits.)

4. **Mga prutas ang tinitinda ng tindera.**
   The saleswoman is selling fruits.
   (Literally, Fruits *marker* selling *marker* saleswoman.)

5. **Sitenta pesos ang isang kilo ng mangga.**
   A kilo of mangoes is seventy pesos.

6. **Matamis ang manggang hinog.**
   Ripe mangoes are sweet.

 Pagsasanay

Practice these questions and answers by both speaking and writing. Use some of the pairs as a guide. Classroom learners can form pairs and ask each other questions.

1. TANONG : **Sino ang bumibili ng mangga?**
   SAGOT : **Bumibili si Juan ng mangga.**

2. TANONG : **Sino ang nagtitinda ng prutas?**
   SAGOT : **Nagtitinda ang tindera ng prutas.**

3. TANONG : **Sino ang bumibili ng pinya?**
   SAGOT : _____.

4. TANONG : **Ano ang binibili mo?**
   SAGOT : **Bumibili ako ng lanzones.**

5. TANONG : **Ano ang binibili ni** _____?
   SAGOT : _____.

6. TANONG : **Ano ang binibili mo sa tindahan?**
   SAGOT   : **Bumibili ako ng** _____.

7. TANONG : _____?
   SAGOT   : **Bumibili si** _____ **ng pinya.**

8. TANONG : _____?
   SAGOT   : _____.

9. TANONG : **Ano ang tinitinda ni** _____?
   SAGOT   : _____ **ang** _____ **ni** _____.

10. TANONG : _____?
    SAGOT   : _____.

11. TANONG : **Magkano ang lanzones?**
    SAGOT   : _____ **ang isang kilo ng lanzones.**

12. TANONG : **Magkano ang** _____?
    SAGOT   : _____ **ang** _____.

13. TANONG : _____?
    SAGOT   : _____.

14. TANONG : **Magkano ang sukli ni Juan?**
    SAGOT   : _____ **ang sukli ni** _____.

15. TANONG : _____?
    SAGOT   : _____.

★ Gawain (Activity)

Classroom learners can play the following game as a role-play. Individual learners can also practice by looking at the dialogue studied at the beginning of the chapter and writing a short dialogue of their own by modifying it as they choose.

Tinda-tindahan (Playing store)

Students play "store" acting as sellers and buyers. The teacher can assign half of the class as sellers (working in pairs), and the other half as buyers (also working in pairs). Each pair of sellers sell a kind of fruit, and determine the price of what they sell.

🔍 Gramatika

I. Conjugating the Verbs **Bili** and **Tinda**

Following the formulas you have learned earlier, let's conjugate the verbs **bili** and **tinda** when the focus is on the subject or the doer of the action.

Completed	Incompleted	Contemplated
Bumili	Bumibili	Bibili
Nagtinda	Nagtitinda	Magtitinda

Now, let's use thse verbs in sentences. The words in parethesis are words whose equivalents in Filipino have not yet been taught. They are there, however, for clarity, so you can imagine the use of the verbs. In Tagalog/Filipino, you will notice that the direct objects (in this case **saging**, **prutas**, **mangga**) are not in plural form. In conversational Filipino, it is not important to specify this.

However, in the English translation, it is important to be specific such that we need to use the plural form (banana*s*, fruit*s*, mango*es*) since in reality, one does not really buy just one banana. When using English terms that have no equivalent in Filipino ("cakes," "cookies"), you can retain the plural form.

Note the use of the marker **ang** before the subject and the marker **ng** before the direct objects.

EXAMPLES: **Bumili ang babae ng saging.**

yesterday (The woman bought bananas.) (literally, Bought *marker* woman *marker* banana.)

Bumibili ang babae ng prutas.

every day (The woman is buying fruits.) (literally, Buying *marker* woman *marker* fruit.)

Bibili ang babae ng mangga.

tomorrow (The woman will buy mangoes.) (literally, Will buy *marker* woman *marker* mango.)

Nagtinda siya ng cake.

yesterday (She sold cakes.) (literally, Sold she *marker* cake.)

Nagtitinda siya ng pastries.

every day (She is selling pastries.) (literally, Selling she *marker* pastries.)

Magtitinda siya ng cookies.

tomorrow (She will sell cookies.) (literally, Will sell she *marker* cookies.)

Now, let us practice these verbs as used when the focus is on the object. Note that there are sometimes two ways of using the verb **tinda**. For example, consider

itinitinda and **tinitinda**. **Itinitinda** is the correct and formal version that you need to use in writing. However, when speaking, you will often hear native speakers just say **tinitinda** without the "**i**" before the word.

Completed	Incompleted	Contemplated
Binili	Binibili	Bibilhin
Itininda/Tininda	Itinitinda/Tinitinda	Ititinda

Let's use these verbs in sentences.

EXAMPLES: **Saging ang binili niya.**

yesterday (literally, Banana *marker* bought she.)

Prutas ang binibili niya.

every day (literally, Fruit *marker* buys she.)

Mangga ang bibilhin niya.

tomorrow (literally, Mango *marker* will buy she.)

II. The Word **Yata**

In the dialogue you read, you may have noticed the use of **yata** by Juan:

JUAN   : **Mawalang galang na ho, kulang ho yata ang sukli niyo.**

Excuse me, perhaps the change is not enough.

TINDERA : **Pasensiya na kayo. Heto ho ang tamang sukli.**

Sorry. Here is the correct change.

Why use **yata?** Because it is the polite way. Remember that politeness is an important aspect in Filipino culture. Thus, it is not proper to accuse the seller. By using **yata** (perhaps), Juan acknowledges that he might be making a mistake and that the seller might also have given him the wrong change unintentionally.

III. The Words **Bili** and **Halaga**

When shopping, the words **bili** and **halaga** both refer to the cost of the item. Let's look at some examples.

EXAMPLES: **Magkano ang bili mo sa mangga?**

How much did you buy the mangoes for? (literally, How much *marker* buy you *preposition* mangoes?)

Magkano ang halaga ng mangga?

How much is the cost of the mangoes? (literally, How much *marker* cost *marker* mango?)

Moreover, you can also choose to delete the words **ang halaga** and simply say:

Magkano ang mangga?

How much are the mangoes? (literally, How much *marker* mango?)

IV. **Iyan** and **'Yan**

You already know the demonstrative pronoun **iyan** meaning that. When speaking, and when writing dialogues, **iyan** becomes **'yan**.

V. The Question Word "**Bakit**" and "**Dahil**"

In the dialogue you read, the **Tindera** (*Saleswoman*) says "**Matamis 'yan!**" (*That's sweet!*) as she urges the Juan to buy the yellow mangoes.

This brings us to the question: how then do we ask and answer questions related to purpose. We use the question word **bakit** (*why*) and the word **dahil** (*because*).

TANONG   : **Bakit bumili si Juan ng dilaw na mangga?**
Why did Juan buy yellow mangoes? (literally, Why bought marker Juan marker yellow linker mango?)

SAGOT   : **Dahil matamis ang dilaw na mangga.**
Because yellow mangoes are sweet. (literally, Because sweet marker yellow linker mangoes.)

OR

SAGOT   : **Dahil gusto ni Juan ng matamis na mangga.**
Because Juan likes sweet mangoes. (literally, Because like marker Juan marker sweet linker mangoes.)

 Pagsasanay

In these sets of questions, the objective is to try to approximate a conversation between you and a "friend." Try to practice the question words you have learned in a practical way. Always think of "follow-up questions" to keep the conversation running. Examples are given for you to analyze and use as a guide.

1. TANONG : **Saan ka bumili ng prutas?**
   SAGOT   : **Bumili ako ng prutas sa Berkeley Bowl.**
   TANONG : **Anong prutas ang binili mo?**
   SAGOT   : **Saging ang binili ko.**
   TANONG : **Magkano ang bili mo sa saging?**
   SAGOT   : **Beinte pesos ang isang kilo ng saging.**
   TANONG : **Bakit ka bumili ng saging?**
   SAGOT   : **Dahil matamis ang saging.**

2. TANONG : **Saan** _____?
   SAGOT   : _____.
   TANONG : **Anong** _____?
   SAGOT   : _____.

TANONG : _____ ?

SAGOT   : _____ **pesos ang** _____ .

TANONG : **Bakit** _____ ?

SAGOT   : **Dahil** _____ .

3. TANONG : _____ ?

   SAGOT   : _____ .

   TANONG : _____ ?

   SAGOT   : _____ .

   TANONG : _____ ?

   SAGOT   : _____ .

   TANONG : _____ ?

   SAGOT   : _____ .

4. TANONG : **Sino ang bumili ng pinya?**

   SAGOT   : _____ .

   TANONG : **Magkano ang halaga ng pinya?**

   SAGOT   : _____ .

   TANONG : **Ilang kilo ng pinya ang binili niya?**

   SAGOT   : _____ .

   TANONG : _____ ?

   SAGOT   : _____ .

5. TANONG : _____ ?

   SAGOT   : **Si** _____ **ang bumili ng** _____ .

   TANONG : _____ ?

   SAGOT   : **Bumili siya ng** _____ **sa** _____ .

   TANONG : **Ano ang halaga ng isang kilo ng** _____ ?

   SAGOT   : _____ **ang isang** _____ **ng** _____ .

   TANONG : _____ ?

   SAGOT   : _____ .

6. TANONG : _____ ?

   SAGOT   : _____ .

   TANONG : _____ ?

   SAGOT   : _____ .

   TANONG : _____ ?

   SAGOT   : _____ .

   TANONG : _____ ?

   SAGOT   : _____ .

Mga Tala Sa Kultura

When buying fruits and produce in the Philippines, one can go to a supermarket or to the more popular **palengke** or open-air "wet market." In Metro Manila, among the most popular **palengkes** are Farmers' Market and Nepa Q-Mart in Quezon City, and Central Market and Divisoria in Manila.

Why is it called a wet market? While most parts of the market are dry, some parts, such as the fish-selling area, are literally wet because of the constant cleaning of the stalls.

Wet markets are known for their fresh items; in most cases fish, shellfish, chicken and meat are delivered at dawn, straight from the ocean or the farms. Prices are also relatively low.

While most sellers sell their items by the kilogram, some also make small piles called the **tumpok**. One **tumpok** for example of chiles can cost a certain amount. Fruit sellers sometimes make sign indicating where the fruit is from, taking advantage of the popularity of a specific town known for a specific fruit. For example, mangoes from Cebu are popular, and the best lanzones comes from Paete. There are also signs that urge the buyer to taste the fruit by saying **"Libre tikim"** (It is free to have a taste of the fruit).

In recent years, the **tiangge** or farmers' market, usually held in parks or other open spaces, has been extremely popular. One of the open-air **tiangges** is the one near the Lung Center. Here, sellers sell all kinds of wares from baked goods, delicacies, meat, herbal medicine, cooked food, and fruits from the sellers' own farms.

In both the **palengke** and the **tiangge**, it is customary to bargain for a better price. The discount is called "**tawad**." For many, it is less about saving money than it is about feeling successful at the art of bargaining.

 ## Pagbabasa

Read the following passage, and then answer the questions that follow. This popular legend (rewritten here using simpler words) was among the many legends, myths, epics, and folklore compiled by Damiana Eugenio in the book *The Myths, Volume II* of the Philippine Folk Literature Series.

Before reading, here are some words that will help you understand the more difficult parts:

Alamat	*Legend*
Hari	*King*
Palasyo	*Palace*
Noong unang panahon	*Once upon a time*
Isang araw	*One day*

Nakita	*Saw*
Nang	here used for contracted two linkers "**na na**"; also used as linker between verbs and adverbs
Sundalo	*Soldiers*
Sinabi	*Said*
Nahulog	*Dropped*
Mula	*From*
Korona	*Crown*

Ang Alamat ng Bayabas

Noong unang panahon, may isang hari. Nakatira ang hari sa isang malaking palasyo. Maraming puno ng mga prutas sa bakuran ng palasyo, pero ayaw ng hari na ibigay ang prutas sa ibang tao. Kanya ang mga prutas; walang ibang tao na kumakain ng mga ito.

Isang araw, nakatayo ang hari sa balkonahe ng palasyo. Nakita niya ang mga ibon at kumakain sila ng mga prutas ng puno. Sabi niya sa mga sundalo, "Paalisin ninyo ang mga ibon!" Ayaw ng mga sundalo dahil gusto nila ang mga ibon. Pero ginawa nila ang sinabi ng hari.

Isang araw, nasa hardin ang hari. Nahulog ang isang buko mula sa puno ng niyog. Wala nang nakakita sa hari.

Isang araw, nakita ng mga tao ang isang puno. May mga prutas ang puno. Maliit at kulay berde ang mga prutas, at may korona ito. Bayabas ang ibinigay nilang pangalan sa prutas.

1. Saan nakatira ang hari?
2. Kanino ang mga prutas?
3. Saan nakatayo ang hari?
4. Bakit ayaw ng mga sundalo na paalisin ang mga ibon?
5. Ano ang nahulog mula sa puno?
6. Ano ang kulay ng mga prutas?
7. Ano ang binigay nilang pangalan sa mga prutas.

✏ Pagsusulat (Writing)

Try writing your own paragraphs about shopping. Use the words on location as well as adjectives to make your own sentences. Read the two examples given, and write about your own shopping experience.

Halimbawa 1 (Example 1):
Ang tindahan ng prutas ay nasa tapat ng Treehouse Restaurant. Bumibili ng mangga si Juan. Sitenta pesos ang isang kilo ng mangga. Matamis ang mangga.

Halimbawa 2
Ang panaderya ay nasa kanan ng bangko. Bumili ng pandesal si Maria. Apat na piso ang isang pandesal. Masarap ang pandesal.

(**Pandesal**: a popular type of bread; literally, bread of salt)

⚑ Paglalagom (Summing Up)

In **Aralin 10**, you have:
1. Learned new words that can be used in shopping and bargaining,
2. Practiced conjugating verbs,
3. Learned more about actor/subject and object focus.

You should now be able to:
1. Do a shopping role-play.
2. Keep up a short conversation using question words such as **ano**, **saan**, **magkano**, and **bakit**.

Pagpunta sa Eskuwelahan (Going to School)

  Diyalogo: Pagpunta sa Eskuwelahan (Going to school)

Read the dialogue below. After completing this chapter, practice this dialogue using your own information.

MARIA : **Pedro! Ano ang hinihintay mo?**
Pedro! What are you waiting for?

PEDRO : **Ang jeepney papuntang unibersidad. Ikaw, saan ka pupunta?**
The jeepney going to the university. What about you, where are you going?

MARIA : **Pupunta ako sa opisina ko sa Makati.**
I am going to my office in Makati.

PEDRO : **Paano ka pupunta sa Makati?**
How are you going to Makati?

MARIA : **Sasakay ako ng tren.**
I will ride the train.

PEDRO : **Magkano ang pamasahe mula rito hanggang Makati?**
How much is the fare from here to Makati?

MARIA : **Trenta pesos.**
Thirty pesos.

PEDRO : **Sige. Heto na ang jeepney ko.**
Okay, bye. Here is my jeepney.

MARIA : **Sige.**
Bye.

Bokabolaryo

Study the following words. Some of them were used in the dialogue you just read and some of them will be useful when you make your own sentences for your dialogues.

Mga Salita Tungkol sa mga Sasakyan (Words about Transportation)

Study the Tagalog/Filipino names of these Philippine fruits. Some of them do not have English names.

Jeepney/Dyip	A uniquely Filipino vehicle made from surplus army jeeps
Bus	*Bus*
Tren	*Train*
Kotse	*Car*
Bisikleta	*Bicycle*
Trak	*Truck*
Traysikel	*Tricycle* (a means of transportation; using either a motorcycle or a bicycle, and a sidecar)
Taksi	*Taxi*
Eroplano	*Airplane*
Bangka	*Small Boat*
Barko	*Large Boat*

Mga Pandiwa Tungkol sa Pagbibiyahe (Verbs used in Travelling)

Biyahe	*Travel*
Pagbibiyahe	*Travelling*
Pumupunta	*Go/Come*
Sumasakay	*Ride*
Nagmamaneho	*Drive*
Naglalakad	*Walk*
Nagbibisikleta	*Ride a bicycle*

Iba Pang mga Salita (Other Words)

Pamasahe	*Fare*
Mula	*From*
Hanggang	*To*
Paano	*Question word; How*
Sige	*Goodbye* (earlier studied to mean, "okay")
Estasyon ng tren	*Train Station*
Paliparan/Airport	*Airport*
Daungan/Pier	*Pier*

Mga Pangungusap

Practice saying these sentences aloud, to get a feel for how this chapter's vocabulary and grammar work in Filipino.

1. **Sumasakay si Pedro ng jeepney papuntang unibersidad.**

   Pedro rides the jeepney going to the university. (literally, Rides *marker* Pedro *marker* jeepney going *marker* university.)

2. **Nagmamaneho si Julian papunta sa opisina.**

   Julian drives to the office. (literally, Drives *marker* Julian going to office.)

3. **Nasa harap ng tindahan ng prutas ang jeepney stop.**

   The jeepney stop is in front of the fruit store. (literally, In front *marker* store *linker* fruit *marker* jeepney stop.)

4. **Trenta pesos ang pamasahe mula dito hanggang Makati.**

   The fare from here to Makati is thirty pesos. (literally, Thirty pesos *marker* fare from here to Makati.)

  Pagsasanay

Practice these questions and answers by both speaking and writing. Use the earlier pairs as a guide. Independent learners should write at least four questions and answers. Classroom learners should work as pairs and ask each other questions.

1. TANONG : **Paano pumupunta si Pedro sa unibersidad?**
   SAGOT : **Sumasakay siya ng jeepney papuntang unibersidad.**

2. TANONG : **Paano pumupunta si** _____ **sa** _____?
   SAGOT : _____.

3. TANONG : _____?
   SAGOT : **Nagbibisikleta siya papuntang** _____.

4. TANONG : **Paano ka pumupunta sa** _____?
   SAGOT : _____.

5. TANONG : _____?
   SAGOT : _____.

6. TANONG : _____?
   SAGOT : _____.

7. TANONG : **Nasaan ang jeepney stop?**
   SAGOT : _____.

8. TANONG : **Nasa anong kalye ang malapit na bus stop sa bahay mo?**
   SAGOT : **Nasa kalye** _____ **ang malapit na bus stop.**

9. TANONG : _____?
   SAGOT : **Nasa kalye** _____ **ang malapit na Estasyon ng tren.**

10. TANONG : _____?
    SAGOT : _____.

11. TANONG : _____?
    SAGOT : _____.

12. TANONG : **Magkano ang pamasahe mula** _____ **hanggang** _____?
    SAGOT : _____ **ang pamasahe mula** _____
    hanggang _____.

13. TANONG : _____?
    SAGOT : _____ **ang pamasahe mula** _____
    hanggang _____.

14. TANONG : _____?
    SAGOT : _____.

15. TANONG : _____?
    SAGOT   : _____.

🔍 Gramatika

Study the information below to improve your Filipino grammar skills.

I. The verbs **sakay**, **lakad**, and **maneho**
    The verbs **sakay** (*ride*), **lakad** (*walk*) and **maneho** (*drive*) are usually used in sentences with the focus on the subject. They can be conjugated this way:

Completed	Incompleted	Contemplated
sumakay	sumasakay	sasakay
naglakad	naglalakad	maglalakad
nagmaneho	nagmamaneho	magmamaneho

Here are examples of how these verbs can be used in sentences. The words in parenthesis are words whose equivalents in Filipino have not yet been taught. However, they are useful in imagining the time line of the action. Note the use of the marker **ang** before the subject and the marker **ng** before the object.

EXAMPLES: **Sumakay ang lalaki ng bus.**
(yesterday) (The man took a bus.) (literally, Rode *marker* man *marker* bus.)
Sumasakay ang babae ng tren.
(every day) (The woman takes the train.) (literally, Rides *marker* woman *marker* train.)
Sasakay siya ng eroplano.
(tomorrow) (He/She will ride a plane.) (literally, Will ride he/she *marker* plane.)
Naglakad ang bata papuntang eskuwelahan.
(yesterday) (The child walked going to school.) (literally, Walked *marker* child going to school.)
Naglalakad ang mga estudyante papuntang eskuwelahan.
(every day) (The students walk to school.) (literally, Walking *marker* students going *marker* school.)
Maglalakad ako papuntang opisina.
(tomorrow) (I will walk to the office.) (literally, Will walk I going to the office.)

Nagmaneho siya ng kotse.
(yesterday) (He/she drove a car.)
Nagmamaneho siya ng Honda.
(every day) (He/she drives a Honda.)
Magmamaneho siya ng trak.
(tomorrow) (He/she will drive a truck.)

The verbs **sakay** and **maneho** can also be used in sentences where the focus is on the object. Affixes such as **in** and **an** are used.

Completed	Incompleted	Contemplated
Sinakyan	Sinasakyan	Sasakyan
Minaneho	Minamaneho	Imamaneho

EXAMPLES: **Bus numero 45 ang sinakyan ko.**
I took Bus number 45. (literally, Bus number 45 *marker* rode I.)
Eroplano ang sinasakyan ko papuntang Pilipinas.
I take the plane going to Philippines. (literally, Plane *marker* ride I going to Philippines.)
Taksi ang sasakyan ko papuntang airport.
I will take a taxi going to the airport. (literally, Taxi *marker* will ride I going to airport.)

II. **Ng and Sa**

Using the words **ng** and **sa** can be confusing because in some cases, they can be used interchangeably. For example, we can say:

EXAMPLES: **Sumakay ako ng taksi papuntang airport.**
I took a taxi going to the airport.
Sumakay ako ng taksi papunta sa airport.
I took a taxi going to the airport.

In the first sentence, the words **papunta** and **ng** are contracted, resulting in the word **papuntang**. But when do we use **ng**, when do we use **sa**, and when are the two interchangeable?

The word **ng** has several uses: as a marker for direct objects when the focus is on the doer of the action; as a marker for the doer of the action when the focus is on the object; to show possession; and as a preposition.

It is for the last use (that of a preposition) that we can interchange **ng** with **sa**. Why? Because **sa** is a preposition that can be used to mean *to, for, at, in, on, over,* and *through.*

Look again at the sample sentences above. Make sure that you contract only **ng (papuntang)** and not **sa**.

III. **Pupunta** and **Papunta**

Because the words **pupunta** and **papunta** seem similar, they can easily be confused by learners. Remember that **pupunta** means *going* and **papunta** is followed by a preposition and then the location. For example:

EXAMPLES: **Pupunta si Pedro sa unibersidad.**
Pedro is going to the university.
Sasakay si Pedro ng bus papunta sa unibersidad.
Pedro will ride a bus going to the university.

  Pagsasanay

Using what you have learned in the grammar section, practice asking and answering questions. Use the earlier pairs as a guide. Independent learners should write their own questions and answers. Classroom learners should work as pairs and ask each other questions.

Remember that the questions can also be grouped to simulate a conversation. This way, you can learn how to ask follow-up questions.

1. TANONG : **Paano ka pumupunta sa opisina?**
   SAGOT : **Sumasakay ako ng bus.**
   TANONG : **Saan ka sumasakay ng bus?**
   SAGOT : **Sumasakay ako ng bus sa tapat ng restawran.**
   TANONG : **Anong bus ang sinasakyan mo?**
   SAGOT : **Sumasakay ako sa bus na 52L.**
   TANONG : **Magkano ang pamasahe mula bahay mo hanggang opisina?**
   SAGOT : _____ .

2. TANONG : **Paano ka pupunta sa airport?**
   SAGOT : _____ .
   TANONG : **Saan ka sasakay ng** _____ ?
   SAGOT : _____ .
   TANONG : **Anong** _____ **ang** _____ **mo?**
   SAGOT : _____ .
   TANONG : _____ ?
   SAGOT : **Isang daang piso ang pamasahe papunta sa airport.**

3. TANONG : _____ ?
   SAGOT   : _____ .
   TANONG : _____ ?
   SAGOT   : _____ .
   TANONG : _____ ?
   SAGOT   : _____ .
   TANONG : _____ ?
   SAGOT   : _____ .

Mga Tala Sa Kultura

One of the most popular means of transportation in the Philippines is the jeepney. Originally made from surplus army vehicles used in World War II, it has in recent years taken on more modern looks from local manufacturers; been built using second-hand Japanese trucks; and even become more green-friendly by using alternative fuel, such as electricity. A jeepney can seat between fourteen to sixteen passengers.

What the jeepney is especially known for, however, is its decoration, which ranges from miniature horses perched on top of hoods, to vibrantly-colored paintings of cartoon characters or the children of the jeepney owner, to elaborately written names or sayings. Occasionally, you may even see religious figurines found near the driver's seat.

Thus, the jeepney is a bearer of "street art," accessible to the masses whether they ride the jeepney or whether they simply enjoy seeing its humor and colorful designs.

  Pagbabasa

Read the following passage, and then answer the questions that follow. Study the words below to better understand the short short story:

Na naman	*Again*
Kaninang umaga	*This morning*
Masayang-masaya	*Very happy*
Biyahe	*Travel*

Biyahe

Mula sa bahay niya, sumakay si Jose ng tricycle papunta sa Philcoa. Doon may mga jeepney papunta ng Quezon Boulevard. Mula sa Quezon Boulevard, sumakay siya ng tren papuntang Pasay, at pagkatapos, sumakay na naman siya ng jeepney. Mula sa kalye, naglakad siya papuntang Ninoy Aquino International Airport.

Kaninang umaga, sumakay ang nanay niya ng eroplano mula sa Hong Kong. Nagtatrabaho doon ang nanay niya. Isa itong "domestic worker." Nakatayo si Jose sa airport. Darating ang nanay niya. Masayang-masaya siya.

1. Ano ang sinakyan ni Jose papuntang Philcoa?
2. Saan siya sumakay ng tren?
3. Saan papunta ang tren?
4. Sino ang sumakay ng eroplano?
5. Saan nakatayo si Jose?

✎ Pagsusulat (Writing)

Try writing your own paragraph using the words you have learned. You may want to talk about how you go to school or to work.

⚑ Paglalagom (Summing Up)

In **Aralin 11**, you have learned:
1. Words you can use to talk about transportation and travelling,
2. How to use the question word **paano**,
3. The use of **ng** and **sa** as prepositions.

You should now be able to:
1. Talk about how you get around the community.
2. Ask and answer questions about travelling.

Pagdating at Pag-alis (Arrivals and Departures)

  Diyalogo: Anong Oras Na? (What Time Is It?)

Read the dialogue below. After completing this chapter, practice this dialogue using your own information.

JUAN : **Mawalang galang na ho, anong oras na po?**
Excuse me, what time is it?

BABAE : **Alas-tres kinse na po ng hapon.**
It is three fifteen in the afternoon.

JUAN : **Salamat ho.**
Thank you.

BABAE : **Wala hong anuman.**
You are welcome.

  Diyalogo: Variation

JUAN : **Mawalang galang na po, anong oras na po?**
Excuse me, what time is it?

BABAE : **Pasensiya na kayo, wala po akong relo.**
Sorry, I don't have a watch.

  Bokabolaryo

Study the following words. Some of them were used in the dialogue you just read and some of them will be useful when you make your own sentences for your dialogues.

Mga Salita Tungkol sa Oras (Words About Time)

There are two ways of telling time in Tagalog/Filipino. The more popular way is to use the Spanish-derived words. The other way is to use indigenous Tagalog words. The Spanish-derived words are on the left and the indigenous words are in the middle.

Ala-una	**Ika-isa**	*One o'clock*
Alas-dos	**Ikalawa**	*Two o'clock*
Alas-tres	**Ikatatlo**	*Three o'clock*
Alas-kuwatro	**Ika-apat**	*Four o'clock*
Alas-singko	**Ikalima**	*Five o'clock*
Alas-sais	**Ika-anim**	*Six o'clock*
Alas-siyete	**Ikapito**	*Seven o'clock*
Alas-otso	**Ikawalo**	*Eight o'clock*
Alas-nuwebe	**Ikasiyam**	*Nine o'clock*
Alas-diyes	**Ikasampu**	*Ten o'clock*
Alas-onse	**Ikalabing-isa**	*Eleven o'clock*
Alas-dose	**Ikalabindalawa**	*Twelve o'clock*
y medya	**kalahati**	*Half* (used for thirty minutes)
menos... para	**bago ang**	*Before* (used for indicating minutes before reaching an hour; for example: **menos singko para alas-onse** or **limang minuto bago ang ikalabing-isa** = five minutes before eleven)

Oras	*Time; hour*
Minuto	*Minute*
Segundo	*Second*
Ng umaga	*In the morning*
Ng tanghali	*At noon*
Ng hapon	*In the afternoon*
Ng gabi	*In the evening*
Madaling-araw	*Dawn*
Hatinggabi	*Midnight*
Makalipas	*After*
Relo	*Watch*
Orasan	*Clock*

Mga Halimbawang Pangungusap

Practice saying these sentences aloud and study the sentence structures.

1. **Alas-tres kinse na ng hapon.**   *It is three fifteen in the afternoon.*
2. **Ika-anim na ng umaga.**   *It is six o'clock in the morning.*
3. **Hatinggabi na.**   *It is midnight.*
4. **Menos kinse na para alas-dos.**   *It is quarter to two.*
5. **Dalawampung minuto na makalipas**   *It twenty minutes past four.*
   ang alas kuwatro.
6. **Wala ho akong relo.**   *I don't have a watch.*

 Pagsasanay

Practice these questions and answers by both speaking and writing. Use the time indicated in parentheses as your guide. Independent learners should write the questions and answers. Classroom learners should work as pairs and ask each other questions.

1. TANONG : **Anong oras na?**
   SAGOT   : **Alas-tres na ng hapon.**

2. TANONG : **Anong oras na?**
   SAGOT   : **Alas-diyes kinse na ng umaga.**

3. TANONG : **Anong oras na?**
   SAGOT   : (*5:30 A.M.*) _____.

4. TANONG : _____?
   SAGOT   : (*2:00 P.M.*)_____.

5. TANONG : _____?
   SAGOT   : (*8:25 P.M.*)_____.

6. TANONG : _____?
   SAGOT   : (*12:00 midnight*)_____.

7. TANONG : _____?
   SAGOT   : (*10:50 A.M.*)_____.

Diyalogo: Sa Estasyon ng Bus (At the bus station)

Read the dialogue below. After completing this chapter, practice this dialogue using your own information.

PASAHERO	:	**Saan po ako sasakay papuntang Los Baños?**
		Where will I "ride" going to Los Baños?
KONDUKTOR	:	**Sa bus na may karatulang "Laguna."**
		On the bus with the sign "Laguna."
PASAHERO	:	**Anong oras po aalis ang bus?**
		What time will the bus leave?
KONDUKTOR	:	**Bandang alas-dos kinse po.**
		Around two fifteen.
PASAHERO	:	**Anong oras po darating ng bus sa Los Baños?**
		What time will the bus arrive in Los Baños?
KONDUKTOR	:	**Bandang alas-kuwatro po. Saan kayo bababa?**
		Around four o'clock. Where will you get off?
PASAHERO	:	**Sa "crossing" po sa U.P. Los Baños.**
		At the cross streets of the University of the Philippines Los Baños.

  Bokabolaryo

Study the following words. Some of them were used in the dialogue you just read and some of them will be useful when you make your own sentences for your dialogues.

Sasakay	*Get on*
Bababa	*Get off*
Karatula	*Sign*
Pasahero	*Passenger*
Konduktor	*Conductor*
Aalis	*Leave*
Darating	*Arrive*
Alis	*Departure*
Dating	*Arrival*
Papuntang	*Going to*
Bandang	*Around*

Dagdag na Bokabolaryo

Study the following words that you can use when talking about a series, for example, "first bus, second bus, third bus." Note the use of the linker **na** when used with a noun.

una	*first*
unang bus	*first bus*
ikalawa/pangalawa	*second*
ikalawang bus	*second bus*
ikatlo/pangatlo	*third*
ika-apat/pang-apat	*fourth*
ikalima/panlima	*fifth*
ika-anim/pang-anim	*sixth*
ika-pito/pampito	*seventh*
ika-walo/pangwalo	*eighth*
ika-siyam/pansiyam	*ninth*
ika-sampu/pangsampu	*tenth*
huli/panghuli	*last*

Mga Halimbawang Pangungusap

Practice saying these sentences aloud, to get a feel for how this chapter's vocabulary and grammar work in Filipino.

1. **Ang dilaw na bus ay papuntang Calamba.** — *The yellow bus is going to Calamba.*
2. **Papuntang Calamba ang dilaw na bus.** — *The yellow bus is going to Calamba.*
3. **Aalis ang bus papuntang Calamba ng bandang alas-dos kinse.** — *The bus going to Calamba will leave at around two fifteen.*
4. **Darating ang bus sa Calamba ng alas-kuwatro ng hapon.** — *The bus arrives in Calamba at around four o'clock in the afternoon.*
5. **Sasakay siya ng bus sa Pasay Bus Terminal.** — *He/she will get on the bus at Pasay Bus Terminal.*
6. **Bababa siya sa Crossing sa U.P. Los Baños.** — *He/she will get off at the "crossing" ((cross street) at U.P. Los Baños.)*

Pagsasanay

Practice these questions and answers by both speaking and writing. Use the earlier pairs as a guide. Independent learners should write the questions and answers. Classroom learners should work as pairs and ask each other questions.

1. TANONG : **Anong oras aalis ang bus papuntang** _____**?**
   SAGOT : **Alas-dose ng hatinggabi aalis ang bus papuntang** _____**.**

2. TANONG : **Anong oras aalis ang bus papuntang** _____**?**
   SAGOT : **Alas-sais aalis ang bus papuntang** _____**.**

3. TANONG : **Anong oras aalis ang bus papuntang** _____**?**
   SAGOT : _____ **aalis ang bus papuntang** _____**.**

4. TANONG : **Saan sasakay si** _____**?**
   SAGOT : **Sasakay si** _____ **sa** _____**.**

5. TANONG : **Saan bababa si** _____**?**
   SAGOT : **Bababa siya sa** _____**.**

6. TANONG : **Saan ka** _____**?**
   SAGOT : _____ **ako sa** _____**.**

7. TANONG : _____**?**
   SAGOT : _____**.**

8. TANONG : _____**?**
   SAGOT : _____**.**

9. TANONG : _____**?**
   SAGOT : _____**.**

10. TANONG : _____**?**
    SAGOT : _____**.**

 Gramatika

Study the following new lessons in Filipino grammar.

I.   **Aalis** (*will leave*), **Darating** (*will arrive*), **Bababa** (*get off*)
     The verbs **aalis** (*will leave*) and **darating** (*will arrive*) are used when asking about departures and arrivals. The verb **bababa** (with the accent on the first syllable) is used to mean "will get off." In Filipino, we can use either the present tense or the future tense. For example:

> EXAMPLES: **Anong oras dumarating ang bus?**
> *What time does the bus arrive?*
> **Anong oras darating ang bus?**
> *What time will the bus arrive?*
> **Saan ka bababa?**
> *Where will you get off?*

For **alis**, **dating** and **baba**, we use the prefix **um**.

Completed	Incompleted	Contemplated
umalis	umaalis	aalis
dumating	dumarating	darating
bumaba	bumababa	bababa

Similarly, we can also use the noun forms of these words: **alis** (*departure*) and **dating** (*arrival*). Thus, we can ask:

> EXAMPLES: **Anong oras ang alis ng bus?**
> *What time does the bus leave?*
> **Anong oras ang dating ng bus?**
> *What time does the bus arrive?*

Note also that in some instances, you will find the verb **darating** spelled or spoken as **dadating**. Bear in mind that this is also acceptable because in the **baybayin** script **d** and **r** are both indicated by a single character. When Filipinos were asked, "How do you know whether to read a letter as **d** or **r**?" they replied that they "simply knew." Ambiguity was not a problem for them.

II. Particles for More Natural Speech

Some particles (**na**, **pa**, and **lang**) have been introduced earlier. Let us review them again and see how we can use them in this lesson to have more natural speech.

> TANONG : **Anong oras na?**
> *What time is it?* (literally, What time already?)
>
> SAGOT : **Alas-kuwarto na.**
> *It is four o'clock.* (literally, Four o'clock already.)
>
> TANONG : **Alas-dos y medya na ba?**
> *Is it two thirty already?* (literally, Two thirty already **ba**?)
>
> SAGOT : **Alas-dos kinse pa lang.**
> *It is only two fifteen.* (literally, Two fifteen also only.)

In studying these sentences, we can observe the following:

A. The fondness for the use of **na** or *already*. Filipino English tends to use the word *already*, even when the word is not necessary.

B. **Pa lang** combines the particles **pa** and **lang** to mean *only*. When used alone, **pa** usually means *also*. However, with **lang**, it just means *only*.

III. Practicing the Imperative and Infinitive Forms

For many verbs such as **sakay**, **baba**, **alis**, and **dating** which all use the **um** prefix, the imperative form of the verb is equivalent to the completed aspect of the verb. The imperative form is used when giving commands, for example, "**Sumakay ka ng bus 35**. (*Ride bus 35.*)"

The infinitive form is usually used when using the verbs with helping verbs such as **gusto** (*like*). In English, it is easy to recognize the infinitive form because of the word *to*—for example, *want to leave* (**gustong umalis**) or *want to get off* (**gustong bumaba**). Note the use of the linker **na**, contracted into **ng**. If using a pronoun, the linker can be attached to the pronoun. Thus we say, "**Gusto kong umalis**" (*Want I* marker *leave*).

Here are some examples:

> TANONG : **Saan ako sasakay ng jeepney?**
> *Where will I ride/take the jeepney?*
>
> SAGOT : **Sumakay ka ng jeepney sa harap ng post office.**
> *Ride the jeepney in front of the post office.*
>
> TANONG : **Saan ako bababa?**
> *Where will I get off?*
>
> SAGOT : **Bumaba ka sa tapat ng parke.**
> *Get off across from the park.*
>
> TANONG : **Anong oras mo gustong umalis ng bahay?**
> *What time do you want to leave the house?*
>
> SAGOT : **Gusto kong umalis ng bahay nang alas-kuwatro.**
> *I want to leave the house at four o'clock.*

TANONG : **Anong oras mo gustong dumating sa airport?**
What time do you want to arrive at the airport?

SAGOT : **Gusto kong dumating sa airport nang alas-siyete.**
I want to arrive at the airport at seven o'clock.

Mga Tala Sa Kultura

The ambiguity that we find in the letters of the **baybayin** alphabet is also present when talking about time in the Philippines. Thus, we have the concept of "Filipino time," which refers to the Filipino stereotype of a person who is always late.

However, it is not a matter of being precise or prompt. We find that "exactness" is not important in Filipino culture. In telling time, we find that the words we use are influenced by indigenous ways of telling time. Look at the following examples of common speech and idiomatic expressions:

1. **Gumising ka na. Mataas na ang araw.** *Wake up. The sun is high in the sky.*
2. **Umuwi ka bago dumilim.** *Go home before it goes dark.*
3. **Pupunta ako sa party nang bandang alas-otso.** *I will go to the party at around eight o'clock. (Go I party at around eight o'clock.)*
4. **Pupunta ako sa party nang mga alas-otso.** *I will go to the party at around eight o'clock. (Go I party at around eight o'clock.)*
5. **Pagputi ng uwak, pag-itim ng tagak.** *When the crow turns white (and) the seagull turns black. ("eternity")*

In the first two sentences, time is told through signs of nature (the sun; the sky turning dark). In the third and fourth sentences, the words **bandang** and **mga** (meaning "around") are used to show indeterminate time. When one says **bandang alas-otso** or **mga alas-otso**, it can mean anywhere from quarter to eight to around eight fifteen.

The fifth sentence is an idiomatic expression, meaning "never" or "forever" depending on the context. When is this used? Let us take a situation where a woman is asked when she plans to give her love to the man courting her. Instead of saying "never" she can say "**Pagputi ng uwak.**" Since the crow will never turn white, she is actually saying "never."

Similarly, in many areas in the country, buses and jeepneys do not leave at exact times. In areas where there are jeepney or bus stops (**paradahan**), where the vehicles wait for passengers, the vehicles usually leave when they become full.

 **Dagdag-Aral**

Two helpful words to know are **susunod** (*next*) and **dapat** (*should*). Study how these words are used in the following questions and answers:

TANONG : **Anong oras ang alis ng susunod na bus papuntang Batangas?**
What time is the departure of the next bus for Batangas?

SAGOT : **Alas-siyete ang alis ng susunod na bus papuntang Batangas.**
The arrival of the next bus going to Batangas is seven o'clock.

TANONG : **Anong oras ang dating ng susunod na eroplano mula sa Las Vegas?**
What time will the next plane from Las Vegas arrive?

SAGOT : **Alas-tres kinse ang dating ng susunod na eroplano mula sa Las Vegas.**
The next plane from Las Vegas arrives at three fifteen.

TANONG : **Anong oras ako dapat umalis ng bahay?**
What time should I leave the house?

SAGOT: : **Dapat umalis ka ng bahay nang alas-otso.**
You should leave the house at eight o'clock.

 Pagsasanay

Study the following information. Then think of possible situations and the questions and answers which may arise from such a situation. Use the first situation as an example. Classroom learners can work in pairs while individual learners should write the answers and questions and try to approximate a role-play.

Destination: Intramuros
Nearest Jeepney Stop: Faculty Center
Best Place to Get Off: Fort Santiago
Fare: 15 pesos
Jeepney Schedule: No schedule

1. TANONG : **Paano ako pupunta sa Intramuros?**
    SAGOT : **Sumakay ka ng jeepney.**
    TANONG : **Saan ako sasakay ng jeepney papuntang Intramuros?**
    SAGOT : **Sumakay ka sa harap ng Faculty Center.**
    TANONG : **Saan ako bababa?**
    SAGOT : **Bumaba ka sa Fort Santiago.**
    TANONG : **Magkano ang pamasahe?**
    SAGOT : **Kinse pesos ang pamasahe.**

Destination: Makati
Best Place to Catch a Train: **kanto ng** EDSA at Quezon Boulevard
Best Place to Get Off: Makati Station
Fare: Twenty pesos
Departure of Train: 5:30 A.M.

2. TANONG : **Paano ako pupunta sa Makati?**
   SAGOT : _____.
   TANONG : **Saan ako....**
   SAGOT : _____.
   TANONG : **Saan ako bababa?**
   SAGOT : _____.
   TANONG : **Magkano** _____?
   SAGOT : _____.

Destination: Baguio
Best Place to Get a Bus: New York Street, Cubao
Departure of Bus: 11:00 P.M.
Departure of Next Bus: 11:30 P.M.
Fare: Three hundred pesos

3. TANONG : **Paano** _____?
   SAGOT : _____.
   TANONG : **Saan ako** _____ **papuntang** _____?
   SAGOT : **Sumakay ka sa** _____.
   TANONG : **Saan ako** _____?
   SAGOT : _____ **ka sa** _____.
   TANONG : _____?
   SAGOT : _____.
   TANONG : _____?
   SAGOT : _____.

Destination: Airport, Davao City
Means of Transportation: Taxi to the airport
Available Flights: Philippine Airlines Flight 234, 10 A.M.
                   Cebu Pacific Flight 112, 2 P.M.
Flight Time: One hour and thirty minutes
Fare: ₱5000 round trip
Travel Time from Mabuhay Hotel to Airport: One hour

4. TANONG : **Paano** _____?
   SAGOT : _____.

TANONG	:	**Anong oras** _____ ?
SAGOT	:	_____ .
TANONG	:	**Anong oras** _____ ?
SAGOT	:	_____ .
TANONG	:	**Magkano** _____ ?
SAGOT	:	_____ .
TANONG	:	**Anong oras ang susunod** _____ ?
SAGOT	:	_____ .
TANONG	:	**Paano ako pupunta sa airport?**
SAGOT	:	_____ .
TANONG	:	**Anong oras ako dapat umalis sa Mabuhay Hotel?**
SAGOT	:	**Umalis ka sa Mabuhay Hotel** _____ .

Diyalogo: Pagbili ng Tiket (Buying a bus ticket)

Study this dialogue. It reviews the words and phrases used in buying and selling that you have learned earlier. This time these words and phrases are used in the context of the situation in this lesson.

PASAHERO	:	**Pabili po ng tiket papuntang Calamba.**
KONDUKTOR	:	**Anong oras po?**
PASAHERO	:	**Alas-kuwatro po.**
KONDUKTOR	:	**Ilang tiket po?**
PASAHERO	:	**Isa lang ho. Magkano po?**
KONDUKTOR	:	**Isang daang piso ho.**
PASAHERO	:	**Heto po ang isang daang piso.**
KONDUKTOR	:	**Heto po ang tiket niyo.**

Pagsasanay

After reading the dialogue above, try to answer the following questions. This is a good way to test your what you have learned so far. Try to navigate between the different aspects of the verb that you have learned.

1. TANONG : **Saan pupunta ang pasahero?**
   SAGOT : _____ .

2. TANONG : **Ilang tiket ang binili niya?**
   SAGOT : _____ .

3. TANONG : **Magkano ang tiket papuntang Calamba?**
   SAGOT   : _____.

4. TANONG : **Anong oras aalis ang bus?**
   SAGOT   : _____.

Now look at the bus schedule below. Classroom learners should use this information by engaging their partners in a roleplay. Individual learners should write their own dialogues to practice.

Destination	Departure	Arrival	Price
Pampanga	8 A.M.	10:00	₱100
Tarlac	8:30	11:00	₱150
Baguio	10 P.M.	4 A.M.	₱300
Dagupan	12 n	4:30 P.M.	₱250
Banaue	11 P.M.	6 P.M.	₱500

  Pagbabasa

Read the following passage, and then answer the questions that follow. To prepare, study the following new words. Also, study again how English words can be used in Filipino by attaching prefixes. A good example is the word "**magpi-picnic**" (to have a picnic).

Burol	*Hill*
Kamukha	*Looks like*
Kasi	*Because*
Kuweba	*Cave*
Naisip	*Thought*
Nakakainis	*Irritating*
Naplano	*Planned*
Ngumiti	*Smiled*
Pelikula	*Movie*
Sarili	*Self*
Tanawin	*View*
Talon	*Waterfalls*

Biyahe Papuntang Sagada

Labindalawang oras ang biyahe mula Maynila hanggang Banaue, dalawang oras mula Banaue hanggang Bontoc, at apatnapu't limang minuto mula Bontoc hanggang Sagada.

May mga tao na mas gusto ang biyahe na Maynila hanggang Baguio, at Baguio hanggang Sagada. Pero mas gusto ni Lillian na sumakay ng bus papuntang Banaue. Mas maganda kasi ang mga tanawin. Nakikita niya ang mga bundok, ang rice terraces, ang mga ilog at mga talon.

Nakaupo si Lillian sa Estasyon ng bus. Dahil alas-diyes ang alis ng bus, dumating siya sa Estasyon nang alas-nuwebe y medya. Hinihintay niya ang nobyo niyang si Ramon.

Alas-nuwebe kwarenta y singko na. May emergency meeting kaya si Ramon? Bakit hindi siya sumasagot sa telepono? Naaksidente kaya siya?

Apat na araw, tatlong gabi. Ito lang ang "vacation leave" niya. Naplano na niya ang lahat. Pupunta sila sa mga kuweba, sa mga talon, sa mga "hanging coffins." Magpi-picnic sila sa isang burol. Magha-hiking sila sa bundok. Ang ganda. Kamukha niya si Hilda Koronel sa vintage 1970s na pelikulang "Kung Mangarap Ka't Magising (If You Should Dream, and then Wake Up)."

Limang minuto bago mag-alas-diyes ng gabi. Aalis na ang bus. Hindi bale. Pupunta pa rin ako sa Sagada, sabi ni Lillian sa sarili. Okay naman. Nakakainis lang ang naghihintay.

Tumatakbo si Ramon. Ngumiti si Lillian. Pagkatapos, naisip niya: Okay naman. Nakakainis lang ang naghihintay.

✏ Pagsusulat (Writing)

Using the vocabulary and grammar you have learned, try writing your own paragraph in Tagalog/Filipino. Try writing it in the aspect (completed, incomplete, contemplated) that you are finding most difficult. The paragraph can be as complex or as simple as you like. Study the examples and use them as a guides.

Halimbawa 1
Bumibili si Juan ng tiket papuntang Los Baños. Alas-kuwatro ang alis ng bus. Alas-sais ang dating nito sa Los Baños. Singkuwento pesos ang isang tiket. Sasakay siya sa Pasay Bus Terminal. Bababa siya sa Crossing ng U.P. Los Baños.

Halimbawa 2

Bibili ako ng tiket papuntang Bohol. Alas-dos ng hapon ang alis ng eroplano. Alas-tres ang dating sa Bohol. Dalawang libong piso ang tiket.

Halimbawa 3

Bibili ako ng tiket _____. _____ ang alis ng

_____. _____ ang dating sa _____.

_____ ang tiket. Sasakay ako sa _____.

Bababa ako sa _____.

⚑ Paglalagom (Summing Up)

In **Aralin 12**, you have learned and practiced:
1. Words and phrases related to time,
2. Words and phrases related to departures and arrivals,
3. Words and phrases related to buying and selling tickets at a station,
4. The imperative and infinitive verb forms.

You should now be able to:
1. Tell the time in both the indigenous Tagalog way and the Spanish-language derived way.
2. Talk about arrivals and departures.
3. Buy tickets at a train station.

Pag-iiskedyul ng Tagpuan
(Scheduling an Appointment)

  Diyalogo: Puwede Ka Ba sa Meeting?
(Can you make it to the meeting?)

Read the dialogue below. After completing this chapter, practice this dialogue using your own information.

PEDRO : **Hello?**

CLARA : **Hello.**

PEDRO : **Puwede bang makausap si Clara?**
May I speak to Clara?

CLARA : **Ito nga si Clara.**
This is Clara.

PEDRO : **Si Pedro ito. Puwede ka ba sa pulong ng grupo natin?**
This is Pedro. Can you make it to the meeting of our group?

CLARA : **Kailan ang pulong?**
When is the meeting?

PEDRO : **Sa Sabado, alas-diyes ng umaga.**
On Saturday, at ten o'clock in the morning.

CLARA : **Hindi ako puwede sa Sabado ng umaga. Nasa klinika ako ng doktor. Puwede kaya sa hapon?**
I can't make it on Saturday morning. I am at the doctor's clinic. Is it possible to have it in the afternoon?

PEDRO : **Anong oras?**
What time?

CLARA : **Alas-dos ng hapon.**
Two o'clock in the afternoon.

PEDRO : **Sige. Baka libre rin sina Juan at Maria.**
Okay. Perhaps Juan and Maria are also free.

CLARA : **Magkita tayo sa Sabado.**
Let us see each other in the afternoon.

PEDRO : **Sige. Salamat.**
Okay. Thanks.

Bokabolaryo

Study the following words. Some of them were used in the dialogue you just read and some of them will be useful when you make your own sentences for your dialogues.

Iskedyul	*Schedule*
Kahapon	*Yesterday*
Ngayon	*Today*
Bukas	*Tomorrow*
Kagabi	*Last night*

Mga Araw sa Isang Linggo (Days in a Week)

Lunes	*Monday*
Martes	*Tuesday*
Miyerkules	*Wednesday*
Huwebes	*Thursday*
Biyernes	*Friday*
Sabado	*Saturday*
Linggo	*Sunday*

Iba Pang Salita sa Diyalogo

Puwede	*Can*
Libre	*Free*
Magkita tayo!	*Let us see each other*
Pulong/Miting	*Meeting*
Grupo/Pangkat	*Group*

Iba Pang Salita

Araw	*Day*
Linggo	*Week*
Buwan	*Month*
Taon	*Year*
Klinika ng doktor	*Doctor's clinic*
Klinika ng dentista	*Dentist's clinic*

Mga Halimbawang Pangungusap

Practice saying these sentences aloud, to get a feel for how this chapter's vocabulary and grammar work in Filipino.

1. **Hindi puwede si Clara sa Sabado ng umaga.**

   Clara cannot make it on Saturday morning. (literally, Cannot be *marker* Clara on Saturday *marker* morning.)

2. **Libre si Clara sa Sabado ng hapon.**

   Clara is free on Saturday afternoon. (literally, Free *marker* Clara on Saturday *marker* afternoon.)

3. **Sa Sabado ng hapon ang pulong.**

   The meeting is on Saturday afternoon. (literally, On Saturday *marker* afternoon *marker* meeting.)

4. **Nasa klinika ng doktor si Clara sa Sabado ng umaga.**

   Clara is at the doctor's clinic on Saturday morning.

5. **Nasa gym si Clara tuwing Lunes at Miyerkules.**

   Clara is at the gym on Mondays and Wednesdays.

6. **Nasa unibersidad si Clara araw-araw.** *Clara is at the university everyday.*

7. **Magkikita sina Pedro at Clara sa Sabado.**

   Pedro and Clara will see each other on Saturday. (Literally, See *marker* Pedro and Clara on Saturday.)

  Pagsasanay

Look at the two appointment books below. Then, answer and ask questions based on the information found on the appointment books. Use the first sets as examples. The third appointment book is yours. Write your schedule on it. Classroom learners should work in pairs to ask about each other's schedule. You may also work in groups and try to arrange a common time when you can have a meeting. Individual learners should write dialogues.

I. **Iskedul ni Dr. Carol Aguilar**

Lunes/Monday:	9:00 **ng umaga; Unibersidad**
Martes/Tuesday:	2:00 **ng hapon; nasa klinika**
	6:00 **ng hapon** – Shirley's Ballroom Dancing Studio
Miyerkules/Wednesday:	8:00 **ng umaga; nasa** gym
Huwebes/Thursday:	2:00 **ng hapon; nasa klinika**
Biyernes/Friday:	9: 00 **ng umaga; nasa unibersidad**
Sabado/Saturday:	10:00 **ng umaga; nasa** tennis court
Linggo/Sunday:	**walang iskedyul**

1. Tanong : **Nasaan si Carol sa Martes nang alas-sais ng hapon?**
    Sagot   : **Nasa Shirley's Ballroom Dancing Studio si Carol sa Martes, alas-sais ng hapon.**

2. Tanong : **Nasaan si Carol sa Sabado nang alas-diyes ng umaga.**
    Sagot   : **Nasa _____ si Carol sa Sabado nang alas-sais ng umaga.**

3. Tanong : **Nasaan si Carol tuwing Lunes, alas-nuwebe ng umaga?**
    Sagot   : **_____ tuwing Lunes at Biyernes, _____.**

4. Tanong : **Nasaan si Carol tuwing Martes at Huwebes ng hapon?**
    Sagot   : **_____.**

5. Tanong : **Anong araw libre si Carol?**
    Sagot   : **Libre si Carol sa araw ng _____.**

6. Tanong : **Kailan libre si Carol sa Sabado?**
    Sagot   : **Libre si Carol sa hapon.**

7. Tanong : **Libre ba si Carol sa Martes ng gabi?**
    Sagot   : **Hindi, hindi siya puwede sa Martes ng gabi.**

8. Tanong : **Kailan siya libre sa gabi?**
    Sagot   : **Libre siya sa _____ ng gabi.**

II. **Iskedyul ni Renato Rodriguez, isang kawani ng bangko**

Lunes/Monday:	8-5 **bangko**
Martes/Tuesday:	8-5 **bangko**
Miyerkules/Wednesday:	8-5 **bangko**; 7:00: Rehearsal Hall
Huwebes/Thursday:	8-5 **bangko**
Biyernes/Friday:	8-5 **bangko**; 7:00 **ng gabi** Manila Jazz Club
Sabado/Saturday:	7:00 **ng gabi** Manila Jazz Club

1. Tanong : **Nasaan si Renato tuwing Lunes ng umaga?**
    Sagot   : **_____.**

2. Tanong : **Nasaan si Renato tuwing Miyerkules ng gabi?**
    Sagot   : **_____.**

3. Tanong : **Nasaan si Renato tuwing Sabado ng gabi?**
    Sagot   : **_____.**

4. TANONG : **Libre ba si Renato sa Huwebes ng gabi?**
    SAGOT   : _____.

5. TANONG : **Anong araw libre si Renato?**
    SAGOT   : _____.

6. TANONG : _____?
    SAGOT   : _____.

7. TANONG : _____?
    SAGOT   : _____.

III. Iskedyul ni _____

Write your name in the blank space above. Then fill out the following "appointment book" with your schedule.

Lunes/Monday		
Martes/Tuesday		
Miyerkules/Wednesday		
Huwebes/Thursday		
Biyernes/Friday		
Sabado/Saturday		
Linggo/Sunday		

IV. Pag-iiskedyul ng Pulong

1. TANONG : **Kailan ka libre para sa pulong?**
    SAGOT   : _____.

2. TANONG : **Puwede ka ba sa _____?**
    SAGOT   : _____.

3. TANONG : **Bakit hindi ka puwede sa_____?**
    SAGOT   : _____.

4. TANONG : **Sino ang puwede sa Lunes ng gabi?**
    SAGOT   : _____.

5. TANONG : **Kailan libre ang mga tao para sa pulong?**
   SAGOT : _____.

6. TANONG : **Puwede ka ba sa Miyerkules ng umaga?**
   SAGOT : _____.

 Dagdag-Aral

Mga Buwan (Months)

Enero	*January*
Pebrero	*February*
Marso	*March*
Abril	*April*
Mayo	*May*
Hunyo	*June*
Hulyo	*July*
Agosto	*August*
Setyembre	*September*
Oktubre	*October*
Nobyembre	*November*
Disyembre	*December*

Mga Panahon

Tagsibol	*Spring*
Tag-araw	*Summer*
Taglagas	*Autumn/Fall*
Taglamig	*Winner*
Tag-ulan	*Rainy season*
Tag-init	*Hot season/Summer season*

Mga Salita Tungkol sa Panahon (Words about the weather)

Ulan	*Rain*
Bagyo	*Storm*
Niyebe	*Snow*
Maulan	*Rainy*
Maaraw	*Sunny*
Malamig	*Cold*
Maulap	*Cloudy*

Iba Pang Salita Tungkol sa Panahon (Other words about time)

Study the following additional useful words for talking about time.

Kanina	*Earlier*
Kaninang umaga	*Earlier this morning*
Kaninang hapon	*Earlier this afternoon*
Mamaya	*Later*
Mamayang gabi	*Later tonight*
Mamayang hapon	*Later this afternoon*
Noong isang linggo	*Last week*
Noong isang buwan	*Last month*
Sa susunod na linggo	*Next week*
Sa susunod na buwan	*Next month*

Rebyu at Pagpapalawak ng Leksiyon sa Mga Pandiwa (Review and Expansion of the Lesson on Verbs)

Earlier, you learned some verbs that are usually used when talking about everyday activities. Review these verbs so you can use them in sentences about the things you do in certain months of the year. Additionally, review new useful verbs; how to form verbs using English words that have no equivalent in Tagalog/Filipino; and Tagalog/Filipino affixes.

Pumunta	*Went*
Pumupunta	*Going*
Pupunta	*Will go*
Pumasok sa klase	*Went to class/Attended class* (literally, entered class)
Pumapasok sa klase	*Go to class*
Papasok sa klase	*Will go to class*
Dumadalo	*Attend*
Nagbabakasyon	*Go on vacation*
Lumalangoy	*Swimming*
Nag-i-iskiing	*Go skiing*
Nag-i-isnowboarding	*Go snowboarding*
Nagsa-skydiving	*Go skydiving*
Naglalaro ng soccer	*Play soccer*
Nagsa-soccer	*Play soccer*
Namimitas	*Picking* (for example, picking apples)

Mga Pangungusap

Study the following sentences about activities you do during particular months of the year. Also pay attention to the use of the prepositions **sa** and **nasa** which are used in answering sentences using the question words **Saan** and **Nasaan**.

1. **Nasa Montreal ako tuwing Enero.**   *I am in Montreal every January.*
2. **Magsi-skiing ako sa buwan ng Enero.**   *I will go skiing in the month of January.*
3. **Pumupunta ako sa Negros tuwing Abril.**   *I go to Negros every April.*
4. **Nagbabakasyon ako tuwing Abril.**   *I take a vacation every April.*
5. **Nasa Berkeley ako mula Setyembre hanggang Disyembre.**   *I am in Berkeley from September to December.*
6. **Nag-aaral ako sa unibersidad mula Setyembre hanggang Disyembre.**   *I study at the university from September to December.*
7. **Naglaro ako ng soccer noong Oktubre.**   *I played soccer last October.*
8. **Mamimitas ako ng mansanas sa Nobyembre.**   *I will pick apples in November.*
9. **Dadalo ako ng kumperensiya (conference) sa Disyembre.**   *I will attend a conference in December.*
10. **Pupunta ako sa Madrid sa tag-araw.**   *I will go to Madrid in the summer.*

 ★ **Gawain**

Look at the following appointment books. The places where the person will be and his/her activities are listed. Then, answer the questions or give the questions to the provided answers. You can use the earlier questions and answers as a guide. The fourth appointment book is yours. Make your own schedule. Classroom learners should ask each other questions. Individual learners should write and answer their own questions.

There are three things you should practice here:

      —habitual action (use the incompleted aspect) and the word **tuwing** (*every*)
      —incompleted aspect
      —contemplated aspect

Thus, look for the month marked with ▶. This is the month the person or you are in. All activities preceding that month are in the past except for habitual activities. All activities after that month are in the future.

I. **Iskedyul ni Trina Santos, isang guro sa isang unibersidad sa Quezon City**

Pebrero (*February*):	**kumperensiya sa San Diego**
Abril (*April*):	**meeting sa New York**
Mayo (*May*):	**bakasyon sa Canada**
▶ **Hunyo** (*June*):	**klase sa Maynila**
Oktubre (*October*):	**workshop sa Baguio**
Disyembre (*December*):	"family reunion" **sa Cebu**

1. TANONG : **Nasaan si Trina sa Mayo?**
   SAGOT : **Nasa Canada si Trina sa Mayo.**
2. TANONG : **Saan pumunta si Trina sa Abril?**
   SAGOT : **Pumunta si Trina sa New York sa Abril.**
3. TANONG : **Ano ang ginawa ni Trina noong Pebrero?**
   SAGOT : **Dumalo si Trina sa isang kumperensiya sa San Diego noong Pebrero.**
4. TANONG : **Ano ang ginagawa ni Trina tuwing Mayo?**
   SAGOT : **Nagbabakasyon si Trina sa Canada tuwing Mayo.**
5. TANONG : **Ano ang ginagawa ni Trina mula Hunyo hanggang Oktubre?**
   SAGOT : **Nagtuturo si Trina mula Hunyo hanggang Oktubre.**
6. TANONG : **Saan pupunta si Trina sa Oktubre?**
   SAGOT : **Pupunta si Trina sa Baguio sa Oktubre.**
7. TANONG : **Ano ang gagawin ni Trina sa Oktubre?**
   SAGOT : **Dadalo si Trina sa workshop sa Oktubre.**
8. TANONG : **Nasaan si Trina sa Disyembre?**
   SAGOT : **Nasa Cebu si Trina sa Disyembre?**
9. TANONG : **Ano ang gagawin ni Trina sa Disyembre?**
   SAGOT : **Dadalo si Trina sa "family reunion" sa Disyembre. Lalangoy si Trina sa dagat sa Disyembre.**

II. **Iskedyul ni Tess, isang estudyante**

Enero (*January*):	**klase; UC Berkeley**
Marso (*March*):	**spring break; skiing sa Switzerland**
Abril (*April*):	**kumperensiya ng mga estudyante**
▶ **Hunyo** (*June*):	**bakasyon sa Hawaii**
Hulyo (*July*):	University of the Philippines Diliman; **dadalo** sa Philippine Studies Summer Program
Agosto (*August*):	**UC Berkeley; klase**
Disyembre (*December*):	**Ilocos; bakasyon sa bahay ng lola**

1. TANONG : **Nasaan si Tess noong Enero?**
   SAGOT : _____.

2. TANONG : **Nasaan si Tess noong Marso?**
   SAGOT : _____.

3. TANONG : **Ano ang ginawa ni Tess noong Marso?**
   SAGOT : _____.

4. TANONG : **Nasaan si Tess noong Abril?**
   SAGOT : _____.

5. TANONG : **Ano ang ginawa ni Tess noong Abril?**
   SAGOT : _____.

6. TANONG : _____?
   SAGOT : **Nasa University of the Philippines Diliman si Tess sa Hulyo.**

7. TANONG : **Ano ang gagawin ni Tess sa University of the Philippines Diliman
             sa Hulyo?**
   SAGOT : _____.

8. TANONG : **Nasaan si Tess mula Agosto hanggang Disyembre?**
   SAGOT : _____.

9. TANONG : _____?
   SAGOT : **Mag-aaral si Tess mula Agosto hanggang Disyembre.**

10. TANONG : _____?
    SAGOT : **Nasa Ilocos si Tess sa Disyembre.**

11. TANONG : _____?
    SAGOT : **Magbabakasyon si Tess sa bahay ng lola niya sa Disyembre.**

III. **Iskedyul ni Mira, isang nars**

    Pebrero (*February*):   **eksamen, Maynila**
▶ **Abril** (*April*):   **bakasyon; Boracay**
    Hunyo (*June*):   **trabaho; Saudi Arabia**
    Oktubre (*October*):   **bisita sa kapatid; Egypt**
    Disyembre (*December*):   **Pilipinas**

1. TANONG : **Kailan ang eksamen ni Mira?**
   SAGOT : _____.

2. TANONG : **Nasaan si Mira noong Pebrero?**
   SAGOT   : _____.

3. TANONG : _____?
   SAGOT   : **Magbabakasyon si Mira sa Boracay sa Abril.**

4. TANONG : _____?
   SAGOT   : _____.

5. TANONG : _____?
   SAGOT   : _____.

6. TANONG : _____?
   SAGOT   : _____.

7. TANONG : _____?
   SAGOT   : _____.

8. TANONG : _____?
   SAGOT   : _____.

IV. **Sariling Iskedyul** (Own Schedule)

Enter your own schedule in the "appointment book" below. It doesn't have to be true in real life. Review the words you have learned and try to use them. Then work with a partner to ask and answer questions. Individual learners can write questions and answers in the spaces provided below.

1. TANONG : _____?
   SAGOT   : _____.

2. TANONG : _____?

    SAGOT   : _____.

3. TANONG : _____?

    SAGOT   : _____.

4. TANONG : _____?

    SAGOT   : _____.

5. TANONG : _____?

    SAGOT   : _____.

6. TANONG : _____?

    SAGOT   : _____.

7. TANONG : _____?

    SAGOT   : _____.

8. TANONG : _____?

    SAGOT   : _____.

9. TANONG : _____?

    SAGOT   : _____.

🔍 Gramatika

Study the following explanations of Filipino grammar.

I.   Review **Saan** and **Nasaan**

In an earlier lesson, you learned that there are two ways of asking *"where"* questions: using **saan** and **nasaan**.

Review these again for this chapter. Remember two things:

First, use **nasa** when answering questions that start with **nasaan**, and use **sa** when answering questions that start with **saan**.

Second, **saan** questions are accompanied by a verb while **nasaan** is not. For example:

EXAMPLES:	
Saan ka pupunta?	*Where are you going?*
Saan pupunta si Maria?	*Where is Maria going?*
Nasaan ka?	*Where are you?*
Nasaan si Maria?	*Where is Maria?*

II. Forming verbs using English words

A good way to expand your vocabulary is to learn how to form verbs using English words that have no equivalent in Filipino. For example, words such as *skiing* and *snowboarding* are not indigenous to the culture (since there is no snow in the Philippines) so they cannot be translated. Also, recently invented machines such as the computer have no Filipino equivalent.

Use the prefixes you have learned. For example:

Completed	Incompleted	Contemplated
nag-i-skiing	nag-i-iskiing	mag-iiskiing
nag-i-snowboarding	nag-iisnowboarding	mag-iisnowboarding
nag-computer	nagko-computer	magko-computer

Notice that when two consonants follow each other such as in the syllables "**ski**" and "**snow**," we use the affix **i-** after **nag-**. However, in spoken Filipino, some native speakers say **nagsi-skiing** and **nagso-snowboarding**. Do not say **nagskiskiing**. Also, use **k** instead of **c**, for **nagko-computer**.

Mga Tala Sa Kultura

Being a tropical country, the Philippines does not have the four seasons of spring, summer, fall, and winter. Instead, there are only two seasons: **tag-ulan** (*rainy*) and **tag-araw** (*summer* or *dry season*). **Tag-araw** is also called **tag-init** (*hot season*).

However, seasons can also be indicated by words that refer to particular activities. For example, rice farmers use words such as **tag-ani** (*harvest season*) and **tagtuyot** (*dry season*). **Sacadas** or seasonal sugarcane workers dread **tiempos muertos** (*dead season*) because this is the time when they do not have work. Students go to school during **pasukan** (*school season*).

In many places in the country where most of the people are Catholics and Christians, **Kapaskuhan** (*Christmas season*) starts as early as October and ends as late as January (to celebrate the day of the Three Kings on January 6). Lent is called **Kuwaresma** or **Semana Santa** (*Holy Week*), referring to weeklong activities of **visita** iglesia (*visiting churches*), **prusisyon** (*procession*) of images of saints, **via crucis** (way of the cross), and **dula** (religious plays), especially on **Biyernes Santo** (*Good Friday*) and **Pasko ng Pagkabuhay** (*Easter Sunday*).

 ## Pagbabasa

Read the following poem, and then answer the questions that follow. Study the following new words to enable you to understand the poem better. Also, you may want to refer to the culture note above. Note that in this particular reading exercise, the objective is not to practice the language but for you to see if you can understand the use of images and metaphors in the language. Thus, you can write your answers in English.

Palaspas	*Dried fronds waved during Holy Sunday*
Tuwa	*Happiness*
Luha	*Tears*
Sabado de Gloria	*Holy Saturday*
Deboto	*Devotee*
Pagdiriwang	*Celebration*

Kuwaresma (Lent)

Ang Kuwaresma ay nagsisimula
sa mga palaspas.
Isang linggo ng luha at tuwa.

Ang Biyernes Santo ay pagluluksa,
Ang Linggo ng Pagkabuhay ay pagdiriwang,
Pero ang Sabado de Gloria ay tahimik
na araw.

Maaaring dumaraan ka lang
sa buhay ko,
parang santo sa prusisyon,
o deboto sa via crucis.

Pero salamat.
Ang Sabado de Gloria,
ay araw ng pagdiriwang
kahit walang mga palaspas.

1. What is the poem about?
2. How are the metaphors of Lent used in referring to the loved one?

✏ Pagsusulat

Read the following short paragraphs that talk about scheduling an appointment. Then write your own paragraph. You can talk about the meetings you scheduled with your classmates or the appointment book that you made for this lesson.

Halimbawa 1
Hindi puwede si Clara sa meeting sa Miyerkules ng umaga. May klase siya. Puwede siya sa Miyerkules ng hapon pero hindi puwede si Juan. Puwede si Juan sa Huwebes ng gabi, kaya sa Huwebes ng gabi ang meeting nina Clara at Juan.

Halimbawa 2
Hindi ako puwede sa _____. May _____ ako.
(Pupunta ako sa _____.) Puwede ako sa _____.
Talata (Paragraph)

⚑ Paglalagom (Summing Up)

In **Aralin 13**, you have:
1. Learned names of months and words and phrases associated with time and seasons,
2. Reviewed questions and answers using **saan** and **nasaan**,
3. Practiced forming verbs using English words and Tagalog/Filipino affixes.

You should now be able to:
1. Schedule an appointment.
2. Talk and write about your weekly and monthly schedule or plans.

14

Pagbibigay Direksiyon (Giving Directions)

  **Diyalogo: Nasaan Ang Philippine Bank?
(Where is Philippine Bank?)**

Read the dialogue below. After completing this chapter, practice this dialogue using your own information.

MARIA	:	**Hello. Ito po ba ang Philippine Bank?**
		Hello. Is this Philippine Bank?
MANAGER	:	**Opo.**
		Yes.
MARIA	:	**Paano po pumunta sa Greenhills branch?**
		How can (one) go to the Greenhills branch?
MANAGER	:	**Nasaan ho kayo?**
		Where are you?
MARIA	:	**Nasa Mabuhay Hotel.**
		At Mabuhay Hotel.
MANAGER	:	**Kumaliwa ho kayo sa Masaya Street. Pagkatapos, kumanan kayo sa unang kanto. Dumiretso kayo. Lumampas kayo sa dalawang stoplight. Nasa kaliwa ninyo ang Philippine Bank.**
		Turn left on Masaya Street. Then turn right on the first corner. Go straight. Go past two stoplights. Philippine Bank will be on your left.

Bokabolaryo

Study the following words and how they were used in the dialogue you just read.

Kanto   *Corner*

Mga Pandiwang Pautos (Imperative or Command verbs)

Kumanan	*Turn right*
Kumaliwa	*Turn left*
Dumiretso	*Go straight*
Umikot	*Go round; go around*
Lumampas	*Go past*
Huminto ka	*Stop*
Bumalik	*Go back*

Mga Halimbawang Pangungusap

1. **Kumaliwa ka papuntang Masaya Street.** *Turn left to go to Masaya Street.*
2. **Kumanan ka sa unang kanto.** *Turn right on the first corner.*
3. **Dumiretso ka.** *Go straight.*
4. **Lumampas ka sa dalawang stoplight.** *Go past two stoplights.*
5. **Umikot ka sa Quezon Memorial Circle.** *Go around Quezon Memorial Circle.*

Laro (*Game*): **Ito ay...** (*This is a ...*)
Have some fun while you learn, by playing this game. The objective of the game is to familiarize you with the following commands:

> **Kumanan ka!**
> **Kumaliwa ka!**
> **Dumiretso ka!**
> **Huminto ka!**

Create a classroom maze using chairs. There should be a starting point and an end point. Then, work in pairs. One student is blindfolded or has his/her eyes shut. Then, the other student gives directions so that his/her partner will not bump into any chairs.

 ## Gawain

Study the map below of an area inside the University of the Philippines in Diliman, Quezon City. Then, give directions on how to go from one building to another. The first items are there as your guide. Classroom learners should work in pairs while individual learners should practice asking and giving directions by writing the directions in the spaces provided.

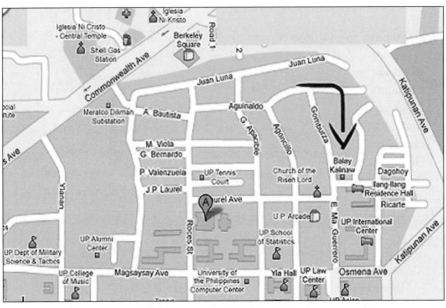

1. TANONG : **Paano ako pupunta sa Church of the Risen Lord mula sa A (Kalayaan Dormitory)?**

   SAGOT : **Mula sa Roces Avenue, kumanan ka sa Laurel Avenue. Lumampas ka sa Apacible at Agoncillo streets. Nasa kaliwa mo ang Church of the Risen Lord.**

2. TANONG : **Paano ako pupunta sa Balay Kalinaw mula sa UP Department of Military Science?**

   SAGOT : _____ **ka sa Magsaysay Avenue.** _____
   ka sa Guerrero. _____ **ka sa Laurel Avenue.**
   _____ **ka sa unang kanto. Nasa** _____
   mo ang Balay Kalinaw.

3. TANONG : **Paano ako pupunta sa UP Alumni Center mula sa Meralco Domain Substation?**

   SAGOT : _____ .

4. TANONG : _____ ?
   SAGOT : _____ .

5. TANONG : _____?
   SAGOT   : _____.

🔍 Gramatika

I. The imperative form of the verb in giving directions
    In English, we use the verbs *go* and *turn* when we give directions. For example, we say "turn right" or "go straight." In Tagalog/Filipino, we form the verb by taking root words such as **kanan** (*right*), **kaliwa** (*left*), **diretso** (*straight*), **lampas** (*past*) and **hinto** (*stop*) and making them into verbs. For these four words, the prefix **um-** is used.
    Thus, we studied the following commands:

EXAMPLES:	**Kumanan ka!**	*Turn right!*
	Kumaliwa ka!	*Turn left!*
	Dumiretso ka!	*Go straight!*
	Lumampas ka sa kalye Mabait.	*Go past Mabait street.*
	Huminto ka!	*Stop!*

II. Inserting honorifics such as **po** and **ho**
    Earlier, you studied honorifics such as **po** and **ho**, which are used for more formal or polite speech. Both mean the same, although the former is considered to be more formal than the latter.
    Many students are confused about the proper placement of **po** and **ho** in the sentence. A common mistake is to say:
    Kumanan kayo po sa Masaya street.
    This is wrong. When using a pronoun, in this case the second-person plural pronoun **kayo**, used to indicate formality, the honorific **po** should be inserted after the verb and before the pronoun.
    Thus, the correct sentence is:
    Kumanan po kayo sa Masaya street.

III. Words in relation to streets, avenues, boulevards, highways
    There are no indigenous words for streets. The Tagalog/Filipino word used is **kalye**, which comes from the Spanish word *calle*. However, in conversational Filipino, when asked where they live, most Filipinos will tend to use "street" instead of **kalye**. Thus, one can say, "**Nakatira ako sa Masaya street.**" (*I live on Masaya street.*)
    Similarly, words such as highways, avenues, boulevards, have no equivalent.

IV. The words **mula** and **galing**

In the dialogue, the manager asks Maria, "**Nasaan ho kayo?** (*Where are you?*)" so that he/she can best give Maria directions. There are two other ways of saying the same thing:

EXAMPLES: **Saan ho kayo magmumula?**
Where will you be coming from?
Saan ho kayo manggagaling?
Where will you be coming from?

The root words are **mula** and **galing** (accent on the first syllable). Both mean *from*. The difference lies in the usage. **Mula** is also used with the word **hanggang** to indicate time. For example, "**Nag-aaral ako mula alas-otso hanggang alas-dose.**" (*I study from eight to twelve o'clock*).

Also, **galing** is more frequently used in situations where two people meet each other and one asks where the other has just come from. For example:

EXAMPLE: **Saan ka galing?**
Where did you come from?

We can conjugate these words and use them as verbs:

Completed	Incompleted	Contemplated
nagmula	nagmumula	magmumula
nanggaling	nanggagaling	manggagaling

Finally, do not confuse **galing** (meaning *from*; the accent is on the first syllable) with **galing** (meaning *good*, referring to one's ability to do something; the accent is on the second syllable).

Dagdag-Aral

Review the old words about coming and going and study the new words, phrases, and sentences below. Remember that in Filipino, there is no difference between the words *come* and *go*, as they have the same equivalent, **punta**. Then study the additional words that refer to streets.

Mga Salita Tungkol sa Pag-alis at Pagpunta (Words about Leaving and Going)

Alis	*Leave*
Punta	*Come, Go*
Mula	*From*
Galing	*From* (accent of "**galing**" is on the first syllable)

Mga Salita Tungkol sa Kalye (Words about Streets)

Kalye	*Street*
Kalsada	*Road*
Eskinita	*Alley*
Daan	*Road; pass*

Mga Ekspresyon at Pangungusap

Alam mo ba....   *Do you know....*

TANONG : **Alam mo ba kung paano pumunta sa Mabuhay Hotel?**
Do you know how to go to Mabuhay Hotel?

SAGOT : **Oo. Alam ko kung paano pumunta sa Mabuhay Hotel.**
Yes. I know how to go to Mabuhay Hotel.

Nasa anong kalye   *On what street...*

TANONG : **Nasa anong kalye ba ang Filipinas Hotel?**
On what street is Filipinas Hotel?

SAGOT : **Nasa General Trias street ang Filipinas Hotel.**
Filipinas Hotel is on General Trias street.

  Pagsasanay

Practice what you have learned about giving directions. In addition, create role-plays using the information given. Use the following vicinity map of Manila, along Taft Avenue. This will be a good opportunity for you to review past lessons so that your dialogues become more natural. Let the first situation serve as your guide.

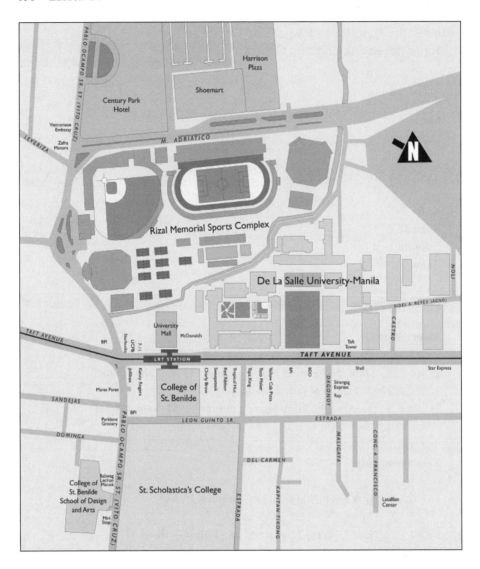

I. Situation 1: Michelle has just left the College of St. Benilde School of Design and Arts. She is walking along the corner of Pablo Ocampo street (formerly Vito Cruz street) and Leon Guinto street, She meets her friend Carlo, who had just come from Tapa King (on Taft Avenue.)

MICHELLE	:	**Kumusta, Carlo?**
CARLO	:	_____. **Ikaw?**
MICHELLE	:	**Mabuti rin.**
CARLO	:	_____.

MICHELLE : **Galing ako sa** _____**. Pupunta ako sa**
_____**. Alam mo ba kung paano pumunta sa**
_____**?**

CARLO : **Oo.** _____**.**

MICHELLE : **Salamat.**

CARLO : _____**.**

II. Situation 2: Cheryl has just left Harrison Plaza. She wants to go to St. Scholastica's College. She meets her classmate Louella on M. Adriatico street. Write a possible dialogue or work with a partner and improvise a scene.

CHERYL : _____.
LOUELLA : _____.
CHERYL : _____.
LOUELLA : _____.
CHERYL : _____.
LOUELLA : _____.
CHERYL : _____.
LOUELLA : _____.
CHERYL : _____.
LOUELLA : _____.

III. Situation 3: Reynaldo is in his house on Del Carmen street. He is going to a party at his friend Vicente's house on Noli street. He calls up his friend to ask for directions. Improvise a scene with your partner or write a dialogue.

REYNALDO : _____.
VICENTE : _____.
REYNALDO : _____.
VICENTE : _____.
REYNALDO : _____.
VICENTE : _____.
REYNALDO : _____.
VICENTE : _____.
REYNALDO : _____.
VICENTE : _____.

Mga Tala Sa Kultura

When Filipinos see each other on the street, they ask not only "How are you?" (**Kumusta ka?**) but also the following: _Where are you going?_ (**Saan ka pupunta?**); _Where did you come from?_ (**Saan ka galing?**); and _Have you eaten?_ (**Kumain ka na ba?**).

This should not be misinterpreted as nosiness, but should instead be viewed as concern for your wellbeing. This concern is similarly reflected in the ways by which Filipino people say goodbye. The formal word **paalam**, meaning *goodbye*, is hardly used, perhaps because it connotes a certain finality. Rather, people will say **Sige** (*Okay*) or **Mag-ingat ka** (*Be careful*).

Two other words provide us with insight on the culture and values of the Filipino people. One is **uwi** (*to go home*). Another is the concept of the **lakaran** (*journey*). In Reynaldo Ileto's *Pasyon and Revolution: Popular Movements in the Philippines 1840-1910*, he writes of the **lakaran** or journey undertaken by Jesus Christ as narrated in the **pasyon** (the Passion, the Christian term for the suffering and death of Jesus) and its similarity to the journey of the revolutionaries as articulated by Andres Bonifacio, founder of the secret society, the Katipunan. In his book, Ileto argues that that the 1896 revolt against the Spanish colonizers was a "journey" for the Filipinos. According to Ileto (105), "The struggle is imagined as an arduous journey on foot, a **lakaran**, toward the 'hills and forests' where for centuries Indios 'fleeing from the bells' found refuge."

These words **uwi** and **lakaran** are useful as heritage learners study more about colonialism, migration, and Filipinos and the diaspora, and as second-language learners strive to know more about the Philippines and its history.

  Pagbabasa

Read the following passage and then answer the questions that follow. Study the new words before reading. Then, answer the questions that follow the short article.

Ibig Sabihin	*Meaning*
Halaman	*Plant*
Pinuno; sa pamumuno	*Leader; led by*
Napapalibutan	*Surrounded*
Sinakop	*Occupied; colonized*
Simbolo	*Symbol*
Makikita	*Will see*
Pasukan	*Entrance*
Gusali	*Building*
Paglubog ng araw	*Sunset*
Rebolusyon	*Revolution*
Lumaban	*Fought*
Nakaaalala	*Remember*
Hitsura	*Looks like*
Nabuhay	*Lived*

Ang Maynila

Ang pinakalumang Maynila, ay ang Maynila ng mga Tagalog, at ang pangalan ng lugar ay galing sa mga salitang "may nila." Ang ibig sabihin, mayroon silang "nila," isang uri ng halaman. Ito ang Maynila ng mga Tagalog at ng mga pinuno nilang sina Rajah Sulayman at Rajah Matanda. Ito rin ang Maynila na sinakop ng Borneo at ng mga Muslim. Ito ang Maynila na nakilala para sa kanyang dagat, ang Manila Bay, at sa kanyang ilog, ang Pasig.

Noong 1571, sinakop ito ng mga Kastila, sa pamumuno ni Miguel Lopez de Lagazpi. Itinayo nila ang isang "walled city" o lungsod na napapalibutan ng pader, ang Intramuros. Galing ang pangalan nito sa wikang Latin: intra at muros, at ibinigay ang pangalan na ito sa Maynila ng mga Kastila. Isang simbolo ang mga pader dahil ang mga Kastila lang ang puwedeng tumira sa loob ng Intramuros.

Ngayon, "tourist destination" na ito. Puwede kang pumunta sa Fort Santiago. Pagkatapos, maglakad ka papunta sa General Luna street. Lampasan mo ang Plaza Moriones at ang Palacio del Gobernador. Makikita mo ang Manila Cathedral.

Maglakad ka pa sa General Luna street. Pagkatapos ng dalawang kanto, kumanan ka. Maglakad ka sa Calle Real. Darating ka sa Puerta de Sta. Lucia. Isa ito sa mga pasukan papunta sa Intramuros. Puwede ka ring pumunta sa iba pang gusali. Nasa General Luna Street din ang San Agustin Church at ang Casa Manila.

Sa labas ng Intramuros, sa Tondo, isinilang ang rebolusyon at ang Katipunan, ang grupo na lumaban sa mga Kastila. Binuo ito sa kanto ng mga kalye na El Cano at Ascarraga (ngayon ay Recto) noong 1892.

Sa panahon ng pananakop ng mga Amerikano, itinayo naman ang mga gusali ng gobyerno. Mga pangalan ng mga Amerikanong mananakop ang ginamit na pangalan ng kalye. May mga bus, kotse, at karitela (horse-drawn carriage) sa daan. Ang mga mayayaman at at mga Amerikano ay nakatira sa Malate, dahil nakikita mula dito ang dagat. Dahil sinakop ng mga Hapon ang Pilipinas mula 1942 hanggang 1945, binomba ng mga Amerikano ang Maynila noong Pebrero hanggang Marso 1945 sa tinatawag na "Battle of Manila."

Para sa ibang Filipino na nabuhay noong 1950s, ang Maynila ay ang Roxas Boulevard kung saan nakikita ang paglubog ng araw sa dagat, ang Rizal Park para sa mga picnic, at ang Escolta at Avenida para sa pamimili. Para sa mga aktibista noong 1960s at 1970s, ang mga lugar ng demonstrasyon at rali ay ang Plaza Miranda, ang Mendiola Bridge (na tinatawag ding Freedom Bridge), at ang Liwasang Bonifacio (sa harap ng post office building). Para sa mga Tsino, ang Maynila ay ang Binondo. Para sa mga estudyante, ang Maynila ang "university belt" sa Recto. Para sa mga Katoliko, ang Maynila ay ang Quiapo Church kung saan maraming deboto (devotees) na makikita.

Iba-iba ang Maynila ng mga taga-Maynila. Lumaki na ang lungsod at naging Greater Manila Area. Wala nang nakaaalala ng hitsura ng "nila." Ang Maynila ay hindi lang Maynila nina Sulayman, Bonifacio, at Rizal. Maynila ito ng lahat ng mga Filipino —Tagalog, Tsino, Kapampangan, at iba pang lahing Filipino na nabuhay sa lungsod na ito.

1. Sino ang mga pinuno ng Maynila bago dumating ang mga Kastila?
2. Ano ang pangalan ng lungsod na itinayo ng mga Kastila?
3. Nasaan ang Katedral ng Maynila?
4. Paano pumunta sa Puerta de Santa Lucia mula sa Katedral ng Maynila?
5. Ano ang mga sasakyan noong panahon ng mga Amerikano?
6. Kailan binomba ng mga Amerikano ang Maynila?
7. Saan namimili ang mga tao noong 1950s?
8. Saan ang mga rallies noong 1960s at 1970s?
9. Saan sa Maynila nakatira noon ang mga Tsino?
10. Anong tulay ang tinatawag na Freedom Bridge?

✏ Pagsusulat

Get a map of your neighborhood. Mark two points on the map. Write directions to go from point A to point B.

⚑ Paglalagom

In **Aralin 14**, you have:
1. Learned words and phrases used in giving directions,
2. Reviewed **saan** and **nasaan**,
3. Practiced the imperative form of the verb.

You should now be able to:
1. Ask directions.
2. Give directions.
3. Talk about places with greater ease.

Pagbabalik-Aral: Pamimili ng Regalo
(Review and Expansion Lesson: Buying a Gift)

  ## Diyalogo: Pagbili ng Blusa (Buying a Blouse)

Read the dialogue below. After completing this chapter, practice this dialogue using
your own information.

JUAN	:	**Patingin nga po ng blusa.**
		Please let me take a look at that blouse.
TINDERA	:	**Aling blusa?**
		Which blouse?
JUAN	:	**Iyong kulay rosas. Saan po yari ang blusa?**
		The pink one. Where was the blouse made?
TINDERA	:	**Dito sa Pilipinas.**
		Here in the Philippines.
JUAN	:	**Magkano po?**
		How much is it?
TINDERA	:	**Isang libo dalawang daang piso.**
		One thousand and two hundred pesos.
JUAN	:	**Bibilhin ko po. Mayroon ba kayong kulay dilaw?**
		I will buy it. Do you have it in yellow?
TINDERA	:	**Opo. Magkapareho po ba ang disenyo?**
		Is the design the same?
JUAN	:	**Opo. Magkapareho ang disenyo pero magkaiba ang kulay.**
		Yes, the design is the same but the colors are different.

  ## Bokabolaryo

Study the following words and phrases. Some of them were used in the dialogue you
just read, a few are words you can use when making sentences for this lesson, have
been introduced in earlier lessons. These words and phrases will be useful when you
make your own sentences for your dialogues.

Yari sa/Gawa sa	*Made in*
Yari sa Pilipinas	*Made in the Philippines*
Magkapareho	*Same*
Magkaiba	*Different*
Bibilhin	*will buy*
Disenyo	*Design*
Malaki	*Big*
Maliit	*Small*
Mahaba	*Long*
Mas Malaki	*Bigger*
Pinakamalaki	*Biggest*
Klase	*Kind* (note: do not confuse with the other meaning of **klase**, *class*)
gusto kong bumili	*Want to buy*
Seda	*Silk*
Tela	*Cloth*
Materyales	*Materials*

Mga Pangungusap

Practice saying these sentences aloud, to get a feel for how this chapter's vocabulary and grammar work in Filipino.

1. **Gusto kong bumili ng bestida.**	*I want to buy a dress.* (subject focus)
2. **Bestida ang gusto kong bilhin.**	*A dress is what I want to buy.* (object focus)
3. **Yari ang bestida sa Tsina.**	*The dress was made in China.*
4. **Kulay rosas ang bestida.**	*The dress is pink.*
5. **Yari sa seda ang bestida.**	*The dress is made of silk.*
6. **Para sa akin ang pantalong ito.**	*This pair of pants is for me.*
7. **Gawa sa faux fur ang coat na bibilhin ko.**	*The coat that I will buy is made of faux fur.*
8. **Magkapareho ang kulay ng mga damit namin ni Cynthia.**	*Cynthia and I have the same color clothes.*
9. **Magkaiba ang disenyo ng sapatos ko sa sapatos niya.**	*The design of my shoes is different from the design of her shoes.*

Pagsasanay 1

Practice these questions and answers by both speaking and writing. Use the sentences in the dialogue and those you have just practiced as guides. For some of the sentences that use expressions of time (such as **noong isang taon** or last year), review past lessons. Also, practice the completed, incompleted, and contemplated forms of the verb "**bili**" or buy.

1. TANONG : **Ano ang gustong bilhin ni Juan?**
   SAGOT : _____.

2. TANONG : **Ano ang gusto mong bilhin?**
   SAGOT : _____.

3. TANONG : **Saan yari ang bestida mo?**
   SAGOT : _____.

4. TANONG : **Ano ang kulay ng bestida mo?**
   SAGOT : _____.

5. TANONG : **Bumili ka ba ng pantalon noong isang taon?**
   SAGOT : _____.

6. TANONG : **Saan ka bumili ng pantalon?**
   SAGOT : _____.

7. TANONG : **Saan yari ang pantalon?**
   SAGOT : _____.

8. TANONG : **Sa anong tela yari ang pantalon?**
   SAGOT : _____.

9. TANONG : **Magkano ang pantalon?**
   SAGOT : _____.

10. TANONG : **Kailan ka bibili ng jacket?**
    SAGOT : _____.

11. TANONG : **Saan ka bibili ng jacket?**
    SAGOT : _____.

12. TANONG : **Gawa sa anong tela o materyales ang jacket na bibilhin mo?**
    SAGOT : _____.

13. TANONG : **Saan gawa ang jacket mo?**
    SAGOT : _____.

 Pagsasanay 2

Practice these questions and answers by both speaking and writing. Use the first situation as a guide. Read the information given about each situation. Classroom learners can work in pairs while individual learners should write and answer questions.

I.   **Pamimili ni Consuelo** (*Consuelo's shopping activity*)

Binibili (*Buying*):	**T-shirt**
Gawa sa (*Made in*):	**Tsina**
Gawa sa (*Made of*):	**Cotton**
Presyo (*Price*):	**₱100**
Kulay (*Color*):	**Asul**
Para kanino:	**Para sa anak niya**

1. TANONG : **Ano ang binibili ni Consuelo?**
   SAGOT : **Bumibili si Consuelo ng T-shirt.**
2. TANONG : **Saan gawa ang T-shirt?**
   SAGOT : **Gawa/Yari ang Tshirt sa Tsina.**
3. TANONG : **Magkano ang T-shirt?**
   SAGOT : **Isang daang piso ang T-shirt.**
4. TANONG : **Ano ang kulay ng T-shirt?**
   SAGOT : **Asul ang T-shirt.**
5. TANONG : **Sa anong tela gawa ang T-shirt?**
   SAGOT : **Gawa sa cotton ang T-shirt.**
6. TANONG : **Para kanino ang T-shirt na binibili ni Consuelo?**
   SAGOT : **Para sa anak ni Consuelo ang T-shirt.**

II. **Pamimili ni Bernard** (*Bernard's shopping activity*)

Binibili:	**Malaking bag**
Gawa sa:	**Italya**
Gawa sa:	**Leather or balat**
Presyo:	**₱15,000**
Kulay:	**Kayumanggi**
Para kanino:	**Para sa asawa**

1. TANONG : **Ano ang binibili ni Bernard?**
   SAGOT   : _____.

2. TANONG : **Saan gawa ang bag?**
   SAGOT   : _____.

3. TANONG : **Sa anong materyales gawa ang bag?**
   SAGOT   : _____.

4. TANONG : **Magkano ang bag?**
   SAGOT   : _____.

5. TANONG : **Ano ang kulay ng bag?**
   SAGOT   : _____.

6. TANONG : **Para kanino ang bag na binibili ni Bernard?**
   SAGOT   : _____.

III. **Pamimili ni Erlinda** (*Erlinda's shopping activity*)

Binibili:	palda
Gawa sa:	bansang Hapon
Gawa sa:	linen
Presyo:	₱2000
Kulay:	abo
Para kanino:	para sa kaibigan niyang si Angela

1. TANONG : _____?
   SAGOT   : **Bumibili si Erlinda ng palda.**

2. TANONG : _____?
   SAGOT   : **Gawa ang palda sa bansang Hapon.**

3. TANONG : _____?
   SAGOT   : **Gawa sa linen ang palda.**

4. TANONG : _____?
   SAGOT   : **Dalawang libong piso ang palda.**

5. TANONG : _____?
   SAGOT   : **Kulay abo ang palda.**

6. TANONG : _____?

    SAGOT   : **Para sa kaibigan niyang si Angela ang palda na binibili ni Erlinda.**

IV. **Pamimili mo** (*Your shopping activity*)

Think of yourself in a department store scene. Choose whatever you want to buy. If you are a classroom learner, work with your partner and create a scene. If you are an individual learner, write down the questions and answers.

1. TANONG : _____?
    SAGOT   : _____.

2. TANONG : _____?
    SAGOT   : _____.

3. TANONG : _____?
    SAGOT   : _____.

4. TANONG : _____?
    SAGOT   : _____.

5. TANONG : _____?
    SAGOT   : _____.

6. TANONG : _____?
    SAGOT   : _____.

🔍 Gramatika

Study the information below to improve your Filipino grammar skills.

I.   Review the verb **bili**

In an earlier lesson, you have learned about the verb **bili**. Here is how we have conjugated this verb. The first row shows the verb with subject focus and the second row, the verb with object focus.

Completed	Incompleted	Contemplated	Infinitive
bumili	bumibili	bibili	gusto kong bumili
binili	binibili	bibilhin	gusto kong bilhin

What many students find confusing is shifting between the use of the verb when the focus is on the subject and when the focus is on the object.

For example, with "**ano**" (*what*) questions, we usually use the object focus.

TANONG	:	**Ano ang binili mo?**
		What did you buy? (literally, What *marker* buy you?)
SAGOT	:	**Blusa ang binili ko.**
		I bought a blouse. (literally, Blouse *marker* bought I.)
TANONG	:	**Ano ang binibili mo?**
		What are you buying? (literally, What *marker* buying you?)
SAGOT	:	**Blusa ang binibili ko.**
		I am buying a blouse. (literally, Blouse *marker* buy I.)
TANONG	:	**Ano ang bibilhin mo?**
		What will you buy? (literally, What *marker* buy you?)
SAGOT	:	**Blusa ang bibilhin ko.**
		I will buy a blouse. (literally, Blouse *marker* will buy I.)
TANONG	:	**Ano ang gusto mong bilhin?**
		What do you want to buy? (literally, What *marker* want you to buy?)
SAGOT	:	**Blusa ang gusto kong bilhin.**
		I want to buy a blouse. (literally, Blouse *marker* want I to *linker* buy).

However, for **sino** (*who*) and **saan** (*where*) questions, the focus is on the subject or the doer of the action.

Thus:

TANONG	:	**Sino ang bumili ng blusa?**
		Who bought the blouse? (literally, Who *marker* bought *marker* blouse?)
SAGOT	:	**Ako ang bumili ng blusa.**
		I was the one who bought the blouse. (literally, I *marker* bought *marker* blouse.)

OR

SAGOT	:	**Bumili ako ng blusa.**
		I bought the blouse. (literally, Bought I *marker* blouse.)
TANONG	:	**Saan ka bumili ng blusa?**
		Where did you buy the blouse? (literally, Where you bought *marker* blouse?)

II. The Pronouns **Ako** and **Ko**, and **Ka** and **Mo**

We have also earlier studied the pronouns **ako** and **ko** (both meaning I), and **ka** and **mo** (both meaning you). At this point, many learners still get confused. When do we use **ako**, and when do we use **ko**? When do we use **ka**, and when do we use **mo**?

We know that **ko** and **mo** are possessive pronouns. Thus we say, **blusa ko** (my blouse) and **blusa mo** (your blouse).

However, why do we have sentences such as:

TANONG : **Ano ang binili mo?**
What did you buy?

SAGOT : **Blusa ang binili ko.**
I bought a blouse.

Why are the following sentences wrong?

TANONG : **Ano ang binili ka?**
(Because this means that the person was the one bought.)

SAGOT : **Blusa ang binili ako.**
(Because this means that the blouse bought the person.)

How do we avoid these mistakes?

By "matching" the pronoun with the "focus" of the sentence.

Remember that when the focus is on the object, use "**mo**" and "**ko**." When the focus is on the actor, use "**ka**" and "**ako**." Also, we use "**ikaw**" instead of **ka**, when we use the second person pronoun at the beginning of the sentence. We use "**ka**" when we use the second person pronoun elsewhere.

Thus, to repeat:

Ako ang bumili ng blusa.

Blusa ang binili ko.

Ikaw ang bumili ng blusa.

Blusa ang binili mo.

Sa Liberty Mall ako bumili ng blusa.

Bumili ako ng blusa sa Liberty Mall

Bumili ka ng blusa sa Liberty Mall.

III. Using **na** for relative pronouns

You may have noticed that when speaking in English, Filipinos tend to make mistakes in using relative pronouns such as *who, what, which, where,* and *when.* This is because the Filipino/Tagalog equivalent of these relative pronouns is only "**na**."

Study the following sentences:

TANONG : **Ano ang coat na bibilhin mo?**
What coat will you buy? (literally, What *marker* coat that will buy you?)

SAGOT : **Gawa sa faux fur ang coat na bibilhin ko.**
The coat that I will buy is made of faux fur. (literally, Made of faux fur *marker* coat that will buy I.)

TANONG : **Sino ang babaeng bumili ng asul na palda?**
Who is the woman who bought the blue skirt? (literally, Who *marker* who bought *marker* blue *linker* skirt?)

SAGOT : **Si Binibining San Miguel ang babae na bumili ng asul na palda.**
Miss San Miguel is the woman who bought a blue skirt. (*Marker* Miss San Miguel *marker* woman who bought *marker* blue *linker* skirt.)

Note that in the second question, the words **babae** and **na** are contracted, resulting in "**babaeng.**"

You will have more practice later in forming complex sentences using "**na.**"

IV. **Magkapareho** and **Magkaiba** (same and different)
The root words of same and different are **kapareho** and **kaiba**. To make sentences, we use the prefix **mag-**. Thus, we can say:

Magkapareho ang kulay ng mga bag namin.
Our bags have the same color. (literally, Same *marker* color *marker* bag our.)
Magkapareho ang kulay ng bag ko at ng bag niya.
The color of my bag and her bag are the same. (literally, Same *marker* color *marker* bag my and *marker* bag her.)
Magkapareho ang kulay ng mga bag ni Sylvia at ni Maureen.
The color of Sylvia and Maureen's bag is the same. (literally, Same *marker* color *marker* bags of Sylvia and of Maureen.)
Magkaiba ang disenyo ng mga blusa namin.
Our blouses have different designs.

Mga Tala Sa Kultura

Bargaining is often expected when shopping in stalls, popular markets such as Divisoria, and **tiangges** (open markets inspired by traditional markets). Although department store prices are usually fixed, most stores will allow customers to bargain. This is called **tawaran**, and interestingly, the root word **tawad** also means *to forgive*. When we want to bargain, we can say, "**Puwede ho bang tumawad?**" (*Can I bargain?*) or "**Patawad naman po.**" In another context, the latter sentence can also be translated into "Please forgive me" although it would actually be phrased differently: "**Patawad na po**" (literally, Forgive [me] already).

The word **tawad** appears to have these two meanings in early dictionaries. In the 1860 work by Juan Jose de Noceda and Pedro de Sanlucar, *Vocabolario de la lengua tagala: composto por varios religiosos doctos y graves* (Manila: Imprente de Ramirez y Gibaudier), the word **tawad** (spelled as **tauad**) is listed as the Tagalog equivalent of both **concertar regateando** (*to haggle* or *to barter*) and **desagraviar** (*to make* *amends*). In *A Tagalog English and English Tagalog Dictionary,* 1904 (Manila: Imp. de Fajardo y comp.) by Charles Nigg it is defined with the following meanings: *bid, immunity,* and *pardon.* It also appears to have these two meanings in Pedro Laktaw's *Diccionario Tag'alog-Hispano* published in 1914 (Manila: Islas Filipinas). These dictionary entries indicate that this indigenous word probably has always had two meanings.

What does it then say about Filipino culture when you have the same word for bargaining and for asking forgiveness? I believe that we need to contextualize this word and how it is used in phrases and sentences with other phrases that convey respect and politeness. For example, "**Mawalang-galang na ho,**" which translates to "excuse me" but literally means "Without respect...". Or the more formal "**Ipagpatawad po ninyo pero...**" which also means "Excuse me," but also literally means "Forgive me but..." Thus, by using the same word for "forgive" in bargaining, Filipinos wish to convey respect and formality.

Diyalogo: Pagsusukat ng Damit (Fitting a dress)

Read the following dialogue. Then try to make a role-play later using this as your guide. Remember that the conversation approximates everyday Filipino in the Metro Manila area. Thus, although some words in English may have translations in Filipino, for exampe "**sukat**" for "*size*" they are taught but may or may not be used in your dialogue practice.

BARBARA : **Ang ganda-ganda! Puwede ko ho bang sukatin ang bestidang ito?**
Can I try this dress on?

TINDERA : **Opo.**
Yes.

BARBARA : **Nasaan ho ang fitting room?**
Where is the fitting room?

TINDERA : **Dumiretso ho kayo. Tapos, kumanan kayo sa dulo. Nasa kaliwa ninyo ang fitting room.**
Go straight. Then, turn right at the end. The fitting room is on your left.

BARBARA : **Maliit ho sa akin at napaka-iksi. Mayroon ba kayong size 8 ng bestidang ito?**
It is too small for me. Do you have this dress in a size 8?

TINDERA : **Opo. Ano pong kulay ang gusto ninyo?**
Yes. What color would you like?

BARBARA : **Kulay itim po.**
Black, please.

TINDERA : **Pasensiya na kayo. Wala na kaming kulay itim na size 8.**
So sorry. We no longer have a black one in a size 8.

BARBARA : **Brown na lang po.**
Just the brown one please.

TINDERA : **Heto po.**
Here.

(Pagkatapos ng ilang minuto).
(After a few minutes).

TINDERA : **Kasya po ba?**
Does it fit?

BARBARA : **Opo. Kukunin ko na ho.**
Yes. I will get it.

  ## Bokabolaryo

Study the following words and how they were used in the dialogue you just read. There are also additional words that you can use when talking about size and length. Many of these words are adjectives, and in this lesson, we shall practice using these adjectives with affixes such as **napaka-** and in combination with words such as **masyadong**.

Mga Salita

Sukat	the verb *"To try on"* (conjugated: **sinukat, sinusukat, susukatin**)
Kasya	*Fits*
Sukat	*Size*
Napaka	*Prefix; too*
Napakaiksi/Masyadong maiksi	*Too short*
Napakahaba/Masyadong mahaba	*Too long*
Napakalaki/Masyadong malaki	*Too big*
Nakapakaliit/Masyadong maliit	*Too small*
Napakaluwang/Masyadong Maluwang	*Too loose*
Napakasikip/Masyadong masikip	*Too tight*
Katamtaman	*Medium; just right*

Note: There are no direct equivalents for small, medium, and large, although sometimes **maliit** (*small*), **katamtaman** (*just right*), or **malaki** (*big*) are used. These English words have been incorporated in everyday Filipino.

Mga Ekspresyon

Study the following expressions. In Filipino/Tagalog, when words are repeated, it is to emphasize them. Thus, by repeating the word, the adjectives that follow mean very beautiful, very small, very big.

Ang ganda-ganda!	*How beautiful!* (literally, *Marker beautiful beautiful*)
Magandang-maganda ang blusa.	*The blouse is very beautiful.*
Ang liit-liit!	*How small!*
Ang laki-laki!	*How big!*

Mga Pangungusap

Practice saying these sentences aloud, to get a feel for how this chapter's vocabulary and grammar work in Filipino.

1. **Gusto kong sukatin ang pulang sapatos.** *I want to try on the red shoes.*
2. **Napakalaki ng kulay abong coat para sa akin.** *The grey coat is too big for me.*
3. **Masyadong maluwang ang pantalon na iyan para kay Jorge.** *Those pants are too loose for Jorge.*
4. **Kasya kay Suzette ang blusang na ito.** *This blouse fits Suzette.*
5. **Size 7 ang sukat ng paa ko.** *My feet are a size 7.*
6. **Size 4 ang sukat ko sa damit.** *I wear a size 4 dress.*
7. **Itim ang gusto niyang kulay.** *Black is the color he/she likes.*
8. **₱500 ang halaga ng T-shirt na binili ni Joey.** *The T-shirt that Joey bought costs ₱500.*
9. **Ang laki-laki ng cardigan na ito.** *This cardigan is so big!*

  Pagsasanay

Study the information given. Then, ask and answer questions. Use the first situation as an example.

I. **Pamimili ni Elena**

   Size: 6
   Kulay: Pula (*red*)
   Presyo: ₱2,500

1. TANONG : **Ano ang gustong sukatin ni Elena?**
   SAGOT : **Sapatos ang gustong sukatin ni Elena.**
2. TANONG : **Kasya ba kay Elena ang size 8 na sapatos? Bakit?**
   SAGOT : **Hindi. Napakalaki ng sapatos para kay Elena.**
3. TANONG : **Anong kulay ang gusto ni Elena?**
   SAGOT : **Pula ang gusto niya.**
4. TANONG : **Ano ang sukat ng paa ni Elena?**
   SAGOT : **Size 6 ang sukat ng paa ni Elena.**
5. TANONG : **Magkano ang sapatos na binili ni Elena?**
   SAGOT : **₱2,500 ang halaga ng sapatos na binili ni Elena.**

II. **Pamimili ni Andy**
   Size: Large
   Kulay: **asul**
   Presyo: ₱3,000

1. TANONG : **Ano ang gustong sukatin ni Andy?**
   SAGOT : _____.

2. TANONG : **Kasya ba kay Andy ang size Small na polo? Bakit?**
   SAGOT : _____.

3. TANONG : **Ano ang sukat ni Andy?**
   SAGOT : _____.

4. TANONG : **Anong kulay ang gusto ni Andy?**
   SAGOT : _____.

5. TANONG : **Magkano ang polo na binili ni Andy?**
   SAGOT : _____.

III. **Pamimili ni Merlinda**
   Size: Small
   Kulay: **Kahel** (*Orange*)
   Presyo: ₱1,500

1. TANONG : **Ano ang gustong sukatin ni Merlinda?**
   SAGOT : _____.

2. TANONG : **Kasya ba kay Merlinda ang size Large na sweater? Bakit?**
   SAGOT : _____.

3. TANONG : **Ano ang sukat ni Merlinda?**
   SAGOT   : _____.

4. TANONG : **Anong kulay ang gusto ni Merlinda?**
   SAGOT   : _____.

5. TANONG : **Magkano ang sweater na binili ni Merlinda?**
   SAGOT   : _____.

IV. **Ang Iyong Pamimili**

Make a stick drawing of yourself. Write down your size, the item you want to buy, and the price of the item. Then, ask and answer questions. Classroom learners should work in pairs while individual learners should write down the questions and the answers.

1. TANONG : _____?
   SAGOT   : _____.

2. TANONG : _____?
   SAGOT   : _____.

3. TANONG : _____?
   SAGOT   : _____.

4. TANONG : _____?
   SAGOT   : _____.

5. TANONG : _____?
   SAGOT   : _____.

⭐ **Gawain**

Using one of the situations in the **Pagsasanay** or Practice section, as well as the dialogue you read earlier, do a role-play.

Classroom learners should work in pairs while individual learners should write a dialogue.

 **Pagbabasa**

Read the following short short story, and then answer the questions that follow. Study the new words and expressions before reading the story. Written in contemporary Filipino, the story uses English words that have been incorporated into everyday life in Metro Manila. Also, this story is informed by a popular urban legend, that of a snake that is said to be the twin of a woman. The snake apparently lives in dressing rooms of a department store.

Ahas	*Snake*
Takot na takot	*Very afraid*
Sayang	*It's a pity*
Nag-iimbita	*Invites*
Tse!	*Expression of disgust*
Matutuklaw	*Will be bitten; refers only to snake bites*
Pagseselos	*Jealousy*

Ahas (Snake)

May urban legend sa Maynila. Mayroon daw ahas sa loob ng fitting rooms ng isang department store.

Takot na takot ako sa loob ng fitting room. Sinusukat ko ang iba't ibang pulang damit. Valentine's Day na sa susunod na linggo at gusto kong isuot ang bestida sa date namin ni Mark.

Bestida no. 1. Strapless, form fitting. Sayang, masyadong masikip.

Bestida no. 2. Plunging neckline. May itim na sinturon.

Sayang, napakaiksi naman.

Bestida no. 3. One-shoulder. Interesante ang disenyo.

At kasyang-kasya sa akin.

Lumalabas na ako sa fitting room nang makita ko siya. Ang ex-girlfriend ng asawa ko. Ang babaeng tumatawag pa rin sa kanya sa telepono. Ang babaeng nag-iimbita sa kanya para magkape o kumain ng tanghalian. Ano bang "friends-friends" lang? Tse. Tse. Tse.

"Hello. Denise, ikaw pala!"

"Vicky! Kumusta?"

Tupperware. Orocan. In other words, plastic moment. Kung hindi, matutuklaw siya ng pagseselos ko.

1. **Nasaan ang ahas sa urban legend ng Maynila?**
2. **Ano ang sinusukat niya?**
3. **Bakit hindi kasya ang bestida no. 1?**
4. **Bakit hindi kasya ang bestida no. 2?**
5. **Sino ang nakita niya sa labas ng fitting room?**

✏ Pagsusulat

Using the vocabulary and grammar you have learned, try writing a paragraph about a recent shopping experience.

⚑ Paglalagom

In **Aralin 15**, you have:
1. Reviewed and studied words and expressions related to shopping,
2. Practiced shifting from the object to subject focus when answering and asking questions,
3. Studied adjectives that refer to size and shape,
4. Reviewed words used when talking about money.

You should now be able to:
1. Go shopping for clothes.
2. Describe nouns better.

Pagpunta sa Salo-salo ng May Kaarawan
(Going to a Birthday Party)

  Diyalogo: Maligayang Kaarawan! (Happy birthday!)

Read the dialogue below. Practice the expressions you can find in this dialogue. After completing this chapter, practice this dialogue using your own information.

JUAN : **Tao po!**
Someone's here!

CLARA : **Ikaw pala, Juan! Tuloy ka!**
It's you, Juan! Come in!

JUAN : **Maligayang kaarawan, Clara!**
Happy birthday, Clara!

CLARA : **Maraming salamat, Juan.**
Thank you, Juan!

JUAN : **Pagpasensiyahan mo na ang maliit na regalo ko.**
Please bear with my small gift./I am sorry for my small gift.

CLARA : **Nag-abala ka pa.**
You shouldn't have bothered.

JUAN : **Hindi ba't ika-labingwalong kaarawan mo ngayon?**
Isn't it your eighteenth birthday?

CLARA : **Naku, hindi. Labinsiyam na ako.**
Oh, no. I am nineteen now.

JUAN : **Ganoon ba?**
Is that so?

Bokabolaryo

Study the following words and expressions. Some of them were used in the dialogue you just read and some are additional words and expressions that will be useful when you make your own sentences for your dialogues talking about life events.

Mga Salita

kaarawan	*birthday*
regalo	*gift*
abala	*bother* (another meaning is *to be busy*)
maligaya/masaya	*happy*
nanalo	*won*
natalo	*lost*
ipinanganak	*born*
nagtapos	*graduated*
elementarya/mababang paaralan	*elementary school*
high school/mataas na paaralan	*high school*
kolehiyo	*college*
gradwadong pag-aaral	*graduate study*
ikinasal	*got married*
namatay/yumao/pumanaw	*passed on; died*

Mga Ekspresyon

Study the following expressions that you can use in certain occasions.

Maligayang kaarawan!	*Happy birthday!*
Maligayang anibersaryo!	*Happy anniversary!*
Binabati kita!	*Congratulations!*
Ikinalulungkot ko.	*I am sad about this.*
Nakikiramay ako.	*My condolences.*
Pagpasensiyahan mo na!	*I am sorry for this.*
Pasensiya ka na.	*Sorry.* (literally, Sorry you.)
Nag-abala ka pa.	*You shouldn't have bothered.* (literally, Bothered you.)
Huwag ka nang mag-abala.	*Please don't bother.*
Ganoon ba?	*Is that so?*
Talaga?	*Really?*

Mga Pangungusap

Study the following sentences that talk about life events.

1. **Ipinanganak ako noong ika-dalawampu't siyam ng Hunyo 1962.**
   I was born on June 29, 1962.

2. **Nagtapos siya sa kolehiyo noong 1990.**
   She graduated from college in 1990.

3. **Ikinasal si Merce noong 2004 kay Julian Romero.**
   Merce got married in 2004 to Julian Romero.

4. **Nagtapos ng gradwadong pag-aaral si Nerissa sa UC Berkeley.**
   Nerissa finished her graduate. studies in UC Berkeley.

5. **Nanalo ang mga estudyante sa high school ng Stella Maris College sa volleyball tournament.**
   The high school students of Stella Maris College won in the volleyball tournament.

6. **Yumao ang guro kong si Ginang Cruz noong 1995.**
   My teacher, Mrs. Cruz, passed away in 1995.

 Pagsasanay 1

Look at the pictures below and read the information on the people featured. Then, ask and answer questions. Use the first situation as an example. Classroom learners can work in pairs while individual learners should write down the questions and the answers.

I. **Si Peter**

Ipinanganak:	Ika-21 ng Oktubre 1961
Nagtapos ng kolehiyo:	1982; Ateneo de Davao
Ikinasal:	1992
Asawa:	Sally
Award:	Businessman of the Year; 2001

1. TANONG : **Kailan ipinanganak si Peter?**
   SAGOT : **Ipinanganak siya noong ika-21 ng Oktubre 1961.**
2. TANONG : **Saan nagtapos ng kolehiyo si Peter?**
   SAGOT : **Nagtapos siya ng kolehiyo sa Ateneo de Davao.**
3. TANONG : **Kailan nagtapos ng kolehiyo si Peter?**
   SAGOT : **Nagtapos siya ng kolehiyo noong 1982.**
4. TANONG : **Kailan ikinasal si Peter?**
   SAGOT : **Ikinasal siya noong 1992.**

5. Tanong : **Kanino ikinasal si Peter?**
   Sagot : **Ikinasal siya kay Sally.**
6. Tanong : **Kailan siya nanalo ng award?**
   Sagot : **Nanalo siya ng award noong 2001.**
7. Tanong : **Ano ang award niya?**
   Sagot : **Businessman of the Year ang award niya.**

II. **Si Ligaya**

Ipinanganak:	ika-3 ng Abril 1981
Nagtapos ng high school:	1998
Nagtapos ng kolehiyo:	2002, University of Santo Tomas
Ikinasal:	2009
Asawa:	Robert
Nanalo:	Palanca Award para sa panitikan 2008

1. Tanong : **Kailan ipinanganak si Ligaya?**
   Sagot : _____.

2. Tanong : **Kailan siya nagtapos ng high school?**
   Sagot : _____.

3. Tanong : **Saan siya nagtapos ng kolehiyo?**
   Sagot : _____.

4. Tanong : **Kailan siya ikinasal?**
   Sagot : _____.

5. Tanong : **Kanino siya ikinasal?**
   Sagot : _____.

6. Tanong : **Kailan siya nanalo ng award?**
   Sagot : _____.

7. Tanong : **Ano ang award niya?**
   Sagot : _____.

III. **Si Monico**

Ipinanganak:	Ika-30 ng Nobyembre 1933
Nagtapos ng gradwadong pag-aaral:	1969 Hindi ikinasal o walang asawa
Nanalo:	Outstanding Teacher Award 1980

1. TANONG : _____?
   SAGOT : _____.

2. TANONG : _____?
   SAGOT : _____.

3. TANONG : _____?
   SAGOT : _____.

4. TANONG : _____?
   SAGOT : _____.

5. TANONG : _____?
   SAGOT : _____.

6. TANONG : _____?
   SAGOT : _____.

IV. **Pangalan mo** (*Your name*): _____

1. TANONG : _____?
   SAGOT : _____.

2. TANONG : _____?
   SAGOT : _____.

3. TANONG : _____?
   SAGOT : _____.

4. TANONG : _____?
   SAGOT : _____.

5. TANONG : _____?
   SAGOT : _____.

6. TANONG : _____?
   SAGOT : _____.

Pagsasanay 2

Practice the expressions you have learned earlier. Take the role of Person B. React to the statement given by Person A. Use the first two exchanges as a guide. Classroom learners can work in pairs while individual learners should write their answers.

1. A : **Kaarawan ko bukas.**
   B : **Maligayang kaarawan!**

2. A : **Nanalo ako sa contest.**
   B : **Binabati kita!**

3. A : **Yumao ang aso ko.**
   B : _____

4. A : **Ikakasal na ako sa susunod na buwan.**
   B : _____

5. A : **Anibersaryo namin ng asawa ko sa isang linggo.**
   B : _____

6. A : **Natalo ang soccer team namin.**
   B : _____

7. A : **Magtatapos ako ng kolehiyo sa Abril.**
   B : _____

 Diyalogo: Ligawan (Courtship)

Read the dialogue below. Practice the expressions you can find in this dialogue. After completing this chapter, practice this dialogue using your own information.

Pedro : **Ano ang binili mo para kay Clara?**
          What did you buy for Clara?
Juan : **Binilhan ko siya ng blusa.**
          I bought her a blouse.
Pedro : **Niiligawan mo ba si Clara?**
          Are you courting Clara?
Juan : **Gusto ko sanang ligawan si Clara.**
          I would like to court Clara. (Literally, Want I hope court marker Clara.)

Pedro : **Sayang. Sana, binigyan mo siya ng pulseras.**
A pity. You could have given her a bracelet. (Literally, Hope gave you her marker *bracelet).*

Juan : **Bakit?**
Why?

Pedro : **Para sabihing, "Mahal kita."**
To say, "I love you." (Literally, Love I you.)

Juan : **Kung singsing kaya?**
How about a ring? (Literally, What if ring?)

Pedro : **"Nangangako akong pakakasalan kita."**
"I promise to marry you." (Literally, Promise I marry I you.)

Bokabolaryo

Study the following words and phrases. Some of them were used in the dialogue you just read; a few are words that have been introduced earlier. These words and phrases will help you make your own sentences.

Binilhan	*Bought (focus on the indirect object or the person to whom the action is directed)*
Nililigawan	*Courting (refers to both "traditional" and "modern" ways of expressing love for another)*
Pulseras	*Bracelet*
Singsing	*Ring*
Kuwintas	*Necklace*
Hikaw	*Earrings*
Alahas	*Jewelry*
Mahal kita.	*I love you. (**Mahal** or "love" is used here to refer to the "beloved," to family, friends, and pets.)*
Iniibig kita.	*I love you. (**Iniibig** or "love") is used here to refer only to the "beloved," and to one's country.)*
Sayang!	*A pity!*
Kung	*If; What about*
Kaya	*(accent on the second syllable) (Expression used to go with **kung**—**kung** + word + **kaya**—to express the conditional "if"*
Kung singsing kaya?	*How about a ring? (Literally, What if ring?)*
Nangangako	*Promise*
Pakakasalan	*Will marry*

Mga Pangungusap

Practice saying these sentences aloud, to get a feel for how this chapter's vocabulary and grammar work in Filipino.

1. **Binilhan ko ng kuwintas ang nanay ko.**	*I bought my mother a bracelet.*
2. **Binigyan kita ng hikaw noong isang buwan.**	*I gave you earrings last month.*
3. **Mahal ko ang pusa ko.**	*I love my pet cat.*
4. **Iniibig ko ang asawa ko.**	*I love my husband.*
5. **Sana, binigyan mo siya ng bulaklak.**	*You could have given her flowers. (Literally, Hope gave you her* marker *flowers).*
6. **Kung rosas kaya?**	*How about roses? (Literally, If roses?/If roses "expression"* **kaya?)**

 Pagsasanay

Study the information given. Then, answer the questions or provide questions to the given answers. The questions and answers are provided in the first situation as examples.

Situation 1: It is your father's birthday. You bought him a necktie.

1. TANONG : **Ano ang binili mo?**
   SAGOT : **Bumili ako ng kurbata.**
2. TANONG : **Sino ang binilhan mo ng kurbata?**
   SAGOT : **Binilhan ko ng kurbata ang tatay ko.**
3. TANONG : **Bakit mo siya binilhan ng kurbata?**
   SAGOT : **Dahil kaarawan niya.**
4. TANONG : **Ano ang gagawin mo mamaya?**
   SAGOT : **Gagawan ko siya ng cake.**
5. TANONG : **Ano ang sasabihin mo sa kanya?**
   SAGOT : **"Mahal kita, Tatay!"**

Situation 2: It is your friend's graduation day. You and your other friends bought her flowers. On the card, you wrote: "Congratulations! We love you, Kathleen!"

1. TANONG : **Ano ang binili ninyo?**
   SAGOT : _____.

2. TANONG : **Sino ang binilhan ninyo ng _____?**
   SAGOT : _____.

3. TANONG : **Bakit niyo siya binilhan ng _____?**
   SAGOT : _____.

4. TANONG : **Ano ang isinulat ninyo sa card?**
   SAGOT : _____.

Situation 3: It is your grandparents' 50th wedding anniversary. You and your brother made a video for them. You will watch the video at the anniversary party.

1. TANONG : _____?
   SAGOT : **Ginawan namin ang lolo at lola namin ng video.**

2. TANONG : _____?
   SAGOT : **Dahil ika-50 anibersaryo nila.**

3. TANONG : _____?
   SAGOT : **Manonood kami ng video sa anniversary party nila.**

4. TANONG : _____?
   SAGOT : **Ginawan namin sila ng video dahil mahal namin sila.**

Gramatika

I. Using the special pronoun **Kita**

In this lesson, the special pronoun **kita** was used in the sentences "**Binabati kita!**" *Congratulations!* (Literally, *Congratulations, I you!*) and "**Mahal kita.**" (*I love you.*)

In the literal meaning of these sentences, the pronouns *I* and *you* come one after the other, resulting in an awkward sentence construction. In Tagalog/Filipino, this would have been "**Binabati ko ka!**" (never used) or "**Binabati ko ikaw!**" (grammatically wrong). Similarly, we do not say "**Mahal ko ka.**" Instead, we say "**Mahal kita.**"

II. Focus on the indirect object or the person to whom the action is addressed

The best way to indicate that the focus is on the indirect object or the person to whom the action is addressed is to look at the markers **ang**, **si** and **sina**.

EXAMPLES: **Binilhan ko ng mga bulaklak ang kaibigan ko.**
I bought my friend flowers.
Bibigyan ko ng cake si Roselle.
I will give Roselle a cake.

To form the verb, we use the affixes **in-** and **-an**. Here are some useful formulas:

Completed: **-in** before the first vowel + root word + **-an**
                binilhan; binigyan
Incompleted: first two syllables of incompleted form + root word + **-an**
                binibilhan; binibigyan
Contemplated: first syllable of root word + root word + **-an**
                bibilhan; bibigyan

But why do we say **binibilhan** instead of **binibilihan**? For ease of speaking, the vowel between **l** and **h** is removed.

Mga Tala Sa Kultura

Humility is important in Filipino culture. In giving a gift or asking someone to dinner, some people apologize by saying that the offering is "not good enough." Two expressions we have learned in this lesson are: "**Pagpasensiyahan mo na ang maliit na regalo ko.** (*Please bear with my small gift./I am sorry for my small gift.*)" and "**Pasensiya ka na.** (*I am sorry.*)" Another similar expression is: "**Ito lang ang nakayanan ko.** (*This is all I can manage.*)"

In dinner situations, the host, who is usually the cook, also tries to diminish the amount of effort he/she has taken in preparing for the meal. Thus, he/she says: "**Pasensiya na kayo at ito lang ang naihanda namin.**" (*So sorry because this is all we have prepared.*" And yet, as one surveys the dinner table, one can see three or four dishes and at least two kinds of dessert.

In response, the gift recipient or the dinner guest can also say the following:

"**Hindi na po kayo dapat nag-abala.** *You shouldn't have bothered.*"

"**Labis-labis naman po ito.** *This is too much.*"

"**Nakakahiya naman sa inyo.** *I am ashamed [that you took so much trouble].*"

This exchange serves an important role in maintaining good relations among neighbors and friends, in a community of interdependent lives.

★ Gawain

If you are a classroom learner, use the dialogue at the beginning of the lesson as a guide and use the words and expressions you have learned to do the following role-plays with your partner. If you are an individual learner, write a dialogue on one of the following situations.

Situation 1: You are attending the wedding anniversary party of Vic and Teresita Mendez. You brought them a wedding gift.

Situation 2: Your friend Francine's father passed on. You are at the funeral home and you have brought a basket of flowers. Francine offers you coffee and some sandwiches.

Situation 3: It is your cousin Flor's 50th birthday party. She looks 40 because she recently got botox and collagen injections.

  Pagbabasa

Read the following short biographies on two heroes during the Spanish colonial period. Then, answer the questions that follow. A vocabulary list precedes the text.

Panahon ng pananakop ng mga Kastila	*Spanish colonial period*
magbasa (accent on the third syllable)	*To read*
Nobela	*Novel*
Sinulat	*Wrote*
Binasa	*Read*
Itinatag	*Established*
Nang	*Used as relative pronoun; here used for "When"*
Sumali	*Join*
Nahati	*Split*

Sina Jose at Andres

Ipinanganak sina Jose Rizal at Andres Bonifacio noong panahon ng pananakop ng mga Kastila; si Jose noong 1861, at si Andres noong 1863. Nag-aral si Rizal sa maraming eskuwelahan: sa Ateneo, Unibersidad ng Santo Tomas, sa Universidad Central de Madrid, sa University of Paris, at University of Heidelberg. Hindi nag-aral sa kolehiyo si Andres pero gusto niyang magbasa.

Dalawang nobela ang sinulat ni Rizal: Ang *Noli me Tangere* (Touch Me Not), 1887 at *El Filibusterismo* (The Subversive), 1891. Binasa ni Andres ang dalawang nobelang ito.

Nang itinatag ni Rizal ang La Liga Filipina sa Maynila noong 1892, sumali si Andres Bonifacio. Ipinatapon ng mga Kastila si Rizal sa Dapitan at nahati ang organisasyon sa mga konserbatibo (conservatives) at mga radikal (radicals). Itinatag ni Andres ang Katipunan sa Maynila noon ding 1892. Rebolusyon ang sagot ng Katipunan sa pananakop ng mga Kastila.

Dalawang bayani ng Pilipinas sina Jose at Andres.

1. **Kailan ipinanganak sina Jose at Andres?**
2. **Anong mga nobela ang sinulat ni Rizal?**
3. **Saan itinatag ang La Liga Filipina?**
4. **Ano ang sagot ng Katipunan sa pananakop ng mga Kastila?**

✒ Pagsusulat

Write a short paragraph on one of the following topics. Remember that writing is a good way to acquire learner-need vocabulary. If you find that you do not know the Filipino equivalent of the words you want to use, get help from a dictionary.

1. A recent birthday party you attended and how you shopped for the gift you brought.
2. A short autobiography.
3. The biography of your grandfather or your grandmother.

⚑ Paglalagom

In **Aralin 16**, you have:
1. Learned words about the life cycle of a person,
2. Studied words and expressions you can use when expressing love and extending congratulations and sympathy,
3. Practiced communicating in situations involving going to an event and receiving guests,
4. Reviewed words used when talking about money,
5. Studied verbs with indirect object focus.

You should now be able to:
1. Write a brief and simple biography or autobiography.
2. Express congratulations and sympathy.

Ang Pang-araw-araw kong Buhay
(My Everyday Life)

  Diyalogo: Ano Ang Ginagawa Mo Tuwing Sabado?
(What do you do on Saturdays?)

Read the dialogue below. After completing this chapter, practice this dialogue using your own information. Remember that in this lesson, we are practicing the incompleted aspect of the verb.

PEDRO : **Hello?**
Hello?

MARIA : **Hello?**
Hello?

PEDRO : **Puwede bang makausap si Maria?**
May I speak to Maria?

MARIA : **Si Maria nga ito.**
This is Maria.

PEDRO : **Gusto mo bang pumunta sa konsiyerto sa Sabado ng gabi?**
Would you like to go to a concert on Saturday evening?

MARIA : **Anong oras?**
What time?

PEDRO : **Alas-sais.**
Six o'clock.

MARIA : **Naku, hindi ako puwede. Dumadalo ako ng pulong ng Philippine Studies Forum tuwing Sabado.**
Oh, I can't make it. I attend the meetings of Philippine Studies Forum on Saturdays.

MARIA : **Anong oras natatapos ang pulong?**
What time does the meeting end?

MARIA : **Nagsisimula ang pulong nang alas-kuwatro at natatapos nang alas-singko. Saan ang konsiyerto?**
The meeting starts at four and ends at five o'clock. Where is the concert?

PEDRO : **Sa Abelardo Hall.**
At Abelardo Hall.

MARIA : **Anong oras ka pupunta?**
What time will you go?

PEDRO : **Mga alas-singko kwarenta. Nagbabasa ako sa library nang Sabado ng hapon.**
Around five forty. I read at the library on Saturday afternoons.

MARIA : **Sige. Pumunta ka sa Vinzon's Hall. Doon ang meeting namin.**
Okay. Go to Vinzon's Hall. Our meeting is there.

PEDRO : **Sige. Dadaanan kita. Magkita tayo sa Sabado.**
Okay. I will pick you up. Let us see each other on Saturday.

 Bokabolaryo

Study the following words. Some of them were used in the dialogue you just read and some of them will be useful when you make your own sentences for your dialogues. Also, a few words have been introduced earlier but need to be reviewed because these are words that you can use in describing your daily activities.

Pumupunta	*Go*
Dumadalo	*Attend*
Pumapasok sa klase	*Attends class/goes to class*
Tumutugtog	*Play* (an instrument)
Naglalaro	*Play* (game)
Nagpapraktis	*Practice* (for example, martial arts)
Gumigising	*Wake up*
Natutulog	*Sleep*
Nagsesepilyo	*Brush* (teeth)
Naghihilamos	*Wash* (face)
Nagsusuklay	*Comb*
Nagba-brush ng buhok	*Brush hair*
Naliligo	*Take a bath/take a shower*
Nagsa-shower	*Take a shower*
Nagbibihis	*Dress up*
Kumakain	*Eats*
Nagbabasa	*Read*
Nagsusulat	*Write*
Nag-aaral	*Studies*
Nagtatrabaho	*Works*
Sumasayaw	*Dance*
Kumakanta/Umaawit	*Sing*
Nag-eensayo	*Rehearse*

Nagluluto	*Cook*
Nanonood	*Watches* (for example, television, movie, game)
Nakikinig	*Listens to* (for example, music, songs, radio)
Nagsisimula	*Starts*
Natatapos	*Ends*
Dadaanan	*Will pass by*
Pulong	*Meeting*
Ensayo	*Rehearsals*
Laro	*Game*
Telebisyon	*Television*
Kanta/Awit	*Song*
Sayaw	*Dance*
Konsiyerto	*Concert*
Dula	*Play*
Sine/Pelikula	*Film*
Radyo	*Radio*
Musika	*Music*
Biyulin	*Violin*
Gitara	*Guitar*
Piyano	*Piano*
Tambol	*Drum*
Almusal	*Breakfast*
Tanghalian	*Lunch*
Hapunan	*Dinner*
Meryenda	*Mid-morning, mid-afternoon, or late-night snack*

Mga Pangungusap

Practice saying these sentences aloud, to get a feel for how this chapter's vocabulary and grammar work in Filipino. These sentences talk about the daily activities of Juan as well as his planned activities this coming Saturday. Note that the daily activities use the incompleted aspect of the verb (for example, **dumadalo** or attend) while the planned activities use the contemplated aspect (for example, **dadalo** or will attend).

1. **Gumigising si Juan nang alas-sais ng umaga.**
   Juan wakes up at six o'clock in the morning.

2. **Naliligo si Juan nang alas-sais y medya ng umaga.**
   Juan takes a bath/takes a shower at six thirty in the morning.

3. **Kumakain si Juan ng almusal nang alas-siyete ng uma.**
   Juan eats breakfast at six o'clock in the morning.

4. **Pumapasok si Juan sa klase nang alas-nuwebe ng umaga.**
   Juan goes to class at nine o'clock in the morning.

5. **Kumakain ng tanghalian sa cafeteria tuwing alas-dose ng tanghali.**
Juan eats lunch at the cafeteria at twelve o'clock noon.

6. **Nagbabasa si Juan sa aklatan mula alas-tres hanggang alas-sais ng hapon.**
Juan reads at the library from three until six o'clock in the afternoon.

7. **Umuuwi si Juan sa bahay nang alas-sais kinse ng gabi.**
Juan goes home at six fifteen in the evening.

8. **Sumasakay si Juan ng bus papunta sa bahay niya.**
Juan rides a bus going to his house.

9. **Nagluluto si Juan ng hapunan nang alas-sais y medya ng gabi.**
Juan cooks dinner at six thirty in the evening.

10. **Sumasayaw si Juan ng tango tuwing Miyerkules.**
Juan dances the tango every Wednesday.

11. **Dumadalo si Juan ng pulong ng Mathematics Society tuwing Huwebes.**
Juan attends the meetings of the Mathematics Society every Thursday.

12. **Tutugtog si Juan ng biyulin sa Sabado.**
Juan will play the violin this Saturday.

13. **Dadalo si Juan ng pulong ng Philippine Studies Forum sa Sabado.**
Juan will attend the meeting of Philippine Studies Forum this Saturday.

14. **Nagsisimula ang pulong nang alas-kuwatro ng hapon.**
The meeting starts at four o'clock in the afternoon.

15. **Natatapos ang pulong nang alas-singko ng hapon.**
The meeting ends at five o'clock in the afternoon.

16. **Natutulog si Juan nang alas-diyes ng gabi.**
Juan goes to sleep at ten o'clock in the evening.

  Pagsasanay

Study the information given. Then, ask and answer questions. Refer to the words and sentences introduced and reviewed in this lesson. Classroom learners can work in pairs while individual learners should write down their answers and questions in the spaces provided.

I.   **Iskedyul ni Katie** (*Katie's schedule*)

7:30 **ng umaga**	**gumigising**
8:00	**nagluluto ng almusal**
9:00	**naliligo**
10:00	**pumupunta sa unibersidad**
11:00	**pumapasok sa klase na Asian American History**
1:00 **ng hapon**	**kumakain sa cafeteria ng sandwich**

3:00	nagbabasa sa aklatan
5:00	kumakanta kasama ang Filipino Choir
7:00 ng gabi	umuuwi ng bahay; sumasakay ng bus
8:00	kumakain ng hapunan
8:30–10:30	nanonood ng telebisyon
11:00	natutulog

1. TANONG : **Anong oras gumigising si Katie?**
   SAGOT : _____.

2. TANONG : **Ano ang ginagawa ni Katie tuwing alas-nuwebe?**
   SAGOT : _____.

3. TANONG : **Saan pumupunta si Katie tuwing alas-diyes ng umaga?**
   SAGOT : _____.

4. TANONG : **Sa anong klase pumapasok si Katie tuwing alas-onse ng umaga?**
   SAGOT : _____.

5. TANONG : **Anong oras kumakain ng tanghalian si Katie?**
   SAGOT : _____.

6. TANONG : **Saan siya kumakain ng tanghalian?**
   SAGOT : _____.

7. TANONG : **Ano ang kinakain niya sa tanghalian?**
   SAGOT : _____.

8. TANONG : **Anong oras nagbabasa si Katie?**
   SAGOT : _____.

9. TANONG : **Saan nagbabasa si Katie?**
   SAGOT : _____.

10. TANONG : **Ano ang ginagawa ni Katie tuwing alas-singko ng hapon?**
    SAGOT : _____.

11. TANONG : **Sino ang kasamang kumanta ni Katie?**
    SAGOT : _____.

12. TANONG : **Paano umuuwi ng bahay si Katie?**
    SAGOT : _____.

13. TANONG : **Anong oras kumakain ng hapunan si Katie?**
    SAGOT : _____.

14. TANONG : **Anong oras nanonood ng telebisyon si Katie?**
    SAGOT : _____.

15. TANONG : **Anong oras natutulog si Katie?**
    SAGOT : _____.

II. **Iskedyul ni Armael** (*Armael's schedule*)

6:30 ng umaga	**gumigising**
6:45	**nagsisipilyo at nagsusuklay**
7:00	**umiinom ng kape**
7:30	**umaalis ng bahay**
8:00	**dumarating sa opisina**
8:00–5:00	**nagtatrabaho sa opisina**
12:00 ng tanghali	**kumakain ng tanghalian sa restawran**
5:00 ng hapon	**umuuwi sa bahay**
5:00–5:30	**nagmamaneho papunta sa bahay**
6:00 ng gabi	**dumarating sa bahay**
6:30	**nagluluto ng hapunan**
7:00	**nanonood ng telebisyon**
9:00	**nagtatrabaho sa computer**
10:30	**naliligo**
11:00	**natutulog**

In some instances, the answers are given so that you can provide the questions. This will help you practice asking questions.

1. TANONG : _____?
   SAGOT : **Gumigising si Armael nang alas-sais y medya ng umaga.**

2. TANONG : _____?
   SAGOT : **Nagsesepilyo at nagsusuklay si Armael nang alas-sais kwarenta y singko ng umaga.**

3. TANONG : _____?
   SAGOT : **Kape ang iniinom ni Armael sa umaga.**

4. TANONG : _____?
   SAGOT : **Dumarating si Armael sa opisina nang alas-otso.**

5. Tanong : _____?

   Sagot   : **Nagtatrabaho siya mula alas-otso ng umaga hanggang alas-singko ng hapon.**

6. Tanong : _____?

   Sagot   : **Kumakain siya ng tanghalian sa restawran.**

7. Tanong : _____?

   Sagot   : **Umuuwi siya ng bahay nang alas-singko ng hapon.**

8. Tanong : _____?

   Sagot   : **Dumarating siya nang bahay nang alas-sais.**

9. Tanong : **Ano ang ginagawa niya tuwing alas-siyete ng gabi?**

   Sagot   : _____.

10. Tanong : **Ano ang ginagawa niya nang alas-nuwebe ng gabi?**

    Sagot   : _____.

11. Tanong : **Anong oras siya naliligo?**

    Sagot   : _____.

12. Tanong : **Anong oras siya natutulog?**

    Sagot   : _____.

III. **Iskedyul ni Rhonda**

11:00 ng umaga	**gumigising**
11:15	**naliligo**
12:00	**nagbibihis**
12:30	**kumakain**
1:00	**umaalis ng bahay**
2:00 ng hapon	**12:00 ng hatinggabi nagtatrabaho sa restawran; nagluluto**
12:15 ng umaga	**umuuwi ng bahay**
12:30	**dumarating sa bahay**
1:45–2:30	**nakikinig ng musika**
2:45	**natutulog**

Work in pairs or write down questions and answers about Rhonda's schedule.

1. Tanong : _____.

   Sagot   : _____.

2. TANONG : _____.
   SAGOT   : _____.

3. TANONG : _____.
   SAGOT   : _____.

4. TANONG : _____.
   SAGOT   : _____.

5. TANONG : _____.
   SAGOT   : _____.

6. TANONG : _____.
   SAGOT   : _____.

7. TANONG : _____.
   SAGOT   : _____.

8. TANONG : _____.
   SAGOT   : _____.

9. TANONG : _____.
   SAGOT   : _____.

10. TANONG : _____.
    SAGOT   : _____.

11. TANONG : _____.
    SAGOT   : _____.

12. TANONG : _____.
    SAGOT   : _____.

★ Gawain "Picture Diary"

Make a picture diary. Start by writing down your daily schedule; use the following heading, and pick a day of the week:

Iskedyul Ko (*My Schedule*) **sa Araw ng** _____.

Then, draw a symbol to signify each of your activities. For example, for reading, you can draw a book. For taking the bus, draw a picture of the bus. Then, using the examples above and below, ask and answer questions. Classroom learners can work in pairs. Individual learners can use the spaces provided to write down questions and answers.

Mga Halimbawa (*Examples*):

TANONG	:	**Ano ang ginagawa mo tuwing alas-siyete ng umaga.**
SAGOT	:	**Kumakain ako ng almusal.**
TANONG	:	**Ano ang ginagawa mo tuwing alas-tres ng hapon?**
SAGOT	:	**Nag-aaral ako ng piyano.**
TANONG	:	**Ano ang ginagawa mo tuwing** _____?
SAGOT	:	_____.

Mga Tanong at Sagot

1. TANONG : _____?
   SAGOT : _____.

2. TANONG : _____?
   SAGOT : _____.

3. TANONG : _____?
   SAGOT : _____.

4. TANONG : _____?
   SAGOT : _____.

5. TANONG : _____?
   SAGOT : _____.

6. TANONG : _____?
   SAGOT : _____.

7. TANONG : _____?
   SAGOT : _____.

8. TANONG : _____?
   SAGOT : _____.

9. TANONG : _____?
   SAGOT : _____.

10. TANONG : _____?
    SAGOT   : _____.

11. TANONG : _____?
    SAGOT   : _____.

12. TANONG : _____?
    SAGOT   : _____.

🔍 Gramatika at Pagsasanay (Grammar and Practice)

I. Conjugating Verbs (Actor focus)

Earlier, you studied how to conjugate verbs using formulas for various affixes. For example, for verbs with the mag prefix:

Completed	Incompleted	Contemplated
nag + root word	first two syllables of completed aspect + root word	**mag** + first syllable of root word + root word

For the **um** prefix:

Completed	Incompleted	Contemplated
um (before the first vowel) + root word	first two syllables of completed aspect + root word	first syllable of root word + root word

For the **na** prefix:

Completed	Incompleted	Contemplated
na + root word	first two syllables of completed aspect + root word	**ma** + first syllable of root word + root word

Using these formulas, list down the verbs you have learned and try to conjugate them by yourself. Do this on a separate piece of paper. Then, check below to see if you did the work correctly. By trying to do this on your own, you will remember the verbs better.

Completed	Incompleted	Contemplated
gumising	gumigising	gigising
naligo	naliligo	maliligo
nagsepilyo	nagsesepilyo	magsesepilyo
nagsuklay	nagsusuklay	magsusuklay
nagbihis	magbibihis	nagbibihis
pumasok	pumapapasok	papasok
nagbasa	nagbabasa	magbabasa
nagsulat	nagsusulat	magsusulat
naglaro	naglalaro	maglalaro
tumugtog	tumutugtog	tutugtog
nagpraktis	nagpapraktis	magpapraktis
nag-ensayo	nag-eensayo	mag-eensayo
kumanta	kumakanta	kakanta
sumayaw	sumasayaw	sasayaw
nagluto	nagluluto	magluluto
nanood	nanonood	manonood
nakinig	nakikinig	makikinig
natulog	natutulog	matutulog

II. Conjugating Verbs (Object Focus)

Some verbs you studied need to be used with direct objects. Thus, you need to know how to conjugate them using the affixes **in** and **an**. This is useful to know for "**ano**" or "what" questions. For example:

TANONG   : **Ano ang kinain mo?**

SAGOT 1 : **Pizza ang kinain ko.**

SAGOT 2 : **Kumain ako ng pizza.**

Note that there are two ways of answering this question. It is actually more natural to say "**Kumain ako ng pizza.**" However, remember that you cannot say "**Ano ang kumain mo?**" because that would be grammatically wrong.

To conjugate, use the following formulas:

Using the **in** affix:

Completed	Incompleted	Contemplated
in (before the first vowel) + root word	first two syllables of completed aspect + root word	first syllable of root word + root word + **in**

(When the word ends with a vowel, insert an **h** between the root word and the affix **in**. This makes you avoid having two vowels together.)

Using the **ni** affix:

Completed	Incompleted	Contemplated
ni + root word	first two syllables of completed aspect + root word	first syllable of root word + root word + **in**

Try to conjugate the following verbs on your own: **laro, basa, sulat, tugtog, sayaw, kanta, ensayo.** Some verbs such as **kain** and **inom** have been studied in earlier lessons. Then compare your verbs to the ones below:

Completed	Incompleted	Contemplated
nilaro	nilalaro	lalaruin
binasa	binabasa	babasahin
sinulat	sinusulat	susulatin
tinugtog	tinutugtog	tutugtugin
inensayo	ineensayo	eensayuhin
niluto	niluluto	lulutuin

The **in-an** affixes are more complicated affixes because when we conjugate the root words **sakay** (as studied earlier), **kinig**, and **aral**, the words change too:

Thus:

Root	Completed	Incompleted	Contemplated
sakay	sinakyan	sinasakyan	sasakyan
aral	pinag-aralan	pinag-aaralan	pag-aaralan

| kinig | pinakinggan | pinakikinggan | pakikinggan |
| nood | pinanood | pinanonood | panoanoorin |

Study how the verb **nood** (*to watch*) was conjugated. When we conjugate **nood**, we say **pinanood, pinanonood,** and **panoanoorin**. Note that the **d** becomes an **r** in the contemplated aspect. To understand this, you need to remember that in the indigenous **baybayin, d** and **r** only has one symbol. **D** is changed into **r** to make the "flow" of the syllables better.

III. Using English words when speaking and writing in Filipino
Some words have been adapted into Filipino because there are no equivalents since the "concept" of the word is not indigenous. For example, the words, *shower* and *brush*. Since Filipinos during precolonial times used to take a bath in rivers or streams, there was no concept of "taking a shower." We take these English words and pair them with the prefix **mag**.

In words, used as sports, we can make the phrases shorter. Instead of saying **naglalaro ng soccer,** we can just say **nagsa-soccer.**

Here are some examples of English words with Filipino affixes:

Completed	Incompleted	Contemplated
nag-shower	nagsa-shower	magsa-shower
nag-brush	nagba-brush	magba-brush
nag-soccer	nagsa-soccer	magsa-soccer

  Pagsasanay

Practice the grammar points you have just learned by asking and answering "what" questions. Review the words for days and time you have learned (**kahapon, bukas,** etc.). Remember that this is just an exercise, so even if you are not reading or cooking something, just pretend you are and use any words or "titles" (of films, books, etc.) that are appropriate. The first few questions and answers are there to serve as your guide. There are also spaces for you to write your own questions and answers.

1. TANONG : **Ano ang binabasa mo?**
   SAGOT : **"Philippine Daily News" ang binabasa ko.**

2. TANONG : **Ano ang sinasayaw mo?**
   SAGOT : **Cha-cha ang sinasayaw ko.**

3. Tanong : **Ano ang tinutugtog mo?**
   Sagot : _____.

4. Tanong : **Ano ang niluluto mo?**
   Sagot : _____.

5. Tanong : **Ano ang pinapanood mo sa telebisyon?**
   Sagot : _____.

6. Tanong : **Ano ang pinapakinggan mo sa radyo?**
   Sagot : _____.

7. Tanong : _____?
   Sagot : **"Bayan Ko" ang kinakanta ko.**

8. Tanong : _____?
   Sagot : **Karate ang pinapraktis ko.**

9. Tanong : _____?
   Sagot : **"Kahapon, Ngayon, at Bukas" ang dula na ineensayo ko.**

10. Tanong : _____?
    Sagot : **Pansit ang niluluto ko.**

11. Tanong : _____?
    Sagot : _____.

12. Tanong : _____?
    Sagot : _____.

13. Tanong : _____?
    Sagot : _____.

Mga Tala Sa Kultura

In Filipino, the English words "to go/return home" is encapsulated in just word, the noun "**pag-uwi.**" The root word "**uwi**" can be conjugated to **umuwi, umuuwi, uuwi**. One does not need to say the location "home." It is implied that the action of "uwi" is to return to one's home.

Filipinos living in the diaspora find themselves asked the following question, "**Kailan ka uuwi?** (*When will you go home?*)" It does not matter if one has been abroad for twenty years, close to retirement, or even if a Filipino American was born in the United States.

Pagbabasa

Read the following snapshot story. Then answer the questions that follow. Study the vocabulary words preceding the story.

Dormitoryo	*Dormitory*
Siyensiya	*Science*
Na naman	*Again*
Alay Sining	name of an organization; literally means "Offer Art"
Nagpipinta	*Paint*

Isang Araw sa Buhay ni Cora

Gumigising nang alas-singko ng umaga si Cora. Naliligo siya, nagsusuklay ng buhok at nagbibihis. Pagkatapos, pumupunta siya sa cafeteria ng dormitoryo para magtrabaho.

Alas-diyes ng umaga. Naglalakad si Cora mula sa dormitoryo hanggang sa kanyang klase. Linguistics ang major niya at nag-aaral siya ng siyensiya ng mga wika. Pagkatapos ng klase, nag-aaral siya sa aklatan.

Sa gabi, nasa cafeteria na naman si Cora at nagtatrabaho. Natatapos siya ng alas-diyes ng gabi. Nag-aaral siya sa kuwarto niya hanggang alas-onse. Pagkatapos, nagsesepilyo siya, naghihilamos, at natutulog.

Tuwing Sabado, dumadalo siya sa pulong at ensayo ng Alay Sining. May mga estudyante na kumakanta, may mga sumasayaw, may mga gumagawa ng dula, at may mga nagpipinta.

---

1. **Anong oras gumigising si Cora?**
2. **Ano ang ginagawa ni Cora pagkatapos gumising?**
3. **Saan nagtatrabaho si Cora?**
4. **Anong oras pumupunta si Cora sa klase?**
5. **Paano siya pumupunta sa klase?**
6. **Ano ang pinag-aaralan ni Cora?**
7. **Ano ang ginagawa niya sa gabi?**

✎ Pagsusulat

Write a short paragraph about your daily activities. Remember two things: first, practice using the incompleted aspect (thus, words like **gumigising**, **natutulog**, etc.); second, use effective linkers (such as **pagkatapos** [meaning *then*, or *afterwards*] and **at** [*and*]). Here is an example.

Halimbawa

Gumigising ako nang alas-sais y medya ng umaga. Pagkatapos, naliligo at nagbibihis ako. Kumakain ako ng almusal ng alas-siyete kinse. Pumupunta ako sa eskuwelahan ng alas-otso. Nag-aaral ako mula alas-otso hanggang alas-onse y medya. Nagbabasa ako ng mga libro, at nagsusulat ng mga report. Pagkatapos, kumakain ako ng tanghalian. Naglalaro ako ng badminton sa hapon. Umuuwi ako ng bahay nang alas-singko. Nanonood ako ng TV. Kumakain ako ng hapunan nang alas-siyete. Natutulog ako nang alas-diyes.

⚑ Paglalagom

In **Aralin 17**, you have:
1. Learned new words describing your daily activities,
2. Practiced the incompleted aspect (which some grammarians refer to in other languages as the present tense),
3. Studied how to conjugate the new verbs you have learned,
4. Learned to use connectors,
5. Reviewed how to use affixes in Filipino when using words derived from English.

You should now be able to:
1. Talk and write about your daily activities.
2. Write sentences and paragraphs that have a better "flow."

Ang Aking Bakasyon (My Holiday)

  Diyalogo: Bakasyon sa Hawaii (Hawaii vacation)

Read the dialogue below. After completing this chapter, practice this dialogue using your own information. Remember that in this lesson we are practicing the completed aspect of the verb.

CLARA : **Maria, kumusta? May pasalubong ako sa iyo.**
Maria, how are you? I have a present for you.

MARIA : **Salamat. Kumusta ang bakasyon mo?**
How was your vacation?

CLARA : **Masaya. Nagpunta ako sa Hawaii.**
Happy. I went to Hawaii.

MARIA : **Sino ang kasama mo?**
Who was with you?/Who were your companions?

CLARA : **Kasama ko ang nanay ko, ang tatay ko, at ang dalawa kong kapatid.**
I was with my mother, my father, and my two siblings.

MARIA : **Ano ang ginawa mo sa Hawaii?**
What did you do in Hawaii?

CLARA : **Lumangoy ako sa dagat. Namasyal kami sa isang taniman ng pinya.**
I swam in the ocean. We went sightseeing at a pineapple plantation.

MARIA : **Ano ang kinain mo?**
What did you eat?

CLARA : **Kumain ako ng macadamia nuts.**
I ate macadamia nuts.

MARIA : **Ano pa ang ginawa mo?**
What else did you do?

CLARA : **Namili ako at nagpamasahe sa spa. Ikaw, saan ka nagbakasyon?**
I went shopping and I asked someone to give me a massage at a spa. What about you, where did you have a vacation?

MARIA : **Dito lang ako sa Oakland.**
I was just here in Oakland.

Bokabolaryo

Study the following words. Some of them were used in the dialogue you just read and some of them will be useful when you make your own sentences for your dialogues. There are also old and new words that can help you express your feelings. The verbs in this lesson practice the completed aspect (which in some languages, grammarians call the past tense.)

Mga Pandiwa (Verbs)

Lumangoy	*Swam*
Sumisid	*Dived*
Namasyal	*Went sightseeing*
Namili	*Went shopping*
Nagbakasyon	*Took a vacation*
Nag-i-scuba-diving	*Went scuba diving*
Nag-i-snorkeling	*Went snorkeling*
Nag-i-iskiing	*Went skiing*
Umakyat	*Climb*
Kumuha ng larawan	*Took pictures*
Nagpahinga	*Rest*
Inempake	*Pack (a suitcase)*
Inihanda	*Prepared*
Humiram	*Borrowed*
Nagsauli	*Returned*
Isinuot	*Wore (completed aspect of* wear*)*
Nagpamasahe	*Have someone to give you a massage*
Nagpagupit	*Have someone cut your hair*
Nagpaluto	*Have someone cook for you*
Nagpa-photocopy	*Have someone make copies for you*

Mga Pangngalan (Nouns)

Taniman	*plantation*
Isla	*island*
Bundok	*mountain*
Pasalubong	*a present you give to a person after going away on a trip*
Ulat/Report	*Report*

Mga Pakiramdam (Feelings)

Masaya	*Happy*
Abala	*Busy*
Pagod	*Tired*
Napagod	*Became tired*
Malungkot	*Sad*

Mga Salitang Nag-uugnay (Connecting Words)

Bago	*Before*
Pagkatapos	*After*

Mga Gabay Na Pangungusap

Practice saying these sentences aloud, to get a feel for how this chapter's vocabulary and grammar work in Filipino.

1. **Nagbakasyon si Clara sa Hawaii.** — *Clara took a vacation in Hawaii.*
2. **Lumangoy siya sa dagat.** — *She swam in the ocean.*
3. **Nagpamasahe siya sa Island Spa.** — *She had someone give her a massage at Island Spa.*
4. **Masaya si Clara dahil sa bakasyon niya.** — *Clara is happy because of her vacation.*
5. **Napagod si Clara sa bakasyon niya.** — *Clara was tired during her vacation.*
6. **Inempake niya ang maleta niya bago siya nagbakasyon.** — *He/she packed his/her suitcase before he/she took a vacation.*
7. **Nagpahinga siya pagkatapos niyang mag-mountain climbing.** — *He/she rested after he/she went mountain climbing.*

 Pagsasanay

Study the following pictures as well as the information given. Then, ask and answer questions. There are three situations here: a recent vacation; a finals week for a student; and a busy week for an office worker. Refer to the words and sentences introduced and reviewed in this lesson as well as in lesson 17. Classroom learners can work in pairs while individual learners should write down their answers and questions in the spaces provided.

I. **Ang Bakasyon ni Edmundo** (*Edmundo's Vacation*)

Saan:	Boracay island
Mga gawain:	**lumangoy sa dagat**
	nagbisikleta sa isla
	nag-i-scuba diving
	nagpamasahe sa Boracay Garden Spa
	kumuha ng larawan
Pagkain:	**lechon** (*roast pig*)
Mga Binili:	T-shirt, **mga pasalubong**
Kasama:	**Asawa**

1. TANONG : **Saan pumunta si Edmundo?**
   SAGOT   : _____.

2. TANONG : **Ano ang mga ginawa niya sa isla?**
   SAGOT   : _____.

3. TANONG : **Saan siya nagpamasahe?**
   SAGOT   : _____.

4. TANONG : **Ano ang kinain niya?**
   SAGOT   : _____.

5. TANONG : **Ano ang mga binili niya?**
   SAGOT   : _____.

6. TANONG : **Sino ang kasama niyang nagbakasyon?**
   SAGOT   : _____.

II. **Ang Linggo ni Debbie** (*Debbie's Week*)

Saan:	**Sa Davao main office ng Filipino Dried Fruits Inc.**
Mga gawain:	**Sumulat ng ulat o report**
	Inihanda ang powerpoint presentation
	Nagpa-photocopy ng report sa Kinko's
Mga Binili:	Folders
Isinuot:	Business suit
Kasama sa trabaho:	**kanyang** assistant

1. TANONG : **Saan nagpunta si Debbie?**
   SAGOT   : _____.

2. TANONG : **Ano ang ginawa ni Debbie bago siya pumunta sa Davao?**
   SAGOT : _____.

3. TANONG : **Ano ang inihanda ni Debbie?**
   SAGOT : _____.

4. TANONG : **Ano ang isinuot ni Debbie para sa pulong?**
   SAGOT : _____.

5. TANONG : **Ano ang binili ni Debbie?**
   SAGOT : _____.

6. TANONG : **Saan siya nagpa-photocopy ng report?**
   SAGOT : _____.

7. TANONG : **Sino ang kasama niya sa trabaho?**
   SAGOT : _____.

III. **Ang Linggo ng Eksamen (*Finals Week*) ni Minnie**

Saan:	**Sa aklatan**
Mga gawain:	**Sumulat ng ulat**
	Nagbasa ng libro
	Nagsauli ng dalawang libro
	Humiram ng tatlong libro
	Nagpa-photocopy ng lumang diyaryo
Kasama sa pag-aaral:	**Mga kaklase**
Pagkatapos mag-aral:	**Uminom ng kape**

1. TANONG : _____?
   SAGOT : _____.

2. TANONG : _____?
   SAGOT : _____.

3. TANONG : _____?
   SAGOT : _____.

4. TANONG : _____?
   SAGOT : _____.

5. TANONG : _____?
   SAGOT : _____.

6. TANONG : _____?
   SAGOT   : _____.

 ★ **Gawain**

Draw a postcard image that represents your most recent vacation. (Or, as an alternative, find a postcard or a photograph that reflects it.) Then, using the examples above and below, ask and answer questions. The incomplete questions and answers below are there as your guide. You can also make your own in the spaces provided. Classroom learners can work in pairs or groups while individual learners should write their questions and answers.

1. TANONG : **Saan ka nagbakasyon?**
   SAGOT   : **Nagbakasyon ako sa** _____.

2. TANONG : **Ano ang ginawa mo sa** _____?
   SAGOT   : _____ **ako sa** _____.

3. TANONG : **Ano ang kinain mo sa** _____?
   SAGOT   : _____ **ako ng** _____.

4. TANONG : **Ano ang** _____ **mo?**
   SAGOT   : _____.

5. TANONG : **Sino ang kasama mo sa** _____?
   SAGOT   : **Si** _____ **ang kasama ko sa** _____.

6. TANONG : _____?
   SAGOT   : _____.

7. TANONG : _____?
   SAGOT   : _____.

8. TANONG : _____?
   SAGOT   : _____.

9. TANONG : _____?
   SAGOT   : _____.

10. TANONG : _____?
    SAGOT   : _____.

 **Gramatika**

Study the information below to improve your Filipino grammar skills.

I.   Conjugating new verbs, subject focus
     In this lesson, you have learned additional verbs. Many of them can be used specifically for talking about a holiday or a recent trip. Before you look at the conjugations below, review the formulas given in previous lessons. Then, conjugate the verbs by yourself and write them in your notebook or on a sheet of paper. This will help you remember the verbs better. Then, check below to see whether you conjugated the verbs correctly.

     Note that the verbs below do not need direct objects, and thus we are only using them with the focus on the subject.

Root	Completed	Incompleted	Contemplated
Langoy	Lumangoy	Lumalangoy	Lalangoy
Sisid	Sumisid	Sumisisid	Sisisid
Pasyal	Namasyal	Namamasyal	Mamamasyal
Bakasyon	Nagbakasyon	Nagbabakasyon	Magbabakasyon
Namili	Namili	Namimili	Mamimili
Pahinga	Nagpahinga	Nagpapahinga	Magpapahinga

II. Conjugating new verbs derived from English words, subject focus
     A quick look at the English words used in Filipino that are introduced in this lesson shows that they start with the letter *s*. The spelling guide of the book *Gabay sa Editing sa Wikang Filipino* (Editing Guide in the Filipino Language) published by the Filipino Language Center of the University of the Philippines Diliman tells us that when an English word starts with the letter *s*, and is followed by a consonant, the sound of the first vowel is repeated when pronouncing the root word.

     Remember, though, that in spoken Filipino, to say **nag-skiing** (*went skiing*) is acceptable. It is only in written Filipino, that we need to standardize spelling. Thus:

Root	Completed	Incompleted	Contemplated
Scuba diving	Nag-i-scuba-diving	Nag-i-iscuba-diving	Mag-i-iscuba diving
Snorkeling	Nag-i-snorkeling	Nag-i-isnorkeling	Mag-i-isnorkeling
Skiing	Nag-i-skiing	Nag-i-iskiing	Mag-i-iskiing

III. Conjugating new verbs that can be used with direct objects

Now let us study the verbs that can be used with subject focus and object focus. Again, try to conjugate the verbs by yourself before looking at the words listed below. The subject focus is on the first line, and the object focus is on the second line.

Root Word	Completed	Incompleted	Contemplated
Akyat	Umakyat	Umaakyat	Aakyat
	Inakyat	Inaakyat	Aakyatin
Kuha (ng larawan)	Kumuha	Kumukuha	Kukuha
	Kinunan	Kinukunan	Kukunan
Empake	Nag-empake	Nag-eempake	Mag-eempake
	Inempake	Ineempake	Eempakihin
Handa	Naghanda	Naghahanda	Maghahanda
	Inihanda	Inihahanda	Ihahanda
Hiram	Humiram	Humihiram	Hihiram
	Hiniram	Hinihiram	Hihiramin
Sauli	Nagsauli	Nagsasauli	Magsasauli
	Isinauli	Isinasauli	Isasauli
Suot	Nagsuot	Nagsusuot	Magsusuot
	Isinuot	Isinusuot	Isusuot

IV. **Nagpa-** and **Pina-** affixes

In this lesson, the **nagpa-** affix is introduced. Attached to the root word, it means to have someone do something for you. Study the following sentences:

EXAMPLES: **Nagpamasahe ako sa Boracay Spa.**
I had someone give me a massage at Boracay Spa.
Nagpapa-photocopy ako sa Kinko's.
I have someone make photocopies for me at Kinko's.
Nagpaluto ako ng adobo sa nanay ko.
I had my mother cook adobo for me.

In the sentences above, you asked someone to do something for you. These sentences answer the following questions:

Kanino ka _____?

Who did you ask to _____?   or

Saan ka _____?

Where did you have someone _____?

To reverse the situation when you are asked to do something by someone, the form of the verb is retained but different pronouns are used. For example:

Nagpaluto ang nanay ko ng adobo sa akin.

(literally, Asked to cook my mother adobo to me.)

To answer the question "**Kanino?**," or for the focus to be on the person doing the action, use the **pina-** affix.

EXAMPLE: TANONG : **Kanino mo pinaluto ang adobo?**

Who did you ask to cook adobo for you?

SAGOT   : **Pinaluto ko ang adobo sa nanay ko.**

I asked my mother to cook the adobo for me.

Pagsasanay

Practice the **nagpa-** affix by asking and answering questions. Remember, the answers need not be true in real life.

Other verbs that can be used for **nagpa-** affixes are the following:

Nagpagupit	*Have someone cut your hair*
Nagpatulong	*Have someone help you*
Nagpakuha ng larawan	*Have someone take your photo*
Nagpakulay (ng buhok)	*Have your hair colored*

1. TANONG : **Saan ka nagpamasahe?**
   SAGOT   : _____.

2. TANONG : **Saan ka nagpa-photocopy?**
   SAGOT   : _____.

3. TANONG : **Saan ka nagpakuha ng larawan para sa passport mo?**
   SAGOT   : _____.

4. TANONG : **Kanino ka nagpatulong sa homework mo?**
   SAGOT   : _____.

5. TANONG : _____?
   SAGOT   : **Nagpaluto ako ng spaghetti kay Maria.**

6. TANONG : _____?
   SAGOT   : **Nagpagupit ako sa Eclipxe Salon.**

7. TANONG : **Kanino ka nagpagupit?**
   SAGOT   : _____ **ako kay** _____.

8. TANONG : _____?
   SAGOT   : _____.

9. TANONG : _____?
   SAGOT   : _____.

10. TANONG : _____?
    SAGOT   : _____.

Mga Tala Sa Kultura

When Filipinos go away on a trip, they buy not only souvenirs, but also **pasalubong**, or gifts for family and friends from the place they visited. This can be anything from food, keychains, scarves, T-shirts or any easy to pack items, that may even be bought in bulk when one is thinking of giving presents to an entire office or a group of friends.

Heritage learners, have you ever wondered why your parents or grandparents bring heavy suitcases when they return to the Philippines? It is because they are somehow expected to bring presents to their relatives and friends. In some instances, they ask and receive lists of expected presents: M&M'S chocolates, Adidas rubber shoes, Dove soap, Jergens lotions, or other signifiers of "abroad."

A recent phenomenon is the "**balikbayan** box" (a box for the "**balikbayan**"— literally, a person returning to his/her country). The boxes come in various sizes ranging from the mini-box (12" x 12" x 12") to the large box (18" x 18" x 24"), and can be shipped from many points in the United States to various regions in the Philippines. The price ranges from 20 to 117 dollars depending on the size of the box and the destination in the Philippines. Since weight is not considered, this method of shipping presents is considered economical.

The "**balikbayan** box phenomenon" has also inspired artwork. On May 8, 2009 the exhibit hall of City Hall in Hong Kong hosted an exhibition entitled "The Box Unfolded" featuring installations, wall displays, and short videos. Among the participating artists are Alwin Reamillo, Dada Docot, Eliza O. Barrios, Felix Bacolor, Arnel S. Agawin, Gene Pendon, Rowena Gonzalez, and Inksurge.

Pagbabasa

Read the following postcard, and then answer the questions that follow. Study the following words before reading the postcard. You have learned some of the words in earlier lessons; they are listed here for you to review. You can also refer to the glossary at the back of the book.

Natanggap	*Received*
Pinadala	*Sent*
Puno ng akasya	*Acacia trees*
Ikinukuwento	*Stories you told*
Kinuha ang larawan	*Took the picture*

Isang Postcard

Kumusta Nanay,

Natanggap ko kahapon ang Balikbayan box na pinadala ninyo sa akin. Salamat. Pasensiya na kayo at nagpabili pa ako ng mga libro sa inyo. Mahal kasi rito ang mga librong iyan.

Ang ganda po ng U.P. Campus, hindi ba? Nandito pa rin ang mga puno ng akasya na ikinukuwento ninyo sa akin. Kinuha ang larawang ito ng propesor ko. Pinagawa ko itong postcard sa Dilimall shopping center.

Masaya naman ako. Nag-aral ako kahapon sa library. Pagkatapos, pumunta kami ng mga kaibigan ko sa Lagoon at namasyal kami. Kagabi, kumain kami ng pasta sa bahay ng kaklase kong si Consuelo.

Kumusta na kayo?

Tonette

---

1. **Ano ang natanggap ni Tonette?**
2. **Ano ang pinabili niya sa nanay niya?**
3. **Nasaan si Tonette?**
4. **Sino ang kumuha ng larawan?**
5. **Saan niya pinagawa ang postcard?**
6. **Saan siya nag-aral kahapon?**

7. **Sino ang kasama niyang namasyal sa Lagoon?**
8. **Ano ang kinain nila sa bahay ni Consuelo?**

✏ Pagsusulat

Using the vocabulary and grammar you have learned, write a paragraph about your recent holiday. The below example paragraph has incomplete sentences but it gives you an idea of how simple or how complicated your paragraph can be.

Halimbawang talata:

Nagbakasyon ako sa _____. Kasama ko _____.
_____ ako sa _____. Kumain ako ng _____.
_____. _____. _____ Masayang-masaya ako.

⚑ Paglalagom

In **Aralin 18**, you have:
1. Practiced the incompleted aspect of the verb,
2. Learned vocabulary related to taking a vacation or a holiday,
3. Studied the **nagpa-** affix.

You should now be able to:
1. Talk about a recent trip.
2. Talk about asking someone to do things for you as well as doing things for someone.
3. Shift from the subject focus to the object focus of the verb with greater ease.

Pagpaplano (Making Plans)

  Diyalogo: Sa Linggo (On Sunday)

Read the dialogue below. After completing this chapter, practice this dialogue using your own information. Remember that in this lesson we are practicing the contemplated aspect of the verb.

JUAN : **Ano ang gagawin mo sa Linggo?**
What will you do on Sunday?

PEDRO : **Maglalaro ako ng tennis. Ikaw?**
I will play tennis. You?

JUAN : **Tatapusin ko ang report ko. Saan ka maglalaro ng tennis?**
I will finish my report. Where will you play tennis?

PEDRO : **Sa campus tennis court.**
At the campus tennis court.

JUAN : **Makikipaglaro ka ba ng tennis kay Ramon?**
Will you play tennis with Ramon?

PEDRO : **Hindi. Tutugtog siya ng piyano sa kasal ng pinsan niya. Kalaro ko si Jose.**
No. He will play the piano at his cousin's wedding. Jose will play tennis with me.

JUAN : **Magluluto ako ng adobo. Gusto mo bang dumaan sa bahay ko?**
I will cook adobo. Would you like to pass by my house?

PEDRO : **Sige. Makikikain ako sa bahay mo dahil ayaw kong magluto.**
Okay. I will eat dinner with you [as a favor] in your house because I don't want to cook.

Bokabolaryo

Review some of the verbs you have studied recently, and then study new verbs used in the dialogue you have just read as well as verbs that can be used in dialogue variations.

Note that words (such as soccer, tennis) that are not indigenous in Filipino have no equivalents and therefore, it is fine to use them in the original English.

We are also introducing here the two affixes **makikipag** and **makiki**. Study how they are used.

Affixes

Makikipag-	*To do something together with someone*
Makiki-	*To do something with someone as a favor*

Mga Pandiwa

Maglalaro	*Will play* (a game)
Makikipaglaro	*Will play with*
Makikipagsayaw	*Will dance with*
Makikipag-away	*Will fight with* (pronounce "ay" in the root word **away** as the long "i" not the long "a")
Makikipagbati	*Will reconcile with*
Makikipag-usap	*Will talk to*
Makikipagkantahan	*Will sing with* (a group of people)
Makikipagtugtugan	*Will play* (instruments) *with* (a group of people)
Tatapusin	*Will finish*
Tutugtog	*Will play a game*
Makikikain	*Will share someone else's food*
Magluluto	*Will cook*
Makikiluto	*Will cook at someone else's house*
Makikiligo	*Will take a bath/shower at someone else's house*
Dadaan	*Will pass by*

Noun

Adobo	*Chicken or pork cooked in vinegar and spices*

Balik-Aral (Review) Sa Mga Relasyon At "Ka"

Earlier, you studied the affix **ka-** and how it indicates relationships. Review the words starting with **ka** that you studied and study new words. These words will be useful when you make your sentences and your dialogues.

Kalaro	*Playmate*
Kaklase	*Classmate*
Kaibigan	*Friend*
Kamag-anak	*Relative*
Kapatid	*Sister/Brother*
Kaaway	*Enemy*
Kasayaw	*Dance Partner*
Kadueto	*Duet partner*

Phrases

gusto kong maglaro	*want to play*
ayaw kong maglaro	*don't want to play*
gusto kong dumaan	*want to pass by*
ayaw kong dumaan	*don't want to pass by*

Mga Halimbawang Pangungusap

Practice saying these sentences aloud, to get a feel for how this chapter's vocabulary and grammar work in Filipino.

1. **Maglalaro ng tennis si Pedro sa Linggo.**   *Pedro will play tennis on Sunday.*
2. **Kalaro ni Pedro sa tennis si Jose.**   *Jose is Pedro's playmate.*
3. **Makikipaglaro ng tennis si Pedro kay Jose.**   *Pedro will play tennis with Jose.*
4. **Magluluto si Juan ng adobo.**   *Juan will cook adobo.*
5. **Kakain si Pedro sa bahay ni Juan.**   *Pedro will eat at Juan's house.*
6. **Makikikain si Pedro sa bahay ni Juan dahil ayaw niyang magluto.**   *Pedro will eat at Juan's house because he doesn't want to cook.*

  Pagsasanay 1

Study the following pictures. Then, ask and answer questions. Refer to the words and sentences introduced and reviewed in this lesson. In this exercise, no additional information is given. Thus, think of the situation and based on the picture, create your own stories. Classroom learners can work in pairs while individual learners should write down their answers and questions in the spaces provided.

I. **Ang Linggo ni Natilou** (*Natilou's Sunday*)

1. TANONG : **Kanino makikipaglaro si Natilou?**
   SAGOT : _____.

2. TANONG : **Kailan makikikain sa bahay ni Natilou ang mga anak at apo niya?**

   SAGOT : _____.

3. TANONG : **Sino ang pupunta sa bahay ni Natilou?**

   SAGOT : _____.

4. TANONG : **Bakit sila makikikain sa bahay niya?**

   SAGOT : _____.

5. TANONG : **Sino ang tutugtog ng piyano?**

   SAGOT : _____.

6. TANONG : **Ano ang sasayawin ng mga bata?**

   SAGOT : _____.

7. TANONG : **Kanino makikipagsayaw si Natilou?**

   SAGOT : _____.

8. TANONG : _____?

   SAGOT : _____.

9. TANONG : _____?

   SAGOT : _____.

10. TANONG : _____?

    SAGOT : _____.

II. Ang Linggo ni Larry

1. TANONG : **Saan pupunta si Larry sa Linggo?**

   SAGOT : _____.

2. TANONG : **Kanino makikipaglaro ng soccer si Larry?**

   SAGOT : _____.

3. TANONG : **Ano ang isusuot ni Larry?**

   SAGOT : _____.

4. TANONG : **Anong oras siya makikipaglaro ng soccer?**

   SAGOT : _____.

5. TANONG : _____?
    SAGOT   : **Makikiligo siya sa shower room ng gym.**

6. TANONG : _____?
    SAGOT   : **Kakain siya sa bahay ng nobya niya sa gabi.**

7. TANONG : _____?
    SAGOT   : **Kakain siya ng roast pork sa bahay ng nobya niya.**

8. TANONG : _____?
    SAGOT   : _____.

9. TANONG : _____?
    SAGOT   : _____.

10. TANONG : _____?
    SAGOT   : _____.

III. **Ang Linggo ni Marilou**

1. TANONG : _____?
    SAGOT   : _____.

2. TANONG : _____?
    SAGOT   : _____.

3. TANONG : _____?
    SAGOT   : _____.

4. TANONG : _____?
    SAGOT   : _____.

5. TANONG : _____?
    SAGOT   : _____.

6. TANONG : _____?
    SAGOT   : _____.

7. TANONG : _____?
    SAGOT   : _____.

8. Tanong : _____?
   Sagot   : _____.

9. Tanong : _____?
   Sagot   : _____.

10. Tanong : _____?
    Sagot   : _____.

🎧 💬 **Pagsasanay 2**

In the box provided, draw a picture of yourself and what you plan to do this Sunday. Then ask and answer questions. Some examples, a few of them with incomplete answers, are given. Independent learners should write the questions and answers. Classroom learners should work as pairs and ask each other questions.

```
┌─────────────────────────────────────────┐
│                                         │
│                                         │
│                                         │
│                                         │
│                                         │
│                                         │
│                                         │
│                                         │
└─────────────────────────────────────────┘
```

1. Tanong : **Ano ang gagawin mo sa Linggo?**
   Sagot   : **Maglalaro ako ng _____.**

2. Tanong : **Ano ang kakainin mo sa _____?**
   Sagot   : _____?

3. Tanong : **Sino ang kalaro mo sa tennis?**
   Sagot   : **Si _____ ang kalaro ko.**

4. Tanong : _____?
   Sagot   : _____.

5. Tanong : _____?
   Sagot   : _____.

6. Tanong : _____ ?
   Sagot : _____ .

7. Tanong : _____ ?
   Sagot : _____ .

8. Tanong : _____ ?
   Sagot : _____ .

9. Tanong : _____ ?
   Sagot : _____ .

10. Tanong : _____ ?
    Sagot : _____ .

📄 Balik-Aral (Review)

Review the months of the year you have studied. Then ask and answer questions about what you plan to do in the coming months.

Mga Buwan

Write down the names of the months. A few months are given to guide you and help you remember.

Enero	*January*	_____	*July*
_____	*February*	**Agosto**	*August*
_____	*March*	_____	*September*
Abril	*April*	_____	*October*
_____	*May*	_____	*November*
_____	*June*	**Disyembre**	*December*

🎧 💬 Pagsasanay

Ask and answer questions about your plans in the coming months. Use the incomplete sentences as your guide, then ask and answer your own questions. If working in pairs, listen to the answers of your partner and practice asking follow-up questions.

1. Tanong : **Ano ang gagawin mo sa Disyembre?**
   Sagot : **Pupunta ako sa _____ sa Disyembre.**

2. TANONG : **Ano ang gagawin mo sa** _____?
   SAGOT : _____?

3. TANONG : **Sino ang kasama mong mamamasyal sa** _____?
   SAGOT : _____.

4. TANONG : _____?
   SAGOT : _____.

5. TANONG : _____?
   SAGOT : _____.

6. TANONG : _____?
   SAGOT : _____.

7. TANONG : _____?
   SAGOT : _____.

8. TANONG : _____?
   SAGOT : _____.

9. TANONG : _____?
   SAGOT : _____.

10. TANONG : _____?
    SAGOT : _____.

🔍 Gramatika

Study the information below to improve your Filipino grammar skills.

I.   The affix **makikipag-** meaning to do something with someone
     As you've been reminded repeatedly, the Filipino/Tagalog language has a complex
     system of affixes. A good example of this is the affix **makikipag-**. When combined
     with the root word of a verb, it connotes the meaning of doing something with
     someone, thus shortening a sentence.
         For example, the sentence "Maria is dancing the fox-trot with Juan" can be
     translated into:
             Sasayaw ng fox-trot si Maria kasama si Juan. (literally, Will dance _marker_
             fox-trot _marker_ Maria with _marker_ Juan.)

However, the sentence becomes clearer and more compact with the use of the prefix **makipag-**:

Makikipagsayaw ng fox-trot si Maria kay Juan.
(literally, Will dance with *marker* fox-trot *marker* Maria *marker* Juan.)

In some instances, the affix **-an** can be found at the end. When is this used? When you are doing something with a group, use **-an** at the end with the **makipag-** prefix. This is best illustrated by the English word *duet*, meaning two people singing together, and its Filipino/Tagalog equivalent "**dueto**," and the word "**makikipagkantahan**" (will sing with). Used in sentences:

Makikipag-dueto si Maria kay Juan.
(literally, Will sing a duet with *marker* Maria *marker* Juan.)
Makikipagkantahan si Maria kina Juan, Pedro, at Clara.
(literally, Will sing with *marker* Maria *plural marker* Juan, Pedro, and Clara.)

Let us now conjugate the **makipag-** verbs we have used in this unit. Again, try to conjugate these verbs on your own using your notebook or a separate sheet of paper. This will allow you to remember the verbs better. Then check what you have against the chart below.

Root word	Completed	Incompleted	Contemplated
Sayaw	Nakipagsayaw	Nakikipagsayaw	Makikipagsayaw
Laro	Nakipaglaro	Nakikipaglaro	Makikipaglaro
Usap	Nakipag-usap	Nakikipag-usap	Makikipag-usap
Away	Nakipag-away	Nakikipag-away	Makikipag-away
Bati	Nakipagbati	Nakikipagbati	Makikipagbati
Dueto	Nakipag-dueto	Nakikipag-dueto	Makikipag-dueto
Kanto	Nakipagkantahan	Nakikipagkantahan	Makikipagkantahan
Tugtog	Nakipagtugtugan	Nakikipagtugtugan	Makikipagtugtugan

II. The affix **nakiki** to connote sharing with someone as a favor

The special affix **nakiki** is a concept that is easier to understand when one contextualizes it in Philippine culture. It is explained further in the cultural note below. It is used when one asks a relative, friend, a roommate, a neighbor, a classmate, or even a stranger to share with what he/she is doing.

When is this used? Let us pretend, for example, that you don't have food for lunch. Your friend asks you to share his/her food because he/she brought two sandwiches. Later, another friend asks you if you have eaten. You can reply by saying:

"Kumain na ako kasama si Maria. Kinain ko ang isang sandwich niya."
I ate already with Maria. I ate one of her sandwiches.

However, you can say this in a clearer and more concise manner by:

"Nakikain na ako sa mga sandwich ni Maria."

Other instances when the affix **nakiki** is applicable would be when you cook in someone else's house as a favor; share a book in class because you forgot your own book; cook at someone else's house because you ran out of gas for your stove; or even take a shower at someone else's house. For people living in some countries, the latter is unthinkable. But, think of this in the Filipino context. It used to be that in remote areas in the countryside, people relied on water pumps for their water supply. What happens when the water pump is broken? **"Makikiligo ka."** (*You will ask to take a shower.*) Or what if you don't have your own pump? **"Makiki-igib ka."** (*You will ask to draw water.*) This is all in the spirit of communal life in a rural village.

Let us now conjugate the words which use the **nakiki-** affix. Again, try to do this on your own before referring to the chart below.

Root word	Completed	Incompleted	Contemplated
Kain	Nakikain	Nakikikain	Makikikain
Sakay	Nakisakay	Nakikisakay	Makikisakay
Luto	Nakiluto	Nakikiluto	Makikiluto
Basa	Nakibasa	Nakikibasa	Makikibasa
Ligo	Nakiligo	Nakikiligo	Makikiligo
Igib (Fetch water)	Naki-igib	Nakiki-igib	Makiki-igib
Damay	Nakiramay	Nakikiramay	Makikiramay

Dagdag na Bokabolaryo

Study the following words that will allow you to talk about problems necessitating the help of others.

Sira	*Broken*
Ayos (accent on the second syllable)	*Fixed*
May problema	*Has a problem*

 **Pagsasanay**

Practice the **nakikipag-** and **nakiki-** affixes by asking and answering questions. Remember to think of follow-up questions to keep the conversation going. Practice the use of **dahil** (*because*) as well as the contemplated aspects of the verbs. Independent learners should write the questions and answers. Classroom learners should work as pairs and ask each other questions.

1. TANONG : **Kanino ka nakikain?**
   SAGOT   : _____.

2. TANONG : **Bakit ka nakikain sa kanya?**
   SAGOT   : _____.

3. TANONG : **Kanino ka makikipagsayaw ng swing sa party?**
   SAGOT   : _____.

4. TANONG : **Kailan tayo makikipagkantahan sa mga kaibigan natin?**
   SAGOT   : _____.

5. TANONG : _____?
   SAGOT   : **Makikiligo ako sa apartment ni Barbara.**

6. TANONG : _____?
   SAGOT   : **Makikiligo ako sa bahay niya dahil sira ang water heater sa apartment ko.**

7. TANONG : _____?
   SAGOT   : **Makikiluto ako ng cake sa bahay ni Ramon.**

8. TANONG : **Bakit ka makikiluto ng cake?**
   SAGOT   : _____.

9. TANONG : _____?
   SAGOT   : _____.

10. TANONG : _____?
    SAGOT   : _____.

Mga Tala Sa Kultura

The communal way of life of indigenous Filipinos is reflected in the affixes **nakikipag-** and **nakiki-**. Even today, those living in rural communities remain interdependent, especially when coping with the difficulties of everyday life and natural disasters.

In this lesson, among the words you studied which use the **naki-** affix are **makikiluto, makikikain, makikiligo, makikibasa** and **makiki-igib**. In an earlier lesson, you also learned the expression "**Nakikiramay ako**." (*My condolences.*)

The noun for of the verb **nakikiramay** is **pakikiramay** (*condolences*). When a family is bereaved, friends and neighbors flock to the house where the wake is held. It is only recently, and only in urban areas, that the wake occurs in funeral parlors.

The relatives and friends need to stay up all night in the belief that they need to "accompany" the dead. Thus, food is abundant. One is served not only coffee and cookies, but also noodles (**pansit**), rice, vegetables, fish, and meat. Children play games and adults gamble using cards or mahjong (a Chinese game).

Meanwhile, the family is never alone. The widow/er or the children continually narrate the circumstances of the death, thereby easing their pain. Grief is thus made communal.

Among the artifacts which depict this communal grief is the Manunggul Jar, one of the burial jars found in the Tabon Caves of Palawan in March 1964. Dating back to around 710 B.C., the jar has a lid with a sculpture of two men rowing, supposedly bringing the spirit of the dead to the afterlife. Thus, the jar depicts not only the indigenous people's belief in life after death, but also that one is never alone, not even in death.

In contemporary popular culture, wake and burial rituals and beliefs are depicted in the feature film ***Ded na si Lolo*** (Grandpa Is Dead) directed by Soxy Topacio in 2009. A comedy, the film was the Philippines's entry to the 2010 Oscar Awards in the foreign film category.

  Pagbabasa

Read the following news item, and then answer the questions that follow. Before reading, study the words below:

Napatay	*Was killed*
Ayon	*According to*
Pinaputok	*Fired*

Karaoke

General Santos, Philippines — **Isang lalaki ang napatay sa Midnight Blue Lounge sa General Santos City kahapon, ika-16 ng Abril. Ayon sa mga taong nakikipagkantahan sa bar, nagsimula ang lahat nang kumanta si Roger Dimalanta ng kantang "My Way."**

Nagsimulang tumawa ang isang lalaking umiinom ng beer. Nakitawa naman ang mga kasama niyang ibang lalaki.

Nagalit ang kaibigan ni Roger na si Elvis. Inilabas niya ang baril niya at pinaputok ito. Napatay niya si Lauro Martinez. Aksidente daw ang nangyari dahil hindi kasama si Lauro sa mga tumatawang lalaki. Nakikipagsaya lang si Lauro sa birthday party ng isang kaibigan sa malayong mesa.

1. **Sino ang napatay?**
2. **Saan nangyari ang insidente?**
3. **Kailan ito nangyari?**
4. **Ano ang kinanta ni Roger Dimalanta?**
5. **Ano ang ginagawa ni Lauro nang nabaril siya?**
6. **Sino ang nakitawa sa lalaking umiinom ng beer?**

🖊 Pagsusulat

Write a paragraph about your plans for this weekend. Remember to use the contemplated aspect of the verb and to try to use the affixes **makikipag-** and **makiki-**.

🚩 Paglalagom

In **Aralin 19**, you have:
1. Practiced how to use verbs in the contemplated aspect,
2. Learned the affixes **nakikipag-** and **nakiki-**,
3. Studied new words related to the communal way of life.

You should now be able to:
1. Talk about future plans.
2. Ask and answer follow-up questions with greater ease.

Mga Bahagi ng Katawan (Parts of the Body)

  Diyalogo: Sa Klinika (At the clinic)

Read the dialogue below. After completing this chapter, practice this dialogue using your own information.

DOKTOR	:	**Ano ho ang nararamdaman niyo?**
(*Doctor*)		*How do you feel?*
PASYENTE	:	**Masakit po ang ulo ko at may lagnat po ako.**
(*Patient*)		*I have a headache and I have a fever.*
DOKTOR	:	**Masakit ba ang lalamunan niyo?**
		Does your throat hurt?
PASYENTE	:	**Hindi po.**
		No.
DOKTOR	:	**Inumin mo ang tabletas na ito nang tatlong beses isang araw.**
		Take these tablets three times a day.
PASYENTE	:	**Puwede ho ba akong pumasok sa klase?**
		Can I go to school?
DOKTOR	:	**Huwag kang pumasok sa klase. Dapat kang magpahinga.**
		Don't go to school. You should rest.
PASYENTE	:	**Salamat po.**
		Thank you.
DOKTOR	:	**Walang anuman. Heto ang reseta.**
		You are welcome. Here is the prescription.

Bokabolaryo

Study the following words. Some of them were used in the dialogue you just read and some of them will be useful when you make your own sentences for your dialogues.

Mga Salita sa Diyalogo (Words in the Dialogue)

Doktor	*Doctor*
Pasyente	*Patient*
Reseta	*Prescription*
Tabletas	*Tablets*
Tatlong beses isang araw	*Three times a day*
Puwede...	*May I....*
Dapat	*Should*
Huwag	*Don't*

Mga Bahagi ng katawan

Ulo	*Head*
Leeg (pronounced as two syllables; le-eg)	*Neck*
Lalamunan	*Throat*
Balikat	*Shoulder*
Likod	*Back*
Dibdib	*Chest/Breast*
Braso	*Arm*
Siko	*Elbow*
Kamay	*Hand*
Daliri	*Finger*
Puso (accent on the first syllable)	*Heart*
Tiyan	*Stomach*
Baywang	*Waist*
Balakang	*Hips*
Puwet	*Buttocks*
Tuhod	*Knee*
Paa	*Feet*
Daliri sa Paa	*Toes*
Balat	*Skin*

Mga Bahagi ng Mukha (Parts of the Face)

Buhok	*Hair*
Noo	*Forehead*

Kilay	*Eyebrow*
Mata	*Eye*
Ilong	*Nose*
Pisngi	*Cheek*
Tenga	*Ear*
Bibig	*Mouth*
Labi (accent on the first syllable)	*Lips*
Ngipin	*Teeth*
Baba	*Chin*

Iba Pang Salita na May Kinalaman sa Sakit at Dahilan ng Sakit (Other words related to illnesses and causes of illnesses)

Ubo	*Cough*
Sipon	*Cold*
Lagnat	*Fever*
Masakit	*Painful*
Sugat	*Wound*
Hiwa	*Cut*
Paso	*Burn*
Nabali ang... (kamay, paa)	*Got Broken* (for example, arm or leg)
Temperatura	*Temperature*
Sumakit, Sumasakit, Sasakit	*Became painful, Is painful, will be painful*
Panis ang pagkain	*Food was rotten/bad*
Naulanan	*Got rained on*
Nahawa	*Got infected*
Nahulog	*Fell*
Nahiwa	*Got cut*
Napaso/Nasunog	*Got burned slightly/Got burned*
Iniresta	*Prescribed*
Gamot	*Medicine*
Bitamina	*Vitamins*
Nagpagamot	*Got treatment*
Nagpatingin sa doktor	*Visited a doctor*
Nag-eehersisyo	*Exercises*
Gumaling	*Got well*
Bawal	*Forbidden*
Sigarilyo	*Cigarettes*
Alak	*Wine*
Baboy	*Pork*

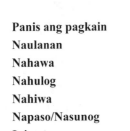

Mga Halimbawang Pangungusap

Practice saying these sentences aloud, to get a feel for how this chapter's vocabulary and grammar work in Filipino.

1. **Masakit ang ulo ng pasyente.**	*The patient's head hurts.*
2. **Mataas ang temperatura niya dahil may lagnat siya.**	*Her/his temperature is high because she/he has a fever.*
3. **Sumakit ang tiyan niya dahil hindi siya kumain ng almusal at tanghalian.**	*He/she had a stomachache because he/she did not eat breakfast and lunch.*
4. **Tableta ang inireseta ng doktor sa pasyente.**	*Tablets are what the doctor prescribed to the patient.*
5. **Dapat kang uminom ng gamot tatlong beses isang araw!**	*You should take your medicine three times a day!*
6. **Puwede siyang uminom ng juice.**	*He/she can drink juice.*
7. **Hindi siya puwedeng uminom ng beer.**	*He/she can't drink beer.*
8. **Bawal sa kanya ang sigarilyo, alak, at baboy.**	*He is forbidden [from having] cigarettes, wine, and pork.*
9. **Huwag kang pumasok sa klase!**	*Do not go to school!*

  Awit

Classroom and individual learners can sing the following song using the basic melody of "Head, Shoulders, Knees, and Toes," a children's song. The lyrics have been translated to refer to body parts in Filipino.

Mata, Tenga, Balikat, Tuhod (*Eye, Ear, Shoulder, Knee*)

Mata, tenga, balikat, tuhod balikat, tuhod.	*Eye, ear, shoulder, knee shoulder, knee.*
Mata, tenga, balikat, tuhod balikat, tuhod.	*Eye, ear, shoulder, knee shoulder, knee.*
Mata, tenga, balikat, tuhod balikat, tuhod.	*Eye, ear, shoulder, knee shoulder, knee.*
Ilong na maganda.	*Beautiful nose.*

★ Gawain

Play a game to remember the body parts. Classroom learners can work in pairs while individual learners can get two dolls or puppets and use them for this exercise.

Laro (*Game*) : Balikat sa Balikat (*Shoulder to Shoulder*)
Two people start the game by being the "it pair." The "it pair" shouts the phrase "**Balikat sa balikat** (*Shoulder to shoulder!*)" The other pairs move quickly to stand shoulder to shoulder. The "it pair" then tries to catch a pair who are NOT standing shoulder to shoulder. If they fail to catch a pair, then they give other directions until they do succeed; the commands are given using the following structure: "**Bahagi ng katawan sa bahagi ng katawan** (*Body part to body part*)." For example, "**Tuhod sa baywang** (*Knee to waist*)." This means that Person A in a pair should bring his/her knee up to Person B's waist.

The game can also be made more challenging by reviewing "**kanan** (*right*)" and "**kaliwa** (*left*)" as part of the command. For example, "**Kanang kamay sa kaliwang balikat** (*Right hand on left shoulder.*)" Thus, one person puts his/her right hand on his/her partner's left shoulder. Note that the partners don't have to mirror each other with both people putting their right hands on the other's left shoulder.

 Pagsasanay 1

Study the situations presented. Then, ask and answer questions. Refer to the words and sentences introduced and reviewed in this lesson. Also, when asked about the doctor's recommendations, or why a person got sick, feel free to improvise your answers. Classroom learners can work in pairs while individual learners should write down their answers and questions in the spaces provided.

I.　**Ang Sakit ni Tonyo** (*Tonyo's Illness*)

1. Tanong : **Ano ang problema ni Tonyo?**
   Sagot : _____.

2. Tanong : _____?
   Sagot : **Nagpunta si Tonyo sa klinika ng doktor.**

3. Tanong : **Bakit sumakit ang tiyan ni Tonyo?**
   Sagot : _____.

4. Tanong : **Saang ospital siya nagpatingin sa doktor?**
   Sagot : _____.

5. TANONG : **Gaano kadalas siya dapat uminom ng tabletas?**
   SAGOT : _____.

6. TANONG (yes or no question) : _____
   SAGOT : **Hindi. Hindi siya puwedeng pumasok sa opisina.**

7. TANONG : **Ano ang dapat niyang inumin?**
   SAGOT : **Dapat siyang uminom ng** _____.

8. TANONG : **Ano ang dapat niyang gawin?**
   SAGOT : _____.

9. TANONG : **Anong gamot ang inireseta ng doktor?**
   SAGOT : _____.

10. TANONG : **Ano ang mga bawal sa kanya?**
    SAGOT : _____.

II. **Ang Sakit ni Maxine** (*Maxine's illness*)

1. TANONG : **Ano ang sakit ni Maxine?**
   SAGOT : _____.

2. TANONG : _____?
   SAGOT : **Nagkasakit siya ng chicken pox dahil nahawa siya sa kaklase niya.**

3. TANONG : _____?
   SAGOT : _____ **ang inireseta ng doktor sa kanya.**

4. TANONG : **Puwede ba siyang pumasok sa klase?**
   SAGOT : _____.

5. TANONG : **Gaano kadalas niya dapat inumin ang gamot?**
   SAGOT : _____.

6. TANONG : **Bakit hindi siya puwedeng pumasok sa klase?**
   SAGOT : _____.

7. TANONG : **May mga bawal ba sa kanya?**
   SAGOT : _____.

8. TANONG : **Gumaling ba siya?**
   SAGOT : _____.

9. TANONG : _____?
   SAGOT : _____.

10. TANONG : _____?
    SAGOT : _____.

III. **Ang Sakit ni Joel** (*Joel's illness*)

1. TANONG : _____?
   SAGOT : **Nabali ang braso ko.**

2. TANONG : **Bakit nahiwa ang balat mo?**
   SAGOT : _____.

3. TANONG : _____?
   SAGOT : _____.

4. TANONG : _____?
   SAGOT : _____.

5. TANONG : _____?
   SAGOT : _____.

6. TANONG : _____?
   SAGOT : _____.

7. TANONG : _____?
   SAGOT : _____.

8. TANONG : _____?
   SAGOT : _____.

9. TANONG : _____?
   SAGOT : _____.

10. TANONG : _____?
    SAGOT : _____.

Pagsasanay 2

Recall the last time you got sick. If you haven't been sick for a long time, you can just make up a story. Classroom learners should work in pairs or groups while individual learners should write down the questions and answers. Remember to make the dialogue flow so that you will sound more natural.

1. TANONG : **Kailan ka nagkasakit?**
   SAGOT   : _____.

2. TANONG : **Ano ang naging sakit mo?**
   SAGOT   : _____.

3. TANONG : **Bakit ka nagkasakit?**
   SAGOT   : _____.

4. TANONG : **Saang klinika ka nagpatingin sa doktor?**
   SAGOT   : _____.

5. TANONG : **Ano ang pangalan ng doktor mo?**
   SAGOT   : _____.

6. TANONG : **Ano ang inireseta ng doktor mo sa iyo?**
   SAGOT   : _____.

7. TANONG : **Gaano kadalas ka dapat uminom ng gamot?**
   SAGOT   : _____.

8. TANONG : **Ano ang mga bawal sa iyo?**
   SAGOT   : _____.

9. TANONG : **Ano ang dapat mong gawin?**
   SAGOT   : _____.

10. TANONG : **Nag-eehersisyo ka ba?**
    SAGOT   : _____.

11. TANONG : **Kailan ka gumaling?**
    SAGOT   : _____.

12. TANONG : _____?
    SAGOT   : _____.

Gramatika

Study the information below to improve your Filipino grammar skills.

I. Verbs in the imperative or command form
    In an earlier unit, you studied verbs in the imperative form when giving directions or commands. For example, "**Kumanan ka!**" (*Turn right!*).

    In most instances, like that for verbs using the **um** affix, the imperative form is similar to the completed aspect of the verb. In other cases, for verbs using the **mag** and **na** affixes, the imperative form is formed by the following formula:

    Mag + root word
    Ma + root word

    Here are the verbs that we studied in this lesson:

Root word	Completed	Imperative
Kain	Kumain	Kumain
Inom	Uminom	Uminom
Pasok	Pumasok	Pumasok
Pahinga	Nagpahinga	Magpahinga
Ehersisyo	Nag-ehersisyo	Mag-ehersisyo
Tulog	Natulog	Matulog

II. Using the word **nang** before adverbs of frequency
    In this unit, we are studying adverbs of frequency. Remember to use the long **nang** instead of the marker **ng** before these adverbs.

    EXAMPLE: **Umiinom ako ng gamot nang tatlong beses isang araw.**
    I take medicine three times a day.

Dagdag-Aral 1 (Additional Study 1)

Study the following words related to frequency. Also, review related words that you have previously learned.

Mga Salita Hinggil sa "Frequency"

Beses	*Times*
Palagi/Lagi	*Always*

Madalas	*Often*
Paminsan-minsan	*Sometimes*
Bihira	*Rarely*
Hindi kailanman	*Never*
Araw-araw	*Every day* or *daily*
Minsan sa isang linggo	*Once a week*
Linggo-linggo	*Every week* or *weekly*
Buwan-buwan	*Every month* or *monthly*
Taon-taon	*Every year* or *annually*

Pagsasanay

Using the words you have just learned, try to answer the following questions. Then, make your own questions. Classroom learners should work in pairs while individual learners should write down their questions and answers.

Remember to use the word **nang** instead of the marker **ng**. Examples are provided through incomplete sentences.

1. TANONG : **Gaano ko kadalas dapat inumin ang gamot?**
   SAGOT : **Dapat mong inumin ang gamot nang _____.**

2. TANONG : **Gaano ka kadalas pumunta sa doktor?**
   SAGOT : **Pumupunta ako sa doktor nang minsan sa isang linggo.**

3. TANONG : **Gaano ka kadalas kumain ng baboy?**
   SAGOT : **Kumakain ako _____.**

4. TANONG : **Madalas ka bang uminom ng alak?**
   SAGOT : **Hindi. _____.**

5. TANONG : **Gaano ka kadalas uminom ng bitamina?**
   SAGOT : _____.

6. TANONG : **Gaano ka kadalas nag-eehersisyo?**
   SAGOT : _____.

7. TANONG : _____?
   SAGOT : _____.

8. TANONG : _____?
   SAGOT : _____.

9. TANONG : _____?

    SAGOT   : _____.

10. TANONG : _____?

    SAGOT   : _____.

📖 Dagdag-Aral 2 (Additional Study 2)

In the dialogue you studied in this lesson, the doctor said:

DOKTOR   :   **Magpahinga ka!** (*Rest!*)

Let us now pretend that someone asked you about your visit to the doctor:

TANONG   :   **Ano ang sabi ng doktor?**
             What did the doctor say?

One way of answering this question is to use the word **daw** or **raw**. Use **daw** when the last letter of the preceding word is a consonant, and use **raw** when the last letter of the preceding word is a vowel. Thus:

SAGOT   :   **Ang sabi ng doktor, magpahinga raw ako.**
            The doctor said to rest.

Now, study the following examples:

TANONG   :   **Ano ang sabi ng nanay mo?**
             What did your mother say?

SAGOT   :   **Ang sabi ng nanay ko, huwag daw akong uminom ng alak.**
            My mother said, don't drink wine/alcohol.

TANONG   :   **Ano ang sabi ng tatay mo?**
             What did your father say?

SAGOT   :   **Ang sabi ng tatay ko, uminom daw ako ng bitamina.**
            My father said, take vitamins.

Practice asking and answering questions using the following pattern:

TANONG   :   **Ano ang sabi** _____?

SAGOT   :   **Ang sabi** _____, _____.

Mga Tala Sa Kultura

Traditional healers have always been present in Filipino society. In precolonial times, the **babaylan** or **baylan**, many of whom were women, performed healing rituals to heal the sick. Usually, this involved the sacrificing of animals such as chicken or pigs. It is believed that by sacrificing the animals the life of the sick person is spared. In the **atang-atang** ritual in Cagayan in northern Philippines that I witnessed in 1987, offerings in the form of food and betel nut were given to the gods as well. Placed in a very small raft, these offerings were set afloat in the river.

In many rural communities where doctors and hospitals are rare, people go to the **albolaryo** or traditional healer. In most cases, the healer uses medicinal plants believed to have healing properties. Among the medicinal plants known to those living in many communities are guava leaves (for wounds); ginger (for sore throats; also anti-fungal and anti-inflammatory); **ampalaya** or bitter melon (for diabetes); **atis** or sugar apple fruit and leaves (for diarrhea).

At times, the **arbolaryo** attributes the sickness to the **aswang** or the **mangkukulam** ("witches" [from a Western perspective]), with the latter having the power to cast spells on his/her victims. Garlic is known to ward off these "witches."

In recent times, packaged tea bags have been manufactured using the traditional knowledge of medicinal plants. Among the most popular teas are **sambong** (for kidney disorders and hypertension), **banaba** (used as a purgative and diuretic), and **lagundi** (for coughs, asthma, and colic).

Pagbabasa

Read the following retelling of a popular story, and then answer the questions that follow. This is a short version of the well-known metrical tale that became popular during the Spanish colonial period. There were two kinds of metrical romances in the Philippines, the **awit** and the **corrido**, both of which were derived from the metrical romances of Spain. Written in narrative poetry form, these metrical romances were set in the Europe in the Middle Ages and spoke of the adventures of princes and princesses as well as the conflict between Christians and Moors. With the exception of Francisco Baltazar's *Florante at Laura*, these metrical romances fueled the anti-Muslim sentiments of Christian Filipinos and thus were considered detrimental to the goal of national unity.

Ibon	*Bird*
Hari	*King*
Dumi	*Manure*
Bato	*Stone*
Ermitanyo	*Hermit*
Kutsilyo	*Knife*
Kalamansi	*Lemon*
Lubid	*Rope*
Hinuli	*Catch*
Binuhos	*Throw* (usually used for liquids)

Ang Ibong Adarna

May sakit si Haring Fernando, ang Hari ng Berbanya. Ang gamot daw sa sakit niya ay ang ibong adarna na nakatira sa gubat.

Tatlo ang anak ng hari at gusto nilang gumaling siya. Unang pumunta sa gubat si Pedro. Napagod siya at nagpahinga siya sa ilalim ng puno. Umawit ang ibong adarna at nakatulog si Pedro. Pagkatapos, nahulog ang dumi ng ibon at naging bato si Pedro.

Umalis din ang ikalawang anak ng hari na si Diego. Pero muli, nagpahinga siya, umawit ang ibon, at nakatulog si Diego. Naging bato rin siya.

Sa huli, umalis si Juan. May nakita siyang ermitanyo. Binigyan niya ito ng pagkain. Itinuro ng ermitanyo sa kanya kung nasaan ang ibong adarna. Binigyan siya nito ng kutsilyo at kalamansi, lubid, at tubig. Nang umawit ang ibon, hiniwa ni Juan ang balat niya para hindi siya matulog. Pagkatapos, hinuli niya ang ibon. Binuhos niya ang tubig sa mga kapatid niya.

Umuwi sila at gumaling ang hari dahil sa ibong adarna.

✏ Pagsusulat

Using the vocabulary and grammar you have learned, write a paragraph about your most recent illness.

⚐ Paglalagom

In **Aralin 20**, you have:
1. Learned words identifying the parts of the body,
2. Learned words you can use when talking about illnesses, reasons for illnesses, and remedies,
3. Reviewed the imperative or command form of the verb,
4. Studied adverbs and words that talk about frequency,
5. Studied words to say "*may I,*" *should* and *shouldn't,*
6. Learned how to repeat what has been said to you.

You should now be able to:
1. Talk about the parts of your body.
2. Talk about illnesses and their remedies.
3. Repeat what someone has said to you.

Pagkain (Food)

  Diyalogo: Sa Restawran (At a restaurant)

Read the dialogue below. After completing this chapter, practice this dialogue using your own information.

WAITER : **Ano ho ang gusto niyang orderin?**
What would you like to order?

PEDRO : **Ano ho ba ang masarap na putahe ninyo?**
What is delicious among your food?

WAITER : **Sinigang na baboy, kare-kare, at inihaw na panga ng tuna.**
Pork in tamarind broth, ox-tail stew, and broiled tuna jaw.

MARIA : **Gusto ko ho ng sinigang na baboy at inihaw na tuna.**
I would like pork in tamarind broth and broiled tuna jaw.

PEDRO : **Kare-kare ang gusto ko.**
I would like ox-tail stew.

WAITER : **Ano ho ang inumin niyo?**
What is the drink you would like?

MARIA : **Buko juice na lang. Puwede ba akong humingi ng isa pang tinidor?**
Just coconut juice. Can I ask for another fork?

WAITER : **Aba, oo. Gusto niyo ba ng panghimagas pagkatapos?**
Of course. Would you like dessert afterwards?

PEDRO : **Leche flan na lang.**
Just leche flan.

Bokabolaryo

Study the following words related to food. Some of them were used in the dialogue you just read and some of them will be useful when you make your own sentences for your dialogues.

Mga Putaheng Filipino na nasa Dayologo (Filipino Dishes in the Dialogue)

Sinigang na baboy	*Pork in soured broth*
Kare-kare	*Ox-tail stew in peanut sauce*
Inihaw na Panga ng Tuna	*Broiled jaw of tuna*
Nilagang Baka	*Boiled beef*
Leche flan	*Egg and milk custard*

Mga Pagkain (Food)

Isda	*Fish*
Hipon	*Shrimp*
Pusit	*Squid*
Alimango	*Crab*
Halaan	*Clams*
Manok	*Chicken*
Baboy	*Pork*
Baka	*Beef*
Kanin	*Cooked rice*
Bigas	*Uncooked rice*
Gulay	*Vegetables*
Prutas	*Fruits*
Sopas	*Soup*
Sabaw	*Broth*
Ulam	*Anything you eat with rice*
Panghimagas	*Dessert*
Ensalada	*Salad*
Inumin (accent on the second syllable)	*Drink*

Mga Paraan ng Pagluluto (Methods of Cooking)

Nilaga	*Boil*
Inihaw	*Broiled*
Pinasingaw	*Steamed*
Prito	*Fry*
Ginisa	*Sauteed*

Mga Kubyertos (Utensils)

Kutsara	*Spoon*
Tinidor	*Fork*
Kutsarita	*Teaspoon*
Plato	*Plate*
Platito	*Small Plate*
Kutsilyo	*Knife*
Baso	*Glass*

Mga Pandiwa

Mag-order	*To order*
Humingi	*Ask*

Other Words

Masarap	*Delicious*
Hapunan	*Dinner*

Mga Halimbawang Pangungusap

Practice saying these sentences aloud, to get a feel for how this chapter's vocabulary and grammar work in Filipino.

1. **Nag-order ang kostumer ng sinigang na baboy at inihaw na tuna.**

   *The costumer ordered **sinigang na baboy** (pork in soured broth) and **inihaw na tuna**.*

2. **Buko juice ang inorder niyang inumin.**

   Coconut juice is the drink he/she ordered.

3. **Leche flan ang kinain niyang panghimagas.**

   Leche flan is the dessert he/she ate.

Pagsasanay

Review the dialogue you read and the new words you studied. Then, ask and answer questions. Use the complete and incomplete sentences below as your guide. Classroom learners can work in pairs while individual learners should write down their answers and questions in the spaces provided.

1. TANONG : **Ano ang inorder ni Pedro?**
   SAGOT   : **Nag-order siya ng sinigang na baboy at inihaw na panga ng tuna.**

2. TANONG : **Ano ang gustong orderin ni Maria?**
   SAGOT   : **Gusto niyang mag-order ng _____.**

3. TANONG : **Ano ang inumin na gusto ni Pedro?**
   SAGOT   : _____.

4. TANONG : **Anong panghimagas ang gusto nila?**
   SAGOT   : **Gusto nila ng _____.**

5. TANONG : **Anong kubyertos ang hiningi ni Maria?**
   SAGOT   : _____.

6. TANONG : **Saang restawran ka kumain?**
   SAGOT   : _____.

7. TANONG : **Anong pagkain ang inorder mo?**
   SAGOT   : _____.

8. TANONG : **Anong inumin ang inorder mo?**
   SAGOT   : _____.

9. TANONG : **Masarap ba ang kinain mo?**
   SAGOT   : _____.

10. TANONG : _____?
    SAGOT   : _____.

★ Gawain (Role-play)

Study the menu below from Cendrillon restaurant. Then, using this lesson's dialogue as an example, do a role-play. Classroom learners should work in pairs or groups of three while individual learners should write down the dialogue.

— APPETIZERS —

Squash soup with crab dumplings $ 9.00
(Cal abaza puree with coconut milk & ginger soup)

Amy's spring roll $ 8.50
w/ achara (pickled green papaya relish)
(Grandmother's recipe of deep fried spring roll with cabbage, stringbeans, tofu, pork, shrimp)

Lumpia Shanghai $ 8.50
with pineapple sweet & sour sauce
(Deep fried spring rolls with pork, carrots, mushrooms & jicama)

Manila clams $ 10.50
with blackbeans, leeks & shitake mushrooms

Beef tapa salad $ 9.50
(thinly sliced air-dried beef marinated in soy, kalamansi & garlic)

Fresh lumpia with tamarind and peanut sauce $ 9.50
(Napa cabbage, beansprouts, jicama, leeks & mushrooms in fresh purple yam wrapper)

Goat curry $ 11.50
with fresh rice pancakes, chutney & plantain

— MAIN COURSES —

Chicken adobo $ 18.50
(braised in rice vinegar, soy, bayleaves, garlic & chilies)

Striped bass with hijiki crust $ 19.50
(panfried filet of bass topped with seaweed, leek & miso crust)

Salt roasted duck $ 21.50
with mango & tomatillo chutney and cellophane noodles

Lamb shank $ 20.50
braised in coconut milk, lemongrass, kaffir lime & galangal

Grilled oxtail kare-kare $ 19.50
with *bagoong* (fermented shrimp paste)
(Oxtail braised in tomatoes & ground peanuts with long beans & eggplant)

— ASIAN GRILL & BBQ —

Romy's spareribs $ 19.50
with mashed taro & sweet potatoes
(marinated in garlic, soy and rice wine & spice-rub; then slow cooked in Chinese smokehouse)

Chicken inasal $ 18.50
(Visayan style barbecue marinated in kalamansi, garlic and achuete)

Grilled trout relleno $ 19.50
stuffed with mushrooms, jicama & leeks in banana leaves

— NOODLES & RICE —

Laksa $ 19.50
with shrimp & udon
(Malaysian curry sauce of coconut milk, lemongrass, curry leaves, chilies)

Spicy rice noodles with tofu $ 17.50
sesame seeds, shiitake mushrooms & watercress

Cellophane noodles $ 17.50
with beansprouts, mushroom, bok choy, snowpeas & lotus root

Black rice paella $ 19.50
with crab, scallops, shrimp & Manila clams
(with green Thai curry, bottleneck gourd, loofah, mushrooms, eggplant)

📄 Balik-Aral Sa Gramatika (Grammar Review)

Using the sentences you have written above, review actor and object focus by writing sentences two ways. Examples are provided.

1. **Kumain ako ng sinigang sa restawran.**
   Sinigang ang kinain ko sa restawran.

2. **Uminom ako ng** _____**.**
   Tsaa ang _____ **ko.**

3. _____ **ako ng tinidor.**
   Tinidor ang _____ **ko.**

4. _____

5. _____

6. _____

7. _____

 ## 💬 Diyalogo: Maalat Ang Sinigang! (The sinigang is too salty!)

Read the dialogue below. After completing this chapter, practice this dialogue using your own information.

MARIA : **Puwede niyo ho bang palitan ang sinigang?**
        Can you please change the pork in tamarind broth?

WAITER : **Ano po ang problema?**
         What is the problem?

MARIA : **Hindi ko ho makain dahil napakaalat.**
        I could not eat it because it is too salty.

WAITER : **Papalitan ko na lang po.**
         I will just change it.

MARIA : **Salamat.**
        Thank you.

 **Bokabolaryo**

Study the following words. Some of them were used in the dialogue you just read and some of them will be useful when you make your own sentences for your dialogues.

Mga Pang-uri Para sa Pagkain (Adjectives to describe food)

Maalat	*Salty*
Matamis	*Sweet*
Maanghang	*Spicy*
Malamig	*Cold*
Mainit	*Hot*
Maasim	*Sour*
Mapait	*Bitter*
Mapakla	*Tangy*
Napaka-alat	*Too salty*
Masyadong maalat	*Too salty*

Mga Pandiwa (Verbs)

Pinalitan	*Changed*
Pinabalik	*Asked to return*

Mga Halimbawang Pangungusap

1. **Hindi makain ni Maria ang sinigang dahil maalat ito.**
   Maria could not eat the pork in sinigang broth because it is salty.
2. **Hindi makain ni Pedro ang sopas dahil malamig ito.**
   Pedro could not eat the soup because it is cold.
3. **Hindi ko makain ang ulam dahil napakaanghang nito.**
   I could not eat the ulam because it is too spicy.
4. **Pinabalik ni Maria sa waiter ang pagkain dahil malamig ito.**
   Maria asked the waiter to return the food because it is cold.
5. **Pinalitan ng waiter ang malamig na sabaw ng mainit na sabaw.**
   The waiter changed the cold soup with hot soup.
6. **Hindi ko makain ang kimchi dahil masyado itong maanghang.**
   I couldn't eat the kimchi because it is too spicy.

Pagsasanay 1

Make a list of some dishes you like and dislike. They do not have to be Filipino. Then in the space provided, use the words you have learned to describe the dish. Use the examples as your guide.

1. *Buffalo wings*   **Maanghang**

2. *Chicken soup*   **Mainit**

3. *Honey*   **Matamis**

4. _____   _____

5. _____   _____

6. _____   _____

7. _____   _____

8. _____   _____

9. _____   _____

10. _____   _____

Pagsasanay 2

Using the words you have learned, as well as the restaurant menu, practice these questions and answers by both speaking and writing. Use the earlier pairs as a guide.

1. TANONG : **Bakit hindi mo makain ang Bicol Express?**
   SAGOT   : **Hindi ko makain ang Bicol Express dahil maanghang ito.**

2. TANONG : **Bakit hindi mo makain ang _____?**
   SAGOT   : **Hindi ko _____ ang _____ dahil**

          _____.

3. TANONG : **Bakit mo pinabalik ang _____?**
   SAGOT   : **_____.**

4. TANONG : _____ ?
   SAGOT : _____ .

5. TANONG : _____ ?
   SAGOT : _____ .

6. TANONG : _____ ?
   SAGOT : _____ .

7. TANONG : _____ ?
   SAGOT : _____ .

8. TANONG : _____ ?
   SAGOT : _____ .

Diyalogo: Ang Sarap! (It's delicious!)

Read the dialogue below. Then, practice this dialogue using your own information.

PEDRO : **Kumusta ang nilagang baka mo?**
How is your boiled beef?

MARIA : **Ang sarap. Gusto mo pa ba ng toyo o patis?**
It is delicious! Would you like soy sauce or fish sauce?

PEDRO : **Ayaw ko ng toyo. Patis na lang.**
I don't like soy sauce. Just fish sauce please.

MARIA : **Gusto ko pang mag-order ng kanin.**
I would like to order more rice.

Bokabolaryo

Study the following words and how they were used in the dialogue you just read. Some of them like **gusto** and **ayaw** have been introduced earlier. Practice them again now, this time talking about food, and using them with verbs.

Mga Pang-uri Para sa Pagkain (Adjectives to describe food)	
Gusto	*Like*
Ayaw	*Dislike*
Sawsawan	*Something to dip food in*
Toyo	*Soy sauce*

Patis	*Fish sauce*
Suka	*Vinegar*
Bagoong	*Fermented shrimp or anchovies*

Mga Halimbawang Pangungusap

Practice saying these sentences.

1. **Nilagang baka ang gustong putahe ni Maria.**
   Boiled beef is the dish that Maria likes.
2. **Gusto ni Pedro ng adobo.**
   Pedro likes adobo.
3. **Ayaw ko ng patis.**
   I don't like patis.
4. **Gusto kong mag-order ng pagkain.**
   I would like to order food.

 Pagsasanay

Practice talking about your food likes and dislikes through the following questions and answers. Use the earlier pairs as a guide. Independent learners should write the questions and answers. Classroom learners should work as pairs and ask each other questions.

1. TANONG : **Ano ang gusto mong sawsawan?**
   SAGOT   : **Gusto ko ng toyo.**

2. TANONG : **Ano ang gusto mong ulam?**
   SAGOT   : **Paborito ko ang sinigang.**

3. TANONG : **Ano ang gusto mong panghimagas?**
   SAGOT   : _____ **ang paborito ko.**

4. TANONG : **Bakit gusto mo ang** _____ **?**
   SAGOT   : **Gusto ko ang** _____ **dahil** _____ **.**

5. TANONG : **Ano ang ayaw mong** _____ **?**
   SAGOT   : **Ayaw ko ng** _____ **.**

6. TANONG : _____ **?**
   SAGOT   : _____ **.**

7. TANONG : _____ **?**
   SAGOT   : _____ **.**

8. Tanong : _____?
   Sagot : _____.

9. Tanong : _____?
   Sagot : _____.

10. Tanong : _____?
    Sagot : _____.

  Diyalogo: Paborito Ko Ang Adobo! (Adobo is my favorite!)

Read the dialogue below. Then, practice this dialogue using your own information.

Juan : **Ano ang paborito mong ulam, Maria?**
    What is your favorite food to eat with rice, Maria?

Maria : **Pinakagusto ko ang adobo.**
    I like adobo best.

Juan : **Anong klaseng adobo?**
    What kind of adobo?

Maria : **Manok at baboy na may kasamang atay. Ikaw?**
    Chicken and pork with liver. And you?

Juan : **Sinigang.**
    Sour soup.

Maria : **Anong klaseng sinigang?**
    What kind of sour soup?

Juan : **Paborito ko ang sinigang na bangus sa bayabas.**
    I like milkfish in soup soured with guavas.

Maria : **Talaga? Mas gusto ko ang ang sinigang na baboy sa sampaloc.**
    Really? I like pork in soup soured with tamarind better.

Juan : **Ganoon ba?**
    Really?

Maria : **Lalo na kapag may gabi.**
    Especially with yam.

Juan : **Bakit?**
    Why?

Maria : **Kasi lumalapot ang sabaw kapag may gabi.**
    Because the broth becomes thick when there is yam.

Bokabolaryo

Study the following words and how they were used in the dialogue you just read.

Mas gusto	*Like better*
Pinakagusto	*Like best*
Pinaka-ayaw	*Like least*
Paborito	*Favorite*
Klase	*Kind of*
Lalo na	*Especially*
Atay	*Liver*
Gabi	*Yam*

Gawain (Role-play)

Sarbey (*Survey*)

Make a survey of the favorite kinds of food of your classmates or friends. Review the words you have learned to talk about meat, seafood, and vegetables. Some examples of questions and answers are provided below. Then make a report (**ulat**) of your findings.

1. TANONG : **Ano ang paborito mong ulam?**
   SAGOT : **Paborito ko ang adobo.**

2. TANONG : **Anong klaseng adobo ang paborito mo?**
   SAGOT : **Gusto ko ng adobong manok at baboy na may kasamang atay.**

3. TANONG : **Anong klaseng sinigang ang gusto mo?**
   SAGOT : **Gusto ko ng sinigang na bangus sa bayabas.**

4. TANONG : **Ano ang paborito mong pagkain?**
   SAGOT : **Paborito ko ang pizza.**

5. TANONG : **Anong klaseng pizza?**
   SAGOT : _____ .

6. TANONG : _____ ?
   SAGOT : _____ .

7. TANONG : _____ ?
   SAGOT : _____ .

Mga Tala Sa Kultura

Filipino food is similar to the cuisines of other countries in Southeast Asia such as Indonesia, Malaysia, and Thailand. However, its history of trade with China as well as its experience of colonization (by Spain and the United States) have also influenced its cuisine.

Several food scholars, including Doreen Fernandez, assert that **sinigang** is perhaps the dish that best reflects Filipino cuisine. It has many variations, depending on the region in the Philippines. In areas near the ocean, it is made with fish or shrimp. It is soured depending on the availability of souring ingredients such as tamarind or guavas.

Adobo, on the other hand, was a popular dish brought by the Spanish colonizers. The meat is stewed in vinegar and spaces, and thus does not spoil easily. Supposedly, it was one way of preserving food for the long journey of Spanish ships to the Philippines. Today, there are several versions of **adobo**: **adobo** made with soy sauce and vinegar, **adobo** with coconut milk, **adobo** with chicken liver sauce, and **adobo** with **patis** instead of soy sauce.

During the Spanish colonial period, introduced Spanish foods became household favorites in upper-class households and were served as delicacies during special occasions such as the **pista** (or the feast of a town's patron saint) in lower-income households.

With American colonization came the introduction of fast food such as hot dogs and hamburgers, as well as canned food. Even today, it is not uncommon for canned goods such as sardines and Spam to be considered special food in the rural household, and thus to be served to guests.

 Pagbabasa

Read the legend below. Study the following words before reading. You have learned some of the words in earlier lessons; they are listed here for you to review. You can also refer to the glossary at the back of the book.

Noong unang panahon	*A long time ago* (literally, in the "first" times)
Tulong	*Help*
Awa	*Pity*
Diyosa	*Goddess*
Tuyong-tuyo	*Very dry*
Lupa	*Earth*
Bumaba	*Went down*
Paligid	*Surroundings*
Dibdib	*Breast*

Pinisil	*Squeeze*
Dugo	*Blood*
Pagkalipas ng panahon	*After some time*
Inani	*Harvested*
Binayo	*Pounded*
Itinanim	*Planted*

Alamat ng Bigas*

Noong unang panahon, walang pagkain ang mga tao sa probinsiya ng Bohol. Humingi sila ng tulong kay Sappia, ang diyosa ng awa. Naawa sa kanila si Sappia at bumaba siya sa lupa.

Nakita ni Sappia na kulay kayumanggi ang lupa. Dahil walang ulan, tuyong-tuyo ang lupa. Namamatay na sa gutom ang mga tao. Damo lang ang nakikita sa paligid.

Inilabas ni Sappia ang kanyang dibdib. Pinisil niya ang dibdib, at lumabas ang gatas. Isa-isa niyang nilagyan ng gatas ang mga damo, pero kulang ang gatas niya. Humingi siya ng mas maraming gatas sa langit pero nang pinisil niya uli ang dibdib, dugo ang lumabas.

Bumalik si Sappia sa langit. Mula sa langit, pinanood niya ang mga damo na mayroon nang mga butil ng palay. Pagkalipas ng panahon, inani ng mga tao ang palay. Nang binayo nila ang palay, marami sa bigas ang kulay puti. May mga bigas din na kulay pula.

Parehong masarap ang bigas na puti at bigas na pula. Itinanim ng mga tao ang ibang palay. Hindi na sila nagutom. Mula sa langit, masayang-masaya si Sappia.

1. Kanino humingi ng tulong ang mga tao?
2. Sino si Sappia?
3. Bakit tuyong-tuyo ang lupa?
4. Ano ang lumabas mula sa dibdib ni Sappia?
5. Nang maubos ang gatas ni Sappia, ano ang lumabas mula sa dibdib niya?
6. Ano ang mga kulay ng bigas?
7. Ano ang lasa ng bigas?

* Based on "The Rice Myth" of Bohol. *Philippine Folk Literature: The Myths.* Edited and compiled by Damiana Eugenio. Quezon City: University of the Philippines Press, 1993. pp. 436–437. Eugenio in turn attributes this to P. C. Malay, *WWM*, Oct. 26, 1956.

✏️ Pagsusulat

Write a paragraph or two about your favorite foods and about a recent trip to a restaurant.

🚩 Paglalagom

In **Aralin 21**, you have:
1. Learned words related to describing food,
2. Reviewed likes and dislikes,
3. Practiced how to order food at a restaurant and how to talk about food.

You should now be able to:
1. Ask and answer questions about food.
2. Describe food.
3. Order at a restaurant.

To Download or Stream Audio Recordings:

1. You must have an internet connection.

2. Type the URL below into your web browser.

https://www.tuttlepublishing.com/tagalog-for-beginners-audio-pdfs

For support email us at info@tuttlepublishing.com.

Pagbibigay ng Instruksiyon (Giving Instructions)

🎧 💬 Diyalogo: Pagluluto ng Turon (Cooking turon)

Read the dialogue below. After completing this chapter, practice this dialogue using your own information.

JUAN : **Paano ba magluto ng turon?**
How does one cook turon [banana spring rolls]?

CLARA : **Maghanda ka lang ng saging, lumpia wrapper, pulang asukal, at langka.**
Just prepare bananas, spring roll wrappers, brown sugar, and jackfruit.

JUAN : **Tapos?**
And then?

CLARA : **Kasunod nito, hiwain mo nang pahaba ang saging. Pagkatapos, ipagulong mo ang mga piraso ng saging sa asukal.**
After this, cut the banana lengthwise. Then, roll the pieces of banana in sugar.

JUAN : **At kapag napagulong ko na?**
And then after I have rolled them?

CLARA : **Sa huli, balutin mo ang saging kasama ang pira-pirasong langka sa lumpia wrapper.**
Finally, wrap the banana with pieces of jackfruit in the spring roll wrapper.

JUAN : **Paano ko pagdidikitin ang dulo ng lumpia wrapper?**
How can I close the ends of the spring roll wrapper?

CLARA : **Kaunting tubig lang ang pandikit diyan.**
Just a little water can be used to then seal it.

JUAN : **Tapos?**
  And then?

CLARA : **Iprito mo ang saging sa mainit na mantika.**
  Fry the banana in hot oil.

JUAN : **Salamat, Clara.**
  Thank you, Clara.

 ## Bokabolaryo

Study the following words. Some of them were used in the dialogue you just read and some of them will be useful when you make your own sentences for your dialogues.

Mga Pandiwang Nag-uutos (Imperative or Command Verbs)

Magluto	*Cook*
Maghanda	*Prepare*
Hiwain	*Cut*
Ipagulong	*Roll*
Balutin	*Wrap*
Pagdikitin	*Seal*
Iprito	*Fry*
Pakuluin	*Boil*
Ihawin	*Broil/grill*
Haluin	*Mix*
Lagyan	*Put*
Dagdagan	*Add*
Tanggalin	*Remove*

Iba Pang Salita (Other Words)

Lumpia	*Spring roll*
Pulang asukal	*Brown sugar* (literally, red sugar)
Pahaba	*Lengthwise*
Hiwain mo nang maliliit	*Cut into small pieces*
Mantika	*Oil*

Mga Halimbawang Pangungusap

Study the following sentences to learn how to give cooking instructions.

1. **Una, hiwain mo nang pahaba ang saging.**
2. **Kasunod nito, ipagulong mo ang saging sa asukal.**
3. **Pagkatapos, balutin mo ng lumpia wrapper ang saging.**
4. **Panghuli, iprito mo ang turon.**

 # Pagsasanay

Study the pictures below. Then write down sentences that describe the steps in making these dishes. Refer to the words and sentences you have just learned.

I.   **Nagluluto si Tess ng spaghetti.**

TANONG : **Paano gumawa ng spaghetti?**
SAGOT   : **Una,** _____ .
_____ .
_____ .
_____ .
_____ .
_____ .

II. Nagluluto si Andrew ng omelette.

TANONG : **Paano magluto ng omelette?**

SAGOT : _____.

_____.

_____.

_____.

_____.

_____.

III. Gumagawa ng cake si Bb. Echave.

TANONG : **Paano gumawa ng cake?**

SAGOT : _____.

_____.

_____.

_____.

_____.

_____.

Mga Tala Sa Kultura

Rice cakes are among the most popular snacks in the Philippines. One kind of rice cake is **suman**, or rice cake wrapped in leaves. How does one make **suman**? Well, there are many answers to that question because there are many varieties of **suman**. It can be wrapped in either banana leaves or coconut palm leaves, it can be sweet, or served with **latik**, which is made of coconut.

Other kinds of rice cakes are **puto** or steamed rice cake and **kutsinta**, a sweet brown rice cake. These are usually eaten with grated coconut. These rice cakes can be eaten for breakfast or as a snack.

 Pagbabasa

Read the following poem, and then answer the questions that follow. Study the following words before reading the poem. You have learned some of the words in earlier lessons; they are listed here for you to review. You can also refer to the glossary at the back of the book.

Nagmamahal	*Love*
Dahan-dahan	*Slowly*
Kamias	*A tropical sour fruit*
Iniipon	*Gather*
Sisidlan	*Container*
Nangangamba	*Afraid*
Makaligtaan	*Forget*
Tinutusok	*Pierce*
Palamigan	*Refrigerator*
Katas	*Juice*
Mag-ingat	*Careful*
Magsugat	*Be wounded*
Balat	*Outer covering; shell; also, skin*
Apoy	*Fire*

Minatamis

Sa ganitong paraan ako nagmamahal,
Dahan-dahan na parang
Gumagawa ng minatamis sa tag-araw.

Iniipon ko ang kamias
Sa isang sisidlan,
Isa-isa na para bang nangangambang
May makaligtaan.

Tinutusok ko ang kamias
Bago iwan sa palamigan
Nang kung ilang araw,
Pagkatapos ay ilalabas
Para pisilin ng mga daliri
At makuha ang katas.
Kailangang mag-ingat
Para huwag magsugat ang balat.

Pinapagulong ko sa asukal ang kamias,
Ibinabalik sa palamigan,
At pag natuyo na'y saka lamang pinapakuluan
Sa arnibal.
Kailangang mabagal at marahan ang apoy
At nang di masunog ang asukal.

Sa ganitong paraan
Din ako magpapaalam.
Ginagawang matamis
Ang asim at pait ng tag-araw.

1. Kailan niya ginagawa ang minatamis?
2. Ano ang iniipon niya sa isang sisidlan?
3. Saan niya iniiwan ang kamias nang ilang araw?
4. Bakit niya pinipisil ang kamias?
5. Bakit kailangang mag-ingat?
6. Saan niya pinapagulong ang kamias?
7. Bakit kailangang mabagal at marahan ang apoy?

✏ Pagsusulat

Share your favorite recipe, by translating it into Filipino.

▶ Paglalagom

In **Aralin 22**, you have:
1. Learned words related to cooking,
2. Reviewed the imperative form of the verb,
3. Practiced how to give step-by-step directions.

You should now be able to:
1. Describe how to cook a dish.
2. Give step-by-step instructions.

Pagbisita sa Bahay ng Kaibigan (Visiting a Friend's House)

  Diyalogo: Pagdalaw sa Maysakit (Visiting a sick person)

This is a review and expansion lesson. As you study the dialogue below, note the words and expressions you already know. Then, try to guess the meaning of the words you don't know through the context. At the end of this lesson, practice this dialogue using your own information.

CLARA : **Kumusta ka na?**
How are you?

MARIA : **Mabuti-buti na ako.**
I am feeling better.

CLARA : **Ano ang naging sakit mo?**
What were you sick of?

MARIA : **Lagnat, sipon at ubo lang.**
Just a fever, runny nose and cough.

CLARA : **Umiinom ka ba ng gamot?**
Do you take medicine?

MARIA : **Oo, dalawang beses isang araw. Gusto mo ba ng turon?**
Yes, two times a day. Would you like some banana spring rolls?

CLARA : **Huwag ka nang mag-abala. Nakakahiya.**
Please don't bother. I feel ashamed.

MARIA : **Sige na.**
Please.

CLARA : **Sige, salamat.**
Okay. Thank you.

Bokabolaryo

Study the following words and how they were used in the dialogue you just read. Other words will also be useful for the exercises in this lesson.

Pagdalaw	*Visit*
Dumalaw	*Visited*
Bisita	*Visitor*
Litrato	*Photograph*
Larawan	*Picture*
Inalagaan	*Took care of*
Mabuti-buti	*Better*
Nakakahiya naman.	*I feel ashamed.* (Expression that actually means "Please don't bother to give me food. It is too much trouble.")
Nag-alok/Inalok	*Offered*
May tubercolosis	*Has tuberculosis*
May kanser	*Has cancer*

Mga Halimbawang Pangungusap

Study the following sentences that narrate Clara's visit to Maria. They will be useful when you practice talking about your visit to a relative or a friend.

1. **Dumalaw si Clara kay Maria.**	*Clara visited Maria.*
2. **May lagnat, sipon at ubo si Maria.**	*Maria has a fever, a cold and a cough.*
3. **Umiinom si Maria ng gamot nang dalawang beses isang araw.**	*Maria takes her medicine twice a day.*
4. **Inalagaan si Maria ng nanay niya.**	*Maria's mother took care of her.*
5. **Inalok ni Maria ng turon si Clara.**	*Maria offered some turon to Clara.*

  Pagsasanay

This exercise has several components. First, study the picture. Who are the people in the picture and how are they related to each other? Second, think of a possible story or narrative about the picture. What is happening? Third, ask and answer questions about the picture with your classmates, or if you are an individual learner, write these questions and answers down. Finally, write as many sentences as you can about the picture. These sentences can describe the people or the place, or narrate the situation. Below are some examples of questions and answers, as well as sentences:

Mga Halimbawang Tanong at Sagot (Examples of questions and answers)

1. TANONG : **Ano ang naging sakit ng lalaki?**

   SAGOT : _____.

2. TANONG : **Gaano siya kadalas uminom ng gamot?**

   SAGOT : _____.

3. TANONG : **Kailan siya nagkasakit?**

   SAGOT : _____.

4. TANONG : **Ano ang kinain niya?**

   SAGOT : _____.

Mga Halimbawang Pangungusap (Examples of sentences)

1. **May isang babae at isang bata sa larawan. Nakasuot ang babae ng _____.**

2. **Dinalaw ni _____ si _____.**

3. **_____ ang sakit ni _____.**

Larawan Blg. 1

Mga Tanong at Sagot

1. TANONG : _____?

   SAGOT : _____.

2. TANONG : _____?

   SAGOT : _____.

3. TANONG : _____?

   SAGOT : _____.

4. TANONG : _____?

   SAGOT : _____.

Mga Pangungusap

1. _____

2. _____

3. _____

4. _____

Larawan Blg. 2

Mga Tanong at Sagot

1. TANONG : _____?
   SAGOT   : _____.

2. TANONG : _____?
   SAGOT   : _____.

3. TANONG : _____?
   SAGOT   : _____.

4. TANONG : _____?
   SAGOT   : _____.

Mga Pangungusap

1. _____

2. _____

3. _____

4. _____

Larawan Blg. 3

Mga Tanong at Sagot

1. Tanong : _____?
   Sagot   : _____.

2. Tanong : _____?
   Sagot   : _____.

3. Tanong : _____?
   Sagot   : _____.

4. Tanong : _____?
   Sagot   : _____.

Mga Pangungusap

1. _____

2. _____

3. _____

4. _____

★ Gawain (Role-play)

Go back to the pictures, and the questions, answers, and sentences you have written about them. Then, using the dialogue you have learned as a guide, do role-plays with your partner. Classroom learners can work in pairs or small groups while individual learners should write down the dialogue.

Mga Tala Sa Kultura

Hiya or the concept of shame is an indicator of Filipino values and has been shaped by indigenous beliefs and practices, as well as by the values of the Christian religion introduced during the Spanish colonial period.

There are many examples to consider; an example we encountered in this lesson is that when one is offered food, one says, "**Nakakahiya naman**" (literally "It is shameful," but actually meaning "I'm shy that you have gone to too much trouble.")

A person who is shy is **mahiyain**, a virtue attributed to well-brought up women during colonial times.

When a son or a daughter has done something the parent considers inappropriate, he/she may be admonished by saying:

"**Nakakahiya ka!**"	*I am ashamed of you!*
"**Hindi ka na nahiya...**"	*You have no shame!*
"**Mahiya ka sa sarili mo!**"	*You ought to be ashamed of yourself!*
"**Nagdadala ka ng kahihiyan sa pamilya natin!**"	*You bring shame to our family!*

One of the worst insults one can give to a person is to say, "**Walanghiya ka!**"

In 2010 a group of Filipino Americans, among them editors Roseli Ilano and Lolan Buhain Sevilla and contributors Eileen Tabios, Reggie Cabico, Emily Lawsin, Adrien Salazar, and Aimee Espiritu, created a literary anthology called *Walang Hiya*. Featuring poetry and fiction, it looks at literature as a liberative practice, and redefines the term and "owns" it, as it "seeks to challenge boundaries and cultural norms."

 Pagbabasa

Read the following diary entry, and then answer the questions that follow. Study the following words before reading. You have learned some of the words in earlier lessons; they are listed here for you to review. You can also refer to the glossary at the back of the book.

Totoo	*Real*
Hukom	*Judge*
Dinismiss	*Got dismissed*
Kumakaway	*Waving*
Detenidong pulitikal	*Political detainee*

Ang Diary ni Trina

Ika-10 ng Hulyo 2015

Dinalaw namin kanina si Tita Beth. Hindi ko siya totoong Tita, pero Tita ang tawag namin sa kanya.

Nagdala kami nina Judy, Shayne, Roland, at Sarah ng mga prutas, puto, bibingka, cake, buko juice, adobo, gulay, at kanin. Tawa kami nang tawa kasi kami rin ang kumain ng dala naming pagkain. Ang sarap ng cheesecake na ginawa ni Shayne!

Mayroon din akong dalang mga libro—gustong-gusto ni Tita Beth na magbasa. Ang sabi niya, araw-araw daw ay nagbabasa siya.

Mabuti-buti na ngayon si Tita Beth. Noong isang linggo kasi, may lagnat siya, sipon, at ubo. Pumunta rin noong isang araw ang doktor niyang si Dr. Beng para bumisita sa kanya.

Sa susunod na linggo, makakalabas na siguro si Tita Beth. Ang sabi ng hukom, wala daw dahilan para ikulong siya. Dinismiss ang lahat ng charges sa kanya.

Alas-kuwatro na ng hapon nang umalis kami sa Camp Crame. Kumakaway sa amin si Tita Beth. Naka-suot siya ng asul na blusa at itim na palda; naka-salamin siya at nakangiti. Isa siyang detenidong pulitikal.

1. Sino ang dinalaw nina Trina, Judy, Roland, Sarah, at Shayne?
2. Ano ang dinala nila?
3. Ano ang lasa ng cheesecake?
4. Ano ang ginagawa ni Tita Beth araw-araw?
5. Ano ang naging sakit ni Tita Beth?
6. Sino ang doktor ni Tita Beth?
7. Ano ang sinabi ng hukom?
8. Anong oras sila umalis sa Camp Crame?
9. Ano ang suot ni Tita Beth?

🖉 Pagsusulat

Write a short paragraph about your recent visit to a friend's or a relative's house.

⚑ Paglalagom

In **Aralin 23**, you have:

1. Practiced words and phrases related to talking about illnesses, frequency, and visiting someone's house,
2. Used visual materials to tell a story,
3. Practiced how to give step-by-step directions.

You should now be able to:

1. Converse better in Filipino when visiting a friend.
2. Write a story based on a picture.

Paggawa ng Reserbasyon (Making Reservations)

  ### Diyalogo: Pagtawag sa University Hotel

Read the dialogue below. After completing this chapter, practice this dialogue using your own information.

Clerk	:	**Hello? University Hotel.**
		Hello? University Hotel.
Pedro	:	**Hello? Nais ko hong magreserba ng kuwarto.**
		Hello? I would like to reserve a room.
Clerk	:	**Ano ho ang pangalan nila?**
		What is your name?
Pedro	:	**Pedro Santos ho.**
		Pedro Santos.
Clerk	:	**Para kailan ho ito?**
		When is this for?
Pedro	:	**Para sa ika-17 ng Disyembre ho.**
		For the 17th of December.
Clerk	:	**Ilang gabi ho?**
		How many nights?
Pedro	:	**Tatlong gabi ho.**
		Three nights.
Clerk	:	**Ano hong klaseng kuwarto?**
		What kind of room?
Pedro	:	**Iyon hong pandalawahan.**
		A room for two people.
Clerk	:	**Uulitin ko ho. Isang kuwartong pandalawahan, mula ika-17 ng Disyembre, para sa tatlong gabi.**
		I will repeat it. One room for two people, from the 17th of December for three nights.
Pedro	:	**Magkano ho ang isang gabi?**
		How much for a night?

CLERK : **Dalawang libong piso ho.**
Two thousand pesos.

PEDRO : **Kasama ho ba ang almusal?**
Is breakfast included?

CLERK : **Oho.**
Yes, sir.

PEDRO : **Sige ho. Salamat.**
Okay. Thank you.

Bokabolaryo

Study the following words and phrases. Some of them were used in the dialogue you just read and some of them will be useful when you make your own sentences for your dialogues. A few words listed are English words that have been incorporated in the Filipino language. Study how they have changed through Tagalog affixes. They are listed so that you know you can use them with your sentences in Filipino.

Heritage learners should try to guess the meaning of the words before looking at the translations; you might be familiar with some of these words.

Magreserba	*To reserve*
Pandalawahan	*For two*
Bawat	*Each*
Uulitin	*Repeat*
Mula _____ hanggang _____	*From _____ to _____*
Kuwartong may tanawin ng dalampasigan	*Room with a view of the beach*
Kuwartong may tanawin ng bundok	*Room with a view of the mountain*
Balkonahe	*Balcony*
Palapag	*Floor*
Suite	*Suite*
Honeymoon Suite	*Honeymoon suite*
Queen Bed	*Queen bed*
King Bed	*King bed*

Balik-Aral

Review the following words you have studied in previous lessons. These words will be useful to you in this chapter. Write them down in the spaces provided.

Mga araw (Days)

Monday   _____
Tuesday   _____
Wednesday   _____
Thursday   _____
Friday   _____
Saturday   _____
Sunday   _____

Mga buwan (Months)

January   _____
February   _____
March   _____
April   _____
May   _____
June   _____
July   _____
August   _____
September   _____
October   _____
November   _____
December   _____

Mga petsa (Dates)

Ika-9 ng Marso   _____
Ika-15 ng Nobyembre   _____
Ika-23 ng Hulyo   _____

Mga Halimbawang Pangungusap

Practice saying these sentences aloud, to get a feel for how this chapter's vocabulary and grammar work in Filipino.

1. **Gusto magreserba ni Pedro ng kuwarto mula ika-17 hanggang ika-20 ng Disyembre.** *Pedro would like to reserve a room from the 17th to the 20th of December.*
2. **Kuwartong pandalawahan ang gusto niya.** *He wants a room for two people.*

3. **Dalawang libong piso bawat gabi ang kuwarto sa University Hotel.**

   A room at the University Hotel costs two thousand pesos for each night.

4. **Nakapagreserba siya ng kuwarto isang buwan bago siya dumating.**

   He was able to reserve a room one month before he arrived.

5. **Natulog siya isang oras pagkatapos niyang dumating sa kuwarto.**

   He slept one hour after he arrived in his room.

 ## Pagsasanay

This exercise has several components. First, study the picture. Who are the people in the picture and how are they related to each other? Second, think of a possible story or narrative about the picture. What is happening? Third, ask and answer questions about the picture with your classmates, or if you are an individual learner, write these questions and answers down. Finally, write as many sentences as you can about the picture. These sentences can describe the people or the place, or narrate the situation. Below are some examples of questions and answers, as well as sentences:

Mga Halimbawang Tanong at Sagot

1. TANONG : **Anong klaseng kuwarto ang gusto niya?**

   SAGOT : **Pang-isahang kuwarto ang gusto niya.**

2. TANONG : **Anong klaseng _____ ang gusto niya?**

   SAGOT : **_____ ang gusto niya.**

3. TANONG : **Kailan niya kailangan ang kuwarto?**

   SAGOT : **Kailangan niya ang kuwarto mula _____ hanggang**

   _____.

4. TANONG : **Magkano ang kuwarto?**

   SAGOT : **_____.**

Mga Halimbawang Pangungusap

1. **Tumawag si _____ sa _____ para _____.**

2. **Nagpareserba siya _____.**

3. **Titigil siya _____.**

4. **_____ ang halaga _____.**

Larawan Blg. 1

Mga Tanong at Sagot

1. TANONG : _____?
   SAGOT   : _____.

2. TANONG : _____?
   SAGOT   : _____.

3. TANONG : _____?
   SAGOT   : _____.

4. TANONG : _____?
   SAGOT   : _____.

5. TANONG : _____?
   SAGOT   : _____.

6. TANONG : _____?
   SAGOT   : _____.

Mga Pangungusap

1. _____

2. _____

3. _____

4. _____

5. _____

6. _____

Larawan Blg. 2

Mga Tanong at Sagot

1. Tanong : _____?
   Sagot : _____.

2. Tanong : _____?
   Sagot : _____.

3. Tanong : _____?
   Sagot : _____.

4. Tanong : _____?
   Sagot : _____.

5. Tanong : _____?
   Sagot : _____.

6. Tanong : _____?
   Sagot : _____.

Mga Pangungusap

1. _____

2. _____

3. _____

4. _____

5. _____

6. _____

Larawan Blg. 3

Mga Tanong at Sagot

1. TANONG : _____?
   SAGOT   : _____.

2. TANONG : _____?
   SAGOT   : _____.

3. TANONG : _____?
   SAGOT   : _____.

4. TANONG : _____?
   SAGOT   : _____.

5. TANONG : _____?
   SAGOT   : _____.

6. TANONG : _____?
   SAGOT   : _____.

Mga Pangungusap

1. _____

2. _____

3. _____

4. _____

5. _____

6. _____

★ Gawain (Role-play)

Review the questions, answers, and sentences you have written. Then, using the dialogue you have learned as a guide, do role-plays with your partner. Classroom learners can work in pairs or small groups while individual learners should write down the dialogue.

🔍 Gramatika

Study the information below to improve your Filipino grammar skills.

I. **Naka** and **Nakapag-** affixes

When attached to a root word, **naka** and **nakapag-** affixes indicate the meaning "have been able to." Here are some examples:

Root word	Completed	Incompleted	Contemplated
Punta	Nakapunta	Nakapupunta	Makapupunta
Reserba	Nakapag-reserba	Nakapag-rereserba	Makapag-rereserba

II. **Bago** and **Pagkatapos** (*Before* and *after*)

The words **bago** (*before*) and **pagkatapos** (*after*) can be useful in making compound sentences. For example:

Kumain ako bago ako pumunta sa unibersidad.

I ate before I went to the university.

Naligo ako pagkatapos kong kumain ng hapunan.

I took a bath after I ate dinner.

Diyalogo: Pagtawang sa Restawran

Read the dialogue below. After completing this chapter, practice this dialogue using your own information.

JUAN : **Gourmet Cafe ho ba ito?**
Is this Gourmet Cafe?

WAITER : **Oho.**
Yes.

JUAN : **Gusto ko hong gumawa ng reserbasyon.**
I would like to make a reservation.

WAITER : **Para kailan ho?**
For when?

JUAN : **Para sa Biyernes.**
For Friday.

WAITER : **Ilang katao ho?**
How many people?

JUAN : **Lima ho kami. May mesa ba kayo malapit sa bintana?**
There are five of us. Do you have a table near a window?

WAITER : **Oho.**
Yes.

Bokabolaryo

Study the following words. Some of them were used in the dialogue you just read and some of them will be useful when you make your own sentences for your dialogues.

Katao	*Number of people*
Mesang malapit sa bintana	*Table near a window*
Mesa sa sulok	*Corner table*
Pribadong kuwarto	*Private room*

⭐ Gawain (Role-play)

Using the words you have learned and the dialogue you just studied, make reservations at a restaurant.

Here are some possible situations you can use in your role-play:

1. Make lunch reservations for a party of five for Tuesday, June 6 at 7:00 P.M.
2. Make reservations for dinner for two for Saturday, February 14 at 8:00 P.M.

3. Make reservations for a private room (**pribadong kuwarto**) for ten people for Easter Sunday brunch (use the word "brunch" because there is no equivalent in Tagalog/Filipino) for April 4 at 10:30 A.M. You need the room for 4 hours.

Mga Talang Sa Kultura

Most Filipinos use spoons and forks as eating utensils. Knives are hardly used at the table because the food is cut up in smaller pieces or is tender enough to be cut without using a knife. Chopsticks are used only in Chinese, Japanese, or Korean restaurants. However, in the provinces, some Filipinos still eat in the indigenous manner—by using their hands.

A return to the use of the hands in eating was made popular in the late 1970s with the proliferation of restaurants advocating the aptly named "**kamayan**" (*using hands*) style. In these restaurants, there are huge clay jars called **banga** where diners can wash their hands.

For a few politicians, eating with one's hands also signifies one's intention to feel for, and be one with the masses. Thus, in several photo opportunities former President Joseph Estrada dined with the less privileged, eating with his hands food served on top of banana leaves. This strategy was also adapted by the next president, Gloria Arroyo, and by other politicians.

  Pagbabasa

Read the following passage, and then answer the questions that follow. Study the following words before reading the story. You have learned some of the words in earlier lessons, so some of them are listed here for you to review. You can also refer to the glossary at the back of the book. This short short story was inspired by Marcia Burnham, a missionary and kidnapping survivor.

Espesyal	*Special*
Tanghaling tapat	*Exactly at noon*
Katimugan	*South*
Naisip	*Thought*
Manggagawa	*Worker*
Mahihirap	*Poor*
Kaya	*That is why* (when the accent is on the first syllable, the meaning of this word is "*Can*")
Bote ng alak	*Bottle of wine*
Magkahawak-kamay	*Holding hands*
Payapa	*Peaceful*
Baril	*Gun*
Bihag	*Prisoner*

Anibersaryo (Anniversary)

Anibersaryo ng kasal namin. Nagreserba ako ng malaking kuwarto sa Oceanview Resort, isa sa pinakamalaking resort sa isla. Mahal ang resort at hindi kami mayaman, pero ang sabi ng mga anak ko: "Mommy, anibersaryo ninyo ng Daddy. Espesyal na araw ito."

Tanghaling tapat nang tumawag ako sa resort. "Gusto ko hong magreserba ng kuwarto," sabi ko.

Mabait ang kausap kong hotel clerk. Sinabi ko sa kanya na anibersaryo namin ng asawa ko. "Ibibigay ko po sa inyo ang pinakamaganda naming cottage."

"Cottage" ang tawag niya sa "bahay kubo" na nasa ibabaw ng tubig. Ganito ang mga bahay ng mga taong Badjao na nakatira sa Sulu sa katimugan ng Pilipinas. Inilalarawan ang mga bahay na ito na "mga bahay na nakatayo sa poste" o "houses on stilts."

Apat na araw, tatlong gabi. Apat na raang dolyar bawat gabi pero kasama na ang almusal, tanghalian, at hapunan. Ang mahal, naisip ko. Siyam na dolyar lang ang suweldo ng isang manggagawa sa Pilipinas. Misyonarya ako, kaya palagi kong naiisip ang mga mahihirap.

Alas-nuwebe ng umaga nang dumating kami ng asawa ko sa resort. Bughaw na bughaw ang dagat, bughaw na bughaw ang langit. May bote ng alak at may mga bulaklak sa kuwarto; regalo ito ng resort sa amin. Mayroon ding coffeemaker, kape, tsaa at minibar sa kuwarto.

Gumawa ng tsaa ang asawa ko. Kinuha ko mula sa bag ko ang chocolate chip cookies na ginawa ng anak ko. Umupo kami ng asawa ko sa balkonahe, umiinom ng tsaa at kumakain ng cookies, tinitingnan ang dagat. Magkahawak-kamay kami, tinitingnan ang dagat, iniisip ang payapa naming buhay na mag-asawa.

Ito ang hindi namin naisip. Noong gabing iyon, dadating ang mga lalaking may baril, isasakay nila kami sa bangka, dadalhin sa malayong isla, at gagawing bihag. At sa biyahe sa gabing iyon, habang may blindfold ang mga mata namin, at takot na takot kami, hindi namin nakikita ang dagat na bughaw.

1. **Sa anong hotel siya nagreserba ng kuwarto?**
2. **Ano ang pinareserba niya?**
3. **Ilang gabi sila titigil sa hotel?**
4. **Ano ang ininom nila ng asawa niya?**
5. **Ano ang kinain nila?**
6. **Saan sila uminom at kumain?**
7. **Bakit sila takot na takot?**

✎ Pagsusulat

Write a paragraph about a recent reservation you made at a hotel or a restaurant.

✎ Paglalagom

In **Aralin 24**, you have:
1. Reviewed words related to days, months, and dates,
2. Learned words related to making reservations,
3. Studied how to describe a room or a table.

You should now be able to:
1. Make reservations.
2. Talk and write about your experience in making reservations.

Pagche-Check In (Checking into a Hotel)

  Diyalogo: Sa University Hotel (At the University Hotel)

Read the dialogue below. After completing this chapter, practice this dialogue using your own information.

CLERK : **Magandang hapon ho.**
Good afternoon.

PEDRO : **Magandang hapon din ho. Nais ko hong mag-check in.**
Good afternoon too. I would like to check-in.

CLERK : **Maaari ko po bang malaman ang pangalan nila?**
May I know your name please?

PEDRO : **Pedro Santos po.**
Pedro Santos.

CLERK : **Kuwartong pandalawahan po ba?**
Is it a room for two people?

PEDRO : **Oho.**
Yes.

CLERK : **Tatlong gabi po, hindi ba?**
Three nights, right?

PEDRO : **Gayon na nga po.**
That's right.

CLERK : **Pakirehistro lang po dito. Pirmahan niyo po ito.**
Please register here. Please sign here.
(Iaabot ang registration card.)
(Gives the registration card.)

PEDRO : **Heto po.**
Here.

CLERK : **Maaari ko po bang makita ang pasaporte nila?**
May I see your passport?

PEDRO : **Heto po.**
Here.

CLERK : **Paano po ninyo gustong magbayad?**
How would you like to pay?

PEDRO : **Sa pamamagitan ho ng credit card ko. Heto po.**
Using my credit card. Here.

CLERK : **Salamat ho. Heto po ang inyong susi, ang inyong pasaporte, at ang inyong credit card.**
Thank you. Here is your key, your passport, and your credit card.

PEDRO : **Salamat po.**
Thank you.

CLERK : **Sana'y magustuhan niyo ang inyong pagtigil sa amin.**
I hope you enjoy your stay with us.

 Bokabolaryo

Study the following words. Some of them were used in the dialogue you just read and some of them will be useful when you make your own sentences for your dialogues.

Nais	*Would like*
Mag-check in	*To check in*
Malaman	*To know*
Pakirehistro	*Please register*
Sa pamamagitan	*Using*
Pagtigil	*To stay*
Pirmahan/Lagdaan	*Sign your name*
Pirma/Lagda	*Signature*
Sana	*Hope*
Magustuhan	*Will like*
Maaari/Puwede	*May*
Makita	*To see*
Ipinakita	*Showed*

Mga Halimbawang Pangungusap

Practice saying these sentences aloud, to get a feel for how this chapter's vocabulary and grammar work in Filipino.

1. **Kuwartong pandalawahan ang inireserba ni Pedro.**
   Pedro reserved a room for two people.

2. **Gusto niyang magbayad sa pamamagitan ng credit card**
   He/she wants to pay using a credit card.

3. **Titigil nang tatlong gabi si Pedro sa hotel.**   *Pedro will stay at the hotel for three nights.*

4. **Pinirmahan niya ang registration card.**   *He/she signed the registration card.*

5. **Ipinakita niya sa hotel clerk ang kanyang California I.D.**   *He/she showed the clerk his/her California identification card.*

6. **Maaari ko bang malaman ang pangalan mo?**   *May I know your name?*

  ## Pagsasanay

Look at the pictures and information in the previous lesson. Then ask and answer questions and write sentences. Use the words and sentences you have studied as a guide. Practice questions that end with "**hindi ba**" (*isn't it?*). Below are some examples of questions and answers, as well as sentences:

Mga Halimbawang Tanong at Sagot

1. TANONG : **Gaano katagal ka sa hotel?**
   SAGOT : **Tatlong gabi ako sa hotel.**

2. TANONG : **Paano mo gustong magbayad?**
   SAGOT : **Gusto kong magbayad sa pamamagitan ng _____.**

3. TANONG : **Kuwartong pandalawahan, hindi ho ba?**
   SAGOT : **Oho, kuwartong pandalawahan.**

Mga Halimbawang Pangungusap

1. **Nagrehistro si _____ sa _____.**
2. **Ipinakita niya ang kanyang school I.D.**
3. **Ibinigay ng clerk ang susi niya sa kanya.**

★ Gawain (Role-play)

Go back to the pictures, and the questions, answers, and sentences you have written. Using the dialogue you have learned as a guide, do role-plays with your partner. Classroom learners can work in pairs or small groups while individual learners should write down the dialogue.

🔍 Gramatika

Study the information below to improve your Filipino grammar skills.

I.   Tag questions
In Filipino, the phrase **hindi ba** (*isn't it*) is used as a tag question.
Here are some examples:

> TANONG : **Dalawampu't isang taong gulang ka na, hindi ba?**
> SAGOT   : **Oo.**
> TANONG : **Sa Manila Hotel ka titigil, hindi ba?**
> SAGOT   : **Hindi. Titigil ako sa Maharlika Hotel.**

II. **Maaari/Puwede**
Maaari and **puwede** (*may*) are used with the infinitive form of the verb:

> EXAMPLES: **Maaari ko bang makita...**   *May I see...*
> **Maaari mo bang isulat/sulatin...**   *Can you write...*
> **Puwede mo bang basahin...**   *Can you read...*

What is the difference between **maaari** and **puwede**? Both words mean the same thing. **Maaari**, being an indigenous Tagalog word, however, can seem to be more formal. In recent times, **puwede** seems to be used more often in everyday life.

💬 Diyalogo: Problema sa Kuwarto

Read the dialogue below. After completing this chapter, practice this dialogue using your own information.

PEDRO : **Hello? Front desk ho ba ito?**
Hello? Is this the front desk?
CLERK : **Oho.**
Yes.
PEDRO : **Sira ho ang aircon ko.**
My air conditioner is broken.
CLERK : **Sandali lang ho. Paakyatin ko ho ang technician namin. Baka puwedeng ayusin.**
Just a moment. I will ask our technician to go up. He might be able to fix it.
PEDRO : **Puwede ho ba akong lumipat ng kuwarto?**
Can I change rooms?
CLERK : **Kung hindi ho maaayos, puwede kayong lumipat sa Room 1240.**
If it is not fixed, you can move to Room 1240.
PEDRO : **Salamat.**
Thank you.

Bokabolaryo

Study the following words. Some of them were used in the dialogue you just read and some of them will be useful when you make your own sentences for your dialogues.

Sira	*Broken*
Ayusin	*Fix*
Paaakyatin	*To ask someone to go up*
Maaayos	*Will be fixed*
Lumipat	*Transfer*

Mga Halimbawang Pangungusap

Practice saying these sentences aloud, to get a feel for how this chapter's vocabulary and grammar work in Filipino.

1. **Sira ang aircon sa kuwarto ni Pedro.**   *The air conditioner in Pedro's room is broken.*

2. **Aakyat ang technician sa kuwarto niya para ayusin ang aircon.**   *The technician will go up to his room to fix the air conditioner.*

3. **Kung hindi maaayos ang aircon, lilipat ng kuwarto si Pedro.**   *If the air conditioner is not fixed, Pedro will transfer rooms.*

  Pagsasanay 1

Study the following pictures as well as the information given. Then ask and answer questions about the pictures. Also, write as many sentences as you can about the picture. These sentences can describe the people involved or the place, or narrate the situation. Below are some examples of questions and answers.

Mga Halimbawang Tanong at Sagot

1. TANONG : **Ano ang problema sa kuwarto?**
   SAGOT : _____ **ang aircon sa** _____ .

2. TANONG : **Kanino siya tumawag?**
   SAGOT : **Tumawag siya sa** _____ .

3. TANONG : **Ano ang ginawa ng manager?**
   SAGOT : _____ .

4. Tanong : **Paano kung hindi maayos ang aircon?**

    Sagot : **Kung hindi maaayos ang aircon, _____.**

Larawan Blg. 1

Sirang Telebisyon (*Broken television*)

Mga Tanong at Sagot

1. Tanong : _____?

    Sagot : _____.

2. Tanong : _____?

    Sagot : _____.

3. Tanong : _____?

    Sagot : _____.

4. Tanong : _____?

    Sagot : _____.

5. Tanong : _____?

    Sagot : _____.

6. Tanong : _____?

    Sagot : _____.

Mga Pangungusap

1. _____

2. _____

3. _____

4. _____

Larawan Blg. 2

Sirang Banyo (*Broken Bathroom*)

Mga Tanong at Sagot

1. TANONG : _____ ?
   SAGOT : _____ .

2. TANONG : _____ ?
   SAGOT : _____ .

3. TANONG : _____ ?
   SAGOT : _____ .

Mga Pangungusap

1. _____

2. _____

3. _____

Larawan Blg. 3

Sirang heater (*Broken heater*)

Mga Tanong at Sagot

1. TANONG : _____?
   SAGOT   : _____.

2. TANONG : _____?
   SAGOT   : _____.

3. TANONG : _____?
   SAGOT   : _____.

Mga Pangungusap

1. _____

2. _____

3. _____

Pagsasanay 2

Practice the following sentence pattern:

Kung hindi _____, _____.

If _____, *then* _____.

★ Gawain (Role-play)

Go back to the pictures, and the questions, answers, and sentences you have written. Then, using the dialogue you have learned as a guide, do role-plays with your partner. Classroom learners can work in pairs or small groups while individual learners should write down the dialogue.

Mga Tala Sa Kultura

One of the oldest and most historic sites in the Philippines is Manila Hotel. Built in 1912, and restored in 1976, among its famous guests were General Douglas MacArthur, Muhammad Ali, and Ernest Hemingway. Built during the American colonial period in the Philippines (1899–1945), and designed by New York architect

William Parsons, the hotel's design was influenced by the architecture of California missions (characterized by solid massive walls, patios, curved pedimented gables, wide projecting eaves and low, sloping tile roofs). The hotel's interior includes a grand lobby, marble floors, chandeliers made of brass, crystal, and seashells, and rooms decorated with handcarved mahogany furniture.

Through the years, Manila Hotel has been the site for the making of history—political speeches delivered, coups d'états staged, and issues discussed. General Douglas MacArthur used it as his residence for seven years (1935–1941), political parties used it for their conventions, and recently, former First Lady Imelda Marcos held her birthday celebration at the hotel. For more than three decades, the hotel has also hosted a **Kapihan** (coffee meet) where guest speakers and the media had informal discussions with audience members while eating breakfast or having coffee.

My own memory of the hotel is my high school senior prom, and through the years it certainly has hosted numerous debuts, weddings, and anniversaries, as it has signified either upper- and middle-class status or yearnings for upper- and middle-class status. A few meters from the hotel, jeepney drivers blare loud music and young children peddle **sampaguita** garlands.

  ## Pagbabasa

Read the following short short story, and then answer the questions that follow. Study the following words before reading the story. You have learned some of the words in earlier lessons, so some of them are listed here for you to review. You can also refer to the glossary at the back of the book.

Mahuhuli	*Will be late*
Ulit	*Again*
Mula noong	*Since*
Nagtapos	*Graduated*
Magkakakilala	*Know each other*
Sarili	*Self*
Salamin	*Mirror*
Nakakatanda	*Make one look old*
Nag-diyeta	*Dieted*
Kumatok	*Knocked*
Nakakainis	*Irritating*
Nagpatuwid	*Had (hair) straightened*
Niyayakap	*Hugs*
Komunidad	*Community*
Nambubugbog	*Person who beats up another*
Nakalimutan	*Forgot*

Blow-Dryer

Sira ang blow-dryer sa kuwarto ni Carmen sa hotel. Tiningnan niya ang relo niya. Alas-sais y medya na. Mahuhuli na siya para sa welcome dinner ng kanilang class reunion.

Tumawag siya ulit sa housekeeping. "Hello? Gusto ko hong i-follow-up iyong hair dryer. Sira ho ang hair dryer sa kuwarto ko. Salamat ho."

Tatlumpung taon na mula noong nagtapos sila ng high school. Pero dahil magkakaklase sila mula kindergarten, mahigit apatnapung taon na silang mag-kakakilala.

Tiningnan niya ang sarili sa salamin. Noong isang linggo, nagpakulay at nagpagupit siya ng buhok sa beauty salon. Ay, salamat. Wala siyang nakikitang puting buhok. Nagsimula siyang maglagay ng make-up. Foundation. Brown eyeshadow. Eyebrow pencil. Blue eyeliner. (Nakakatanda raw kasi ang itim.) Mascara. Blush-on. Sana nagpa-botox injections ako, naisip niya. Parang marami siyang wrinkles. Nakakainis.

Nagbihis siya. Asul at berdeng damit na may geometric prints ang isusuot niya. Maganda ito, naisip niya, hindi nakikita ang extra pounds. Sayang, sana nag-diyeta bago pumunta sa reunion. Sana mas payat siya.

May kumatok sa pintuan. "Heto na ho ang blow dryer ninyo."

Nilagyan niya ng anti-frizz gel ang buhok niya at nagsimula siyang mag-blow dry ng buhok. Naiinis siya sa buhok niya. Bakit ba siya may kulot na buhok? Curly tops nga ang tawag sa kanya noong high school ng kaibigan niyang si Terry. Sana tuwid na lang ang buhok ko, naisip niya. Sana nagpatuwid ako ng buhok sa beauty salon.

Alas-siyete ng gabi nang pumasok siya sa restaurant. Sa isang table, tumatawa ang isang grupo ng mga babae habang kumakain ng appetizers. Sa may bar, nag-uusap ang tatlong babae habang nag-oorder ng drinks. Sa reception area, nakatayo ang dalawang babae na nagbibigay ng mga name tags.

"Carmen!" Nakangiti si Menchie, ang organizer ng reunion. Niyayakap siya ni Macon, ang seatmate niya noong high school. Kumakaway sa kanya si Marlo, ang partner niya sa chemistry lab. Nandoon silang lahat—si Terry, si Erlinda, si Ruth, si Lily, si Maan, si Celine, si Yeng, si Odette, si Iris, sina Camille at Elvira... mga classmates niya.

May tumaba, may pumayat. Mayroong brown na—light brown, medium brown, o dark brown—ang kulay ng buhok. Buong gabi silang nagkukuwento, tumatawa, nagkukuwento, tumatawa. May classmate na nagrereport para sa fund-raising project ng mga madre para sa isang mahirap na komunidad. May nagsalita tungkol sa kanilang cookbook project, *The Blue and White Kitchen*. May nag-distribute ng gift bags—may stationery, may ballpens, may chocolates.

Ipinapakita ni Natilou ang mga larawan ng mga apo niya. Ikinukuwento ni Gina ang divorce niya sa asawang nambubugbog. Binabati nina Anicia at Marj si Ging dahil natapos na nito ang kanyang Ph.D.

At nakalimutan ni Carmen ang wrinkles sa mukha, ang extra pounds, at ang kulot na buhok na ayaw tumuwid.

1. Ano ang problema sa hotel room ni Carmen?
2. Saan pupunta si Carmen?
3. Sino-sino ang mga kaklase ni Carmen?
4. Ano-ano ang mga projects nila?
5. Ano ang ginagawa ng mga babae sa reception area?

🖉 Pagsusulat

Write a paragraph about a problem at a hotel room and how it was solved. You can use the examples given earlier or talk about your own experience.

Halimbawa

Nag-check in ako sa _____ . _____ na kuwarto ang kinuha ko. Tumigil ako doon ng _____ . Nagbayad ako sa pamamagitan ng _____ .

🚩 Paglalagom

In **Aralin 25**, you have:
1. Learned words and phrases related to staying at a hotel,
2. Learned how to talk about a problem,
3. Practiced tag questions,
4. Practiced the sentence pattern, "If... then...",
5. Studied words to say "*may I*," *should* and *shouldn't*,
6. Learned how to repeat what has been said to you.

You should now be able to:
1. Use Filipino when checking into a hotel.
2. Negotiate with the hotel in case there is a problem.

26

Pag-arkila ng Sasakyan (Renting a Vehicle)

 Diyalogo: Sa Quezon Memorial Circle (At the Quezon Memorial Circle)

Read the dialogue below. After completing this chapter, practice this dialogue using your own information.

PEDRO : **Magkano ho ang arkila ng bisikleta?**
How much does it cost to rent a bicycle?
LELAKI : **Tatlumpung piso ho isang oras.**
Thirty pesos for an hour.
PEDRO : **Magkano ho kung tatlong oras?**
How much for three hours?
LELAKI : **Otsenta pesos lang kung tatlong oras. Nakapag-arkila ka na ba rito?**
Eighty pesos for three hours. Have you rented here?
PEDRO : **Noong una ho akong magbakasyon dito.**
When I first took a vacation here.
LELAKI : **Aling bisikleta ang gusto mo?**
Which bicycle would you like?
PEDRO : **Iyon hong nasa dulo.**
The one at the end.

  Bokabolaryo

Study the following words. Some of them were used in the dialogue you just read and some of them will be useful when you make your own sentences for your dialogues.

Arkila	*Rent*
Dulo	*End*
Isasauli	*Will return*
Kailangan	*Need*
Nakatipid	*Saved money*

Mga Halimbawang Pangungusap

Practice saying these sentences aloud, to get a feel for how this chapter's vocabulary and grammar work in Filipino.

1. **Gustong mag-arkila ni Pedro ng bisikleta.** *Pedro wants to rent a bicycle.*
2. **Tatlumpung piso isang oras ang arkila ng bisikleta.** *The rent for the bicycle is thirty pesos for an hour.*
3. **Ang bisikletang nasa dulo ang gusto ni Pedro.** *Pedro wants the bicycle at the end.*
4. **Aarkilahin niya ang bisikleta nang tatlong oras.** *He/she will rent the bicycle for three hours.*
5. **Isasauli niya ang bisikeleta nang ala-una ng hapon.** *He/she will return the bicycle at one o'clock in the afternoon.*
6. **Kailangan niyang mag-arkila ng malaking kotse.** *He/she needs to rent a big car.*
7. **Kasya sa mini-van na ito ang anim na tao.** *This mini-van fits six people.*
8. **Nakatipid siya ng isang libong piso dahil inarkila niya nang isang linggo ang mini-van.** *He/she saved one thousand pesos because he/she rented the van for a week.*
9. **Kailangan niya ng drayber para magmaneho para sa kanya.** *He/she needs a driver to drive for her.*

  Pagsasanay

Study the information below from a car rental company in the Philippines. Then ask and answer questions. Also, write as many sentences as you can about the situation. These sentences can describe the people or the place, or narrate the situation. Below are some examples of questions and answers, as well as sentences:

Mga Halimbawang Tanong at Sagot

1. TANONG : **Ano ang gustong arkilahin ni _____?**
   SAGOT : **_____ ang gustong arkilahin ni _____.**

2. TANONG : **Magkano ang arkila ng bisikleta?**
   SAGOT : **_____ isang araw ang arkila ng _____.**

3. TANONG : **Magkano ang arkila kung isang linggo?**
   SAGOT : **_____.**

4. TANONG : **Aling bisikleta ang gusto niya?**
   SAGOT : _____.

Mga Halimbawang Pangungusap

1. **Gustong pumunta ni** _____ **sa** _____.

2. **Kailangan niya ng** _____.

3. **Nag-arkila siya ng** _____ **dahil** _____.

Car Group A			
Car Features	**Daily / 24 hrs**	**Weekly**	**Monthly**
Toyota Corolla XL	Php 1,200 - Self Driven - add 200 ten	Php 8,400	Php 33,000

Car Group B			
Car Features	**Daily / 24 hrs**	**Weekly**	**Monthly**
Honda City	Php 1,600 - S	Php 10,500	Php 38,000
Toyota Corolla XE	Php 1,400 - S	Php 9,800	Php 38,000

Car Group C			
Car Features	**Daily / 24 hrs**	**Weekly**	**Monthly**
Honda Civic LXI	Php 1,800	Php 11,800	Php 42,000
Honda City (Automatic Transmission)	Php 1,800	Negotiable	Negotiable
Toyota Corolla GLI	Php 1,800	Php 11,800	Php 42,000
Toyota Corolla TRD	Php 1,800	Php 11,800	Php 42,000
Honda Civic Vtec	Php 2,000	Php 11,800	Php 42,000
2004 Honda City (Dual Transmission)	Php 2,500	Negotiable	Negotiable
	Php 2,500	Negotiable	Negotiable

Situation 1

Mr. and Mrs. Lopez need a car for a week because their car is at the repair shop. They only need a small car. However, they need an automatic car because they don't know how to drive using a stick shift.

Mga Tanong at Sagot

1. TANONG : _____?
   SAGOT : _____.

2. TANONG : _____?
   SAGOT : _____.

3. TANONG : _____?
   SAGOT : _____.

4. TANONG : _____?
   SAGOT : _____.

5. TANONG : _____?
   SAGOT : _____.

6. TANONG : _____?
   SAGOT : _____.

Mga Pangungusap

1. _____

2. _____

3. _____

4. _____

5. _____

6. _____

Situation 2

The Romero family is in Manila for a month. They would like a big car or a mini-van so that they can go sightseeing in neighboring cities and towns with their three children. They are open to renting either an automatic or a stick shift car.

Mga Tanong at Sagot

1. TANONG : _____?
   SAGOT : _____.

2. TANONG : _____?
   SAGOT : _____.

3. TANONG : _____?
   SAGOT : _____.

4. TANONG : _____?
   SAGOT : _____.

5. TANONG : _____?
   SAGOT : _____.

6. TANONG : _____?
   SAGOT : _____.

Mga Pangungusap

1. _____

2. _____

3. _____

4. _____

5. _____

6. _____

Situation 3

Ms. See is in Manila on business for three days. She needs a car and driver because she needs to visit several offices in a day. Her company will reimburse her for her expenses and they want her to rent a medium-priced car.

Mga Tanong at Sagot

1. Tanong : _____?
   Sagot   : _____.

2. Tanong : _____?
   Sagot   : _____.

3. Tanong : _____?
   Sagot   : _____.

4. Tanong : _____?
   Sagot   : _____.

5. Tanong : _____?
   Sagot   : _____.

6. Tanong : _____?
   Sagot   : _____.

Mga Pangungusap

1. _____

2. _____

3. _____

4. _____

5. _____

6. _____

★ Gawain (Role-play)

Go back to the information provided, and the questions, answers, and sentences you have written. Then, using the dialogue you have learned as a guide, do role-plays with your partner. Classroom learners can work in pairs or small groups while individual learners should write down the dialogue.

Mga Tala Sa Kultura

Although renting a car is not as common in the Philippines as it is in other countries, renting "smaller" things is. There are two Tagalog/Filipino words for the word *rent*. When one rents or leases a house or an apartment, we say "**umuupa ng bahay**." However, renting a bicycle or a vehicle is "**arkila**." One can usually rent a bicycle at a park, a **bangka** or small boat (with someone rowing it) at a beach resort, and comic magazines at the neighborhood **sari-sari** store (variety store).

However, in many rural neighborhoods, what is more common is **hiraman** or borrowing. A neighbor drops by another's house to borrow a cup of sugar or some vinegar. Children are asked by their parents to go to a friend's house to ask for some banana leaves for cooking. At wedding feasts, neighbors bring their plates to the house of the bride, who needs these plates because of the huge number of guests she is expecting.

In these farming and fishing communities where everyone knows everyone, families are interdependent on each other and learn the value of **pakikisama** (*adapting to others*) and **pakikipagkapwa-tao** (*treating other people well*).

To read more about **pakikipagkapwa-tao**, you may want to look into Katrin de Guia's *Kapwa, The Self in the Other* (Anvil Publishing, 2005), as well as articles on the subject written by Virgilio Enriquez, considered to be the pioneering scholar on Filipino psychology, and by Leny Mendoza Strobel.

  Pagbabasa

Read the following poem, and then answer the questions that follow. Study the following words before reading the story. You have learned some of the words in earlier lessons, so some of them are listed here for you to review. You can also refer to the glossary at the back of the book.

Paglalakbay	*Journey*
Pagsinta	*Love*
Paglalayag	*Sail*
Pinakatuktok	*Highest point*
Pag-asa	*Hope*

Pananalig	*Faith*
Tandaan	*Remember*
Hagurin	*Massage*
Gilid	*Side*
Paroroonan	*Destination*
Mangingibig	*One who loves*

Paglalakbay

Bawat pagsinta'y paglalakbay.
Paglalayag sa malawak na dagat,
Pag-akyat sa pinakatuktok ng bundok.

Sumasakay ka sa pag-asa,
Humahawak sa pananalig.
Bawat pagsinta'y paglalakbay.

Tandaan.
Huwag kaybagal at baka may hindi maabutan.
Huwag kaybilis at baka may malampasan.

Sa gitna nitong paglalakbay,
Saglit na tumigil.
Punasan ang noo,
Hagurin ang talampakan.
Kumustahin ang sarili,
Na minsa'y nakakalimutan sa gilid ng daan.

Huwag hayaang mapagod ang puso
Sa bawat paglalakbay.
Ngunit huwag,
Huwag ring magpapapigil sa pangamba
Kahit ang paroroona'y di tiyak.

Walang huling biyahe sa mangingibig
Na handang maglakbay
Nang may pananalig.

1. Sa anong mga imahe (images) inihahambing (compare) ang paglalakbay?
2. Bakit hindi dapat mabagal ang paglalakbay?
3. Bakit hindi dapat mabilis ang paglalakbay?

4. **Ano ang dapat gawin sa gitna ng paglalakbay?**
5. **Ano ang dapat mayroon ang mangingibig sa paglalakbay?**

✏ Pagsusulat

Write a short paragraph about renting (a bicycle, a car, skis, a **bangka** or small boat). You can use the information and role-play you worked on in this chapter, or you can talk about your own experience.

⚑ Paglalagom

In **Aralin 26**, you have:
1. Learned words and phrases related to renting,
2. Practiced using words related to money,
3. Practiced the **nakapag-** affix,
4. Practiced **Kung**... (*if...*) and **Kailangan**... (*need*).

You should now be able to:
1. Rent a vehicle.
2. Express your needs when renting something.

Pagpunta sa Bangko (Going to a Bank)

  Diyalogo: Sa Bangko (At a Bank)

Read the dialogue below. After completing this chapter, practice this dialogue using your own information.

PEDRO : **Gusto ko hong magpapalit ng dolyar.**
I would like to exchange dollars.

BANK TELLER : **Magkano ho ba?**
How much?

PEDRO : **Isang daang dolyar ho. Ano ho ang palitan?**
A hundred dollars. What is the exchange rate?

BANK TELLER : **Singkwenta pesos ho sa isang dolyar. Kailangan ko hong tingnan ang inyong pasaporte.**
Fifty pesos to a dollar. I need to look at your passport.

PEDRO : **Heto ho ang isang daang dolyar at ang aking pasaporte.**
Here is a hundred dollars and my passport.

BANK TELLER : **Heto ho ang limang libong piso at ang inyong pasaporte.**
Here is five thousand pesos and your passport.

Bokabolaryo

Study the following word and phrases. Some of them were used in the dialogue you just read and some of them will be useful when you make your own sentences for your dialogues.

Magpapalit	*Exchange*
Tingnan	*Look*
Kailangan kong tingnan	*Need to look*
Palitan	*Exchange rate*
Pasaporte	*Passport*

Mga Halimbawang Pangungusap

Practice saying these sentences aloud, to get a feel for how this chapter's vocabulary and grammar work in Filipino.

1. **Gustong magpapalit ni Pedro ng dolyar.** *Pedro wants to exchange dollars.*
2. **Singkuwenta pesos ang palitan ng dolyar sa piso.** *The exchange rate from dollar to pesos is fifty pesos.*
3. **Isang daang dolyar ang pinalitan ni Pedro.** *Pedro exchanged one hundred dollars.*
4. **Kailangang tingnan ng teller ang pasaporte ni Pedro.** *The teller needs to see Pedro's passport.*
5. **May limang libong piso na ngayon si Pedro.** *Pedro now has five thousand pesos.*

  Pagsasanay

Study the information below from a money exchange stall in the Philippines. Then ask and answer questions. Also, write as many sentences as you can about the situation. These sentences can describe the people or the place, or narrate the situation. Below are some examples of questions and answers, as well as sentences:

Mga Halimbawang Tanong at Sagot

1. Tanong : **Ano ang palitan ng dolyar sa peso?**
   Sagot : _____.

2. Tanong : **Magkano ang gusto papalitan ni _____?**
   Sagot : _____.

3. TANONG : **Magkano ang pera ngayon ni** _____?

   SAGOT   : _____.

Mga Halimbawang Pangungusap

1. **May** _____ **si** _____.

2. _____ **ang palitan ng** _____ **sa** _____.

3. **Kailangan ng** _____ **ang** _____.

4. **Mayroon na siya ngayong** _____.

Situation 1

Jina studies in Japan. She brought home 120,000 yen. She wants to exchange her money into pesos. She went to a money changer and she was asked to show her identification card.

Mga Tanong at Sagot

1. TANONG : _____?

   SAGOT   : _____.

2. TANONG : _____?

   SAGOT   : _____.

3. TANONG : _____?

   SAGOT   : _____.

4. TANONG : _____?

   SAGOT   : _____.

5. TANONG : _____?

   SAGOT   : _____.

Mga Pangungusap

1. _____

2. _____

3. _____

4. _____

5. _____

Situation 2

Mila is on her last day of her visit to the Philippines. She wants to buy souvenirs only, so she needs to exchange just 50 dollars into pesos.

Mga Tanong at Sagot

1. TANONG : _____?
   SAGOT : _____.

2. TANONG : _____?
   SAGOT : _____.

3. TANONG : _____?
   SAGOT : _____.

4. TANONG : _____?
   SAGOT : _____.

5. TANONG : _____?
   SAGOT : _____.

Mga Pangungusap

1. _____

2. _____

3. _____

4. _____

5. _____

Situation 3

Francis lives and works in the Philippines but he is going to the United States for a conference for a week. He needs to change some currency because he will be paying the conference fee (five hundred dollars) in cash. He also wants to buy some books.

Mga Tanong at Sagot

1. TANONG : _____?
   SAGOT   : _____.

2. TANONG : _____?
   SAGOT   : _____.

3. TANONG : _____?
   SAGOT   : _____.

4. TANONG : _____?
   SAGOT   : _____.

5. TANONG : _____?
   SAGOT   : _____.

Mga Pangungusap

1. _____

2. _____

3. _____

4. _____

5. _____

★ Gawain (Role-play)

Go back to the information provided, and the questions, answers, and sentences you have written. Then, using the dialogue you have learned as a guide, do role-plays with your partner. Classroom learners can work in pairs or small groups while individual learners should write down the dialogue.

Mga Tala Sa Kultura

The Filipino communities formed by labor migration have resulted in the creation of pockets of Filipino culture abroad—comfortable spaces where they can speak their language, eat familiar food and buy or rent Filipino music and movies. For many domestic workers, these places away from the homes of their employers is what they can consider "home."

Philippine banks with branches in Japan give service to their customers on Sundays. They can be found outside churches or buildings which serve as churches, catering to the needs of Filipinos who want to send money to their families in the Philippines.

In Singapore, Taiwan, and Hong Kong, banks and other remittance companies can be found in shopping malls patronized by Filipinos. On Sundays, Filipinos go on a one-stop trip to these malls—they eat Filipino food, go grocery shopping for Philippine food items, send money and even give or get a manicure.

According to the Philippine Overseas Employment Agency, there are 1,236,013 documented overseas Filipino workers as of December 2008. Among the top destinations are Saudi Arabia (275,933), United Arab Emirates (193,810), Qatar (84,342), Hong Kong (78,345) and Singapore (41,678). Among the top jobs are household service workers (50,082); waiters, bartenders, and related workers (13,911); charworkers, cleaners, and related workers (11,620); nurses (11,495); and caregivers/caretakers (10,109).

It is therefore not surprising that the Philippine economy survives because of the help it gets through the remittances of these household workers. The top five sources of remittances as of 2008 are: United States ($7,825,607,000); Saudi Arabia ($1,387,120,000); Canada ($1,308,692,000); United Kingdom ($776,354,000), Italy ($678,539,000) and United Arab Emirates ($621,232,000). In looking at these figures, we should note that although there are fewer documented overseas workers in the United States, the colonial history of the Philippines accounts for decades-long immigration of many Filipinos to the United States.

In recent years, the internet has also replaced malls and banks as the site of remittance transactions. Through these online companies, money can be picked up by the recipient, delivered to an office or a residence, or transferred to a bank account.

To read more about Filipino culture outside the Philippines, consider reading the following books: *Locating Filipino Americans: Ethnicity and the Politics of Space* by Rick Bonus (Philadelphia: Temple University, 2000); *Pinoy Capital: The Filipino Nation in Daly City* by Benito M. Vergara (Philadelphia: Temple University, 2009); and *Ating Kalagayan (The Social and Economic Profile of Filipinos)* by Peter Chua (Woodside: National Bulosan Center, 2010).

Pagbabasa: Isang Liham (A Letter)

Read the following letter, and then answer the questions that follow. Study the following words before reading the story. You have learned some of the words in earlier lesson; they are listed here for you to review. You can also refer to the glossary at the back of the book.

Kalagayan	*Condition*
Programa	*Program*
Bumaha	*Got flooded*
Agad	*At once*
Magpapadala	*Send*

Liham ni Clara sa kanyang Lola

Ika-15 ng Agosto 2010

Mahal kong Lola,

Kumusta na po kayo?

Mabuti naman ang kalagayan ko dito sa Quezon City. Nakatira na po ako ngayon sa bahay nina Tito Boy at Tita Baby. Tapos na po ang Philippine Studies summer program namin sa unibersidad. Sa huling linggo ng programa, pumunta kami sa Boracay Island ng mga kaklase ko.

Alam po ba ninyo ang nangyari noong isang linggo? Malakas ang bagyo dito sa Maynila. Bumaha sa Marikina at nasira ang bahay nina Tita Mila. Dito sila tumira sa bahay nina Tita Baby nang isang linggo.

Pumunta agad kami ni Tita Baby sa bangko at nagpapalit ako ng dalawang daang dolyar. Ibinigay ko ito kay Tita Mila para makatulong sa kanila.

Magpapadala po ba kayo ng pera? Mas mabilis siguro kung sa pamamagitan ng internet. Puwedeng tumulong sa inyo si Nanay.

Sa Disyembre po ay pupunta ako sa Los Angeles. Kasal po ng kaibigan ko. May problema pa ako sa tiket ko at susulat uli ako kapag sigurado na ang petsa ng dating ko.

Magkita po tayo pagbisita ko riyan.

Nagmamahal,
Clara

✏ Pagsusulat (Writing)

Write a letter to a family member or a friend. Study the following words, phrases, and expressions that might be useful to you.

Mga Salitang Maaaring Gamitin Sa Liham
(Words you can use in your letter): **Mga Pagbati** (Greetings)

Mahal kong...,	*Dear...,*
Minamahal kong...,	*Dear...,*
Mahal na Gng Cruz:	*Dear Gng. Cruz:*
Mga Panahon: Tagsibol,	*Seasons: Spring,*
Tag-araw, Taglagas,	*Summer, Fall,*
Taglamig	*Winter*
Pupunta ako sa...	*I will go to...*
Mag-aaral ako ng...	*I will study...*
Maglalaro ako ng...	*I will play...*
Manonood ako ng...	*I will watch...*
May problema pa ako sa...	*I have a problem with...*
Magkita tayo	*Let us see each other*
Manood, maglaro, kumain	*Watch, play, eat*

Mga Pagtatapos (Endings)

Nagmamahal,	*Love,*
Sumasaiyo,	*Yours,*

⚑ Paglalagom

In **Aralin 27**, you have:
1. Practiced words related to money and numbers,
2. Learned words related to exchanging currency,
3. Practiced writing a letter.

You should now be able to:
1. Exchange currency at a bank or a money changer.
2. Write a letter.

Paglalarawan ng Tao (Describing a Person)

  ## Diyalogo: Unang Pagkikita (First meeting)

Read the dialogue below. Review the words and phrases you can use in describing a person. After completing this chapter, practice this dialogue using your own information.

MARIA : **Magandang hapon. Puwede ho bang makausap si Nena?**
Good afternoon. Can I speak to Nena?

NENA : **Si Nena nga ito. Sino po sila?**
This is Nena. Who is this please?

MARIA : **Nena, si Maria ito. Ako ang susundo sa iyo sa paliparan ng Detroit.**
Nena, this is Maria. I am the person who will pick you up at the airport in Detroit.

NENA : **Paano kita makikilala?**
How will I recognize you?

MARIA : **Nakasuot ho ako ng pulang blusa at itim na palda. Payat ako at matangkad. Ikaw?**
I am wearing a red blouse and a black skirt. I am slim and tall. And you?

NENA : **Ako nama'y nakasuot ng kulay abong bestida. Mahaba at tuwid ang buhok ko. Maliit ako at medyo malaki ang pangangatawan.**
I am wearing a gray dress. My hair is long and straight. I am petite and a little bit heavy.

MARIA : **Sige. Magkita na lang po tayo bukas.**
Okay. Let us see each other tomorrow.

NENA : **Sige. Maraming salamat sa pagsundo mo sa akin.**
Okay. Thank you for picking me up at the airport.

Bokabolaryo

Study the following words. Some of them were used in the dialogue you just read and some of them will be useful when you make your own sentences for your dialogues.

Sundo	*Pick up*
Hatid	*Take someone to a place*
Paliparan	*Airport*

Pagbabalik-Aral at Pagpapalawak (Review and Expansion)

Review past lessons and list the Tagalog/Filipino equivalents of the English words on the left. Also, study the new words. These words are useful in describing a person.

Red	**Pula**
Blue	**Asul/Bughaw**
Green	_____
Yellow	_____
Violet/Purple	_____
White	_____
Brown	_____
Black	_____
Gray	_____
Orange	_____
Pink	_____

Mga Kulay ng Buhok

Study the following new words. The words to describe hair colors are slightly different. For example, in everyday life, one does not really use **kayumanggi** or **kulay kape** to refer to hair. One simply uses **brown**. See how the following words differ from the ones you studied earlier.

Kulay mais (the color of corn)	*Blond*
Brown	*Brown*
Itim	*Black*
Puti	*Gray/White*
Uban	*Special word to refer to gray/white hair*

Mga Kasuotan (Clothes)

Dress	**Damit/Bestida**
Blouse	**Blusa**
Pants	_____
Skirt	_____
Tie	_____
Suit	_____
Shoes	_____
Sandals	_____

Mga Bahagi ng Katawan (Parts of the body)

Hair	**Buhok**
Eyes	_____
Face	**Mukha**

Mga Salitang Naglalarawan ng Hitsura at Pangangatawan (Words that describe what a person looks like)

Round face	**Bilugan ang mukha**
Square face	**Kuwadrado ang mukha**
Heart-shaped face	**Hugis-puso ang mukha**
Small/petite	**Maliit**
Medium build	**Katamtaman ang pangangatawan**
Tall	**Matangkad**
Thin/slim	**Payat**
Wears glasses	**Naka-salamin**
Fat	**Mataba/Medyo malaki** (Note: Refrain from using **mataba** because it can cause offense. Instead, use **medyo malaki** (a little bit big).)

Mga Halimbawang Pangungusap

Practice saying these sentences aloud, to get a feel for how this chapter's vocabulary and grammar work in Filipino.

1. **Susunduin ni Nena si Maria sa paliparan ng Detroit.** — *Nena will pick up Maria at the airport in Detroit.*
2. **Nakasuot ng pulang blusa at itim na palda si Maria.** — *Maria is wearing a red blouse and a black skirt.*

3. **Nakasuot ng kulay abong bestida si Nena.**   *Nena is wearing a gray dress.*

4. **Payat at matangkad si Maria.**   *Maria is thin and tall.*

5. **Maliit si Nena pero malaki ang pangangatawan.**   *Nena is petite but has a heavy body.*

 Pagsasanay

Study the following pictures as well as the information given. Then ask and answer questions about the pictures. Also, write as many sentences as you can about the pictures. These sentences can describe the people or the place, or narrate the situation.

Larawan Blg. 1

Mga Tanong at Sagot

1. TANONG : _____?
   SAGOT   : _____.

2. TANONG : _____?
   SAGOT   : _____.

3. TANONG : _____?
   SAGOT   : _____.

4. TANONG : _____?
   SAGOT   : _____.

5. TANONG : _____?
   SAGOT   : _____.

Mga Pangungusap

1. _____

2. _____

3. _____

4. _____

5. _____

6. _____

Larawan Blg. 2

Mga Tanong at Sagot

1. TANONG : _____?
   SAGOT   : _____.

2. TANONG : _____?
   SAGOT   : _____.

3. TANONG : _____?
   SAGOT   : _____.

4. TANONG : _____?
   SAGOT   : _____.

5. TANONG : _____?
   SAGOT   : _____.

Mga Pangungusap

1. _____

2. _____

3. _____

4. _____

5. _____

Larawan Blg. 3

Mga Tanong at Sagot

1. TANONG : _____?
   SAGOT   : _____.

2. TANONG : _____?
   SAGOT   : _____.

3. TANONG : _____?
   SAGOT   : _____.

4. TANONG : _____?
   SAGOT   : _____.

5. TANONG : _____?
   SAGOT   : _____.

Mga Pangungusap

1. _____

2. _____

3. _____

4. _____

5. _____

⭐ Mga Gawain (Activities)

Role-play 1

Mag-iskedyul ng pagtatagpo sa isang taong di pa nakikita. (Schedule a meeting with someone you have not met before.)

Role-play 2

Pagbabalik-aral sa "kilalanan" sa unang pagtatagpo. Pagkikita ng bagong magkakilala. (Review "greetings" dialogue for people meeting each other for the first time.)
Magsimula sa "Kumusta? Ako si …" (Start with "How are you? I am ….")

Mga Tala Sa Kultura

Have you ever wondered why relatives and friends sending off or picking up travellers are not allowed inside the international airport in Manila? Only those with plane tickets and passports are allowed inside the building. This is because **paghatid** (taking someone to another place) and **pagsundo** (picking up or fetching someone to bring to another place) is a custom in the Philippines.

I remember a photograph from the 1960s when my cousin Margaret left for the United States to work as a nurse. Around a dozen family members, parents, siblings, aunts, uncles, and cousins went to the airport to send her off. She had a bouquet of flowers in her arms, and an orchid corsage pinned to her chest, proofs of how momentous the occasion was for the family. Similarly, it is not uncommon for families to even rent jeepneys just to bring their relatives to the airport when they leave for abroad, or to pick them up when they return.

"Sunduan" (fetching someone) is celebrated in several cities of Rizal, such as Tanay and Parañaque, and Pampanga, through a street pageant. Young men fetch young women from their homes, and dressed in national costumes, they parade and dance in the streets of the city.

The Open University of the University of the Philippines also uses this concept and, in May, celebrates its graduating students and incoming freshmen with a "Sunduan."

Pagbabasa

Read the following passage, and then answer the questions that follow. Study the following words before reading the story. You have learned some of the words in earlier lesson; they are listed here for you to review. You can also refer to the glossary at the back of the book.

Kalaban	*Adversary*
Pulitika	*Politics*
Pauwi	*On his way home*
Lumapag	*Landed*
Bigla	*Suddenly*
Pumutok	*Fired*
Baril	*Gun*
Tunay	*Real*

Ang Lalaking Nakaputi

Nakasuot ng puti ang lalaking naka-upo sa loob ng eroplano. Maiksi ang buhok niya at may salamin siya sa mata. Mayroon siyang hawak na bag.

Galing ng Hong Kong ang lalaki. Bago pumunta ng Hong Kong, nakatira ang lalaki sa Newton, Massachussetts dahil mayroon siyang "fellowships" sa Harvard University at Massachussetts Institute of Technology. Doon, nagbigay ng mga lektyur at sumulat ng mga libro ang lalaki. Dating bilanggong pulitikal o "political prisoner" ang lalaki dahil kalaban niya sa pulitika ang Pangulo.

Pauwi na ang lalaki sa kanyang bayan. Maraming tao sa airport para sunduin siya. Nakasuot ang marami sa kanila ng mga damit na kulay dilaw. Nagsabit din sila ng mga dilaw na ribbon. Inspirasyon nila para dito ang kantang "Tie a Yellow Ribbon."

Lumapag sa paliparan ng Maynila ang eroplano. Tumayo ang lalaki para lumabas ng eroplano. Pababa na ng eroplano ang lalaki nang may biglang pumutok na baril.

Bumagsak ang lalaki.

Sa kanyang passport, nakasulat ang pangalang "Marcial Bonifacio." Ninoy Aquino ang tunay niyang pangalan.

1. **Ano ang suot ng lalaking naka-upo sa eroplano?**
2. **Saan galing ang lalaki?**
3. **Bakit tumira ang lalaki sa Massachusetts?**
4. **Ano ang mga ginawa ng lalaki sa Massachusetts?**

5. **Ano ang suot ng mga tao sa airport na sumundo sa lalaki?**
6. **Ano ang nangyari sa lalaki nang pababa siya sa eroplano?**
7. **Ano ang nakasulat na pangalan sa passport ng lalaki?**
8. **Ano ang tunay niyang pangalan?**

✏ Pagsusulat

Write a paragraph about meeting someone at the airport. You can use the information in the situations you studied in this lesson or you can talk about a recent experience.

⚑ Paglalagom

In **Aralin 28**, you have:
1. Reviewed words you can use when describing a person,
2. Practiced greeting a person for the first time.

You should now be able to:
1. Describe a person.
2. Engage someone you have just met in a conversation with greater ease.

Aralin
Lesson **29**

Pag-upa ng Bahay (Renting a House)

  Diyalogo: Ang Bahay (The House)

Read the dialogue below. After completing this chapter, practice this dialogue using your own information.

JUAN	:	**Ito ho ba ang pinauupahang bahay?**
		Is this the house for rent?
GNG. RAMOS	:	**Ito nga ho. Interesado ho ba kayo?**
		Yes it is. Are you interested?
JUAN	:	**Oho. Ilang kuwarto ho ito?**
		Yes. How many rooms does it have?
GNG. RAMOS	:	**Tatlong kuwarto ho at dalawang banyo. Malaki ho ang master's bedroom. Maraming bintana kaya mahangin.**
		Three rooms and two bathrooms. The master's bedroom is big. There are many windows; that's why it's windy.
JUAN	:	**Kailan ho natayo ang bahay?**
		When was the house built?
GNG. RAMOS	:	**Noon hong 1980.**
		In 1980.
PEDRO	:	**Malayo ho ba ang estasyon ng tren?**
		Is it far from the train station?
GNG. RAMOS	:	**Puwede hong lakarin. Kumanan kayo pagdating sa kanto. Maglakad ng dalawang kalye. Puwede rin hong sumakay ng tricycle.**
		You can walk. Turn right when you get to the corner. Walk two blocks. You can also ride a tricycle.
PEDRO	:	**Hindi ho ba madilim sa kalye sa gabi?**
		Isn't it dark on the street at night?
GNG. RAMOS	:	**Hindi ho. Maliwanag ho dito dahil maraming ilaw.**
		No. It is bright because there are many lights.
PEDRO	:	**Magkano ho ang upa dito?**
		How much is the rent (here)?

GNG. CRUZ	:	**Beinte mil ho isang buwan. Dalawang buwan ho ang deposito at isang buwan ang paunang bayad.**
		Twenty thousand a month. The deposit is two months and the advance payment is one month.
PEDRO	:	**Kasama ho ba ang kuryente at tubig?**
		Does that include electricity and water?
GNG. CRUZ	:	**Kasama ang tubig. Hiwalay ang kuryente.**
		That includes water. Electricity is separate.

  Bokabolaryo

Study the following words. Some of them were used in the dialogue you just read and some of them will be useful when you make your own sentences for your dialogues.

Mahangin	*Windy*
Natayo	*Was built*
Tricycle	*A motorcycle or a bicycle with a sidecar*
Deposito	*Deposit*
Paunang bayad	*Advance payment*
Kasama	*Included*
Hiwalay	*Separate*

Pagbabalik-Aral at Pagpapalawak (Review and Expansion)

Review the following groups of words you have learned. They will be useful for you in this lesson.

Mga Pang-uri na Naglalarawan ng Lugar (Adjectives that describe a place)

Malaki	*Big*
Maliit	*Small*

Madilim	*Dark*
Maliwanag	*Bright*
Maluwang	*Wide*
_____	*Windy*

Mga Salita at Pangungusap na Ginagamit sa Pagbibigay ng Direksiyon (Words and sentences used in giving directions)

Malapit	*Near*
_____	*Far*
Kumanan ka	*Turn right*
Katabi	*Beside*
_____	*Behind*

Mga Halimbawang Pangungusap

Practice saying these sentences aloud, to get a feel for how this chapter's vocabulary and grammar work in Filipino.

1. **Ang pinauupahang bahay ni Gng. Cruz ay may tatlong kuwarto at dalawang banyo.**
   The house that Mrs. Cruz is renting has three rooms and two bathrooms.
2. **Natayo ang bahay noong 1980.**
   The house was built in 1980.
3. **Malapit ang bahay sa estasyon ng tren.**
   The house is near the train station.
4. **Beinte mil ang upa ng bahay isang buwan.**
   The rent for the house is twenty thousand pesos a month.

 ★ **Gawain**

Role-play

Look for a specific house or apartment. In the classroom, one student or a pair of students walks around the room, looking for rental units. They talk to owners and/or company representatives renting out the houses or apartments that are described below. Other students are assigned the roles of owners or company representatives. Independent learners should write down the dialogues.

To prepare yourself for the role-play, study/review the following words, questions, answers, and sentences:

Mga Salita

Malapit	*Near*
Malayo	*Far*
Libre	*Free*
Balkonahe	*Balcony*
Paligid	*Surroundings*
Pag-aari	*Owned*
Kasama	*Included* (other meanings of the word are *companion* and *comrade*)
Tricycle	*Motorcycle or bicycle with a side car for passengers*
Pampublikong transportasyon	*Public transportation*
Kalahating buwan	*Half a month*
Kasangkapan	*Appliances and furniture*

CAMPUS APARTMENTS—dalawang kuwarto, isang banyo, malapit sa estasyon ng bus, may malalaking bintana, ₱10,000 isang buwan, kailangan ng isang buwang deposito, isang buwang advance, libre ang tubig, hiwalay ang kuryente.

LUXURY APARTMENTS—tatlong kuwarto, tatlong banyo, may swimming pool at gym, may balkonahe, ₱20,000 isang buwan, kailangan ng dalawang buwang deposito, isang buwang advance, malapit sa shopping center, hiwalay ang tubig at kuryente, libre ang internet

FAIRVIEW APARTMENTS—isang kuwarto, isang banyo, malayo sa unibersidad, malayo sa bus station, maraming puno sa paligid (many trees around the complex), ₱5,000 isang buwan, kalahating buwang deposito, isang buwan advance, hiwalay ang tubig, kuryente at internet, libre ang cable TV.

BAHAY SA MAPAYAPA VILLAGE—pag-aari ni Ginang Lumbera, apat na kuwarto, dalawang banyo, may maid's room, malaki ang hardin, malaki ang kusina, malapit sa simbahan, ₱25,000 isang buwan, dalawang buwang deposito, isang buwang advance, hiwalay ang tubig, kuryente, internet at cable TV. May tricyle na puwedeng sakyan papunta sa Estasyon ng tren.

U.P. VILLAGE STUDIO—pag-aari ni Ginoong Tolentino, studio apartment, isang banyo, kailangang sumakay ng tricycle papunta sa estasyon ng tren, ₱7,000 isang buwan, libre ang tubig, internet, at cable TV. Hiwalay ang kuryente. Mayroong airconditioner sa studio. Mayroon na ring mga kasangkapan ang studio.

Mga Tanong at Sagot

1. Tanong : **Ilan po ang kuwarto ng bahay/apartment?**
   Sagot : _____ **ang kuwarto ng bahay.**

2. Tanong : **Ilan po ang banyo ng bahay/apartment?**
   Sagot : _____ **ang banyo ng bahay.**

3. Tanong : **Saan po malapit ang bahay/apartment?**
   Sagot : **Malapit ang bahay/apartment sa** _____.

4. Tanong : **Ano po ang kailangang deposito at advance?**
   Sagot : **Kailangan po ng** _____ **buwang deposito at** _____
   buwang advance.

5. Tanong : **Magkano po ang upa sa bahay sa isang buwan?**
   Sagot : **₱** _____ **ang upa sa bahay sa isang buwan.**

6. Tanong : **Kasama na po ba sa upa ang kuryente, tubig, at internet?**
   Sagot : **Kasama na ang** _____. **Hiwalay ang** _____
   at _____.

7. Tanong : **Malapit po ba ang** _____ **sa pampublikong transportasyon?**
   Sagot : _____.

Mga Pangungusap

1. **Maganda ang apartment/bahay na ito dahil maraming puno sa paligid.**
   This apartment/house is good because there are many trees around it.

2. **Maganda ang apartment/bahay na ito dahil may swimming pool at gym sa apartment complex/village.**
   This apartment/house is good because there is a swimming pool and a gym in the apartment complex/village.

3. **Kailangang sumakay/maglakad papunta sa estasyon ng tren.**
   You need to ride/walk going to the train station.

4. **Malapit/malayo ang bahay/ apartment sa** _____.
   The house/apartment is near/far from _____.

5. **Kailangan mong magbayad ng** _____ **deposito at** _____ **na advance.**
   You need to pay _____ *deposit and* _____ *advance (payment).*

6. **Kumpleto/walang kasangkapan ang bahay/apartment.**

The apartment has complete/no appliances/furniture.

Mga Tala Sa Kultura

There are several customs associated with moving to a new house. One is to make sure that one brings in salt and rice first. Another is to shower coins during the "house warming party." Both customs are supposed to give luck to the people living in the house.

Some people also count the steps in the house, saying, "**Oro, plata, mata.**" These words refer to gold coins, silver coins, and to shrubs, which symbolize the working class. One is supposed to avoid houses with stairs ending in "**mata,**" as one will be poor.

Other popular beliefs include hanging garlic to ward off evil spirits; making sure that the master bedroom faces east; and counting the steps on the stairs to ensure that no stairs have thirteen steps, a number that signifies bad luck.

Why are Filipinos superstitious? This may be attributed to early times when people felt they had to find a way to explain things which at that time did not have scientific explanations available.

 Pagbabasa

Read the following short short story, and then answer the questions that follow. Before reading, review/study the following words.

Manananggal	*Mythological creature in the Philippines, described to be a beautiful woman with bat-like wings and whose body can separate into two parts*
Buntis	*Pregnant*
Nahahati	*Divide*
Lumilipad	*Fly*
Naghahanap	*Looks for*
Bubong	*Roof*
Dila	*Tongue*
Sumisigaw	*Shout*
Rebelde	*Rebel*
Sundalo	*Soldiers*
Takot	*Afraid*

Ang Manananggal*

Buntis si Sherlyn. Humiga siya sa kama sa ilalim ng kulambo. Hindi siya makatulog. Mula sa kama, nakikita niya ang bintana. Madilim sa labas ng bahay, kahit na bilog na bilog ang buwan sa labas.

May narinig siyang ingay. Tik. tik. tik. Natakot si Sherlyn. Manananggal kaya?

Ito ang kuwento ng lola niya tungkol sa manananggal. Sa gabi, nahahati ang katawan ng manananggal. Lumilipad ito at naghahanap ng mga buntis na babae. Pumupunta ang manananggal sa bubong ng bahay. Pagkatapos, lalabas ang mahabang dila nito, at kukunin ng dila ang sanggol sa loob ng babae. Dahil dito, naglalagay ng bawang sa iba't ibang kuwarto ng bahay ang mga tao. Ang sabi ng lola niya, kapag nilagyan ng bawang, asin, o abo ang kalahating katawan ng mananggal, hindi na makakabalik ito sa katawan.

Bang. Bang. Bang.

Sa labas, nagpapaputok ng baril ang mga sundalo. Sumisigaw ang kapitbahay. "Hindi po ako rebelde! Hindi po ako rebelde!"

Tumayo si Sherlyn. Pumunta siya sa bintana. Nakita niya ang dalawang babae na kinukuha ng mga sundalo.

Takot na takot si Sherlyn. Nasaan na ba ang bawang?

1. Ano ang pangalan ng babaeng buntis?
2. Ano ang narinig niya?
3. Bakit lumilipad ang manananggal?
4. Saan pumupunta ang manananggal?
5. Paano kinukuha ng mananggal ang sanggol?
6. Sino ang kinukuha ng mga sundalo?

🖊 Pagsusulat

Practice your skills in giving summaries by completing the below paragraph about Pedro's search for an apartment.

Then, write a paragraph about your own search for a house or apartment.

---

* If you want to read more fiction on folklore creatures, consider *Mananggal Terrorizes Manila & Other Stories* by Jessica Zafra (Anvil Publishing, 1992) and *Spooky Mo* by Marivi Soliven Blanco (Milflores Publishing, 2008). If you want to learn more about militarization and human rights, read the Karapatan Alliance for the Advancement of People's Rights Reports found at http://www.karapatan.org/

Gustong umupa ng bahay ni Pedro. Gusto niya ng bahay na may _____.
Gusto niya ng _____. Ang badyet niya ay _____.
    May pinapaupahang bahay si Ginang Cruz. May _____ ang bahay.
_____ ang bahay sa _____.
_____. Kailangan ng _____. Kasama ang _____;
_____.

🏳 Paglalagom

In **Aralin 29**, you have:
1. Reviewed and expanded your knowledge about words that describe a place,
2. Learned new words related to renting a house or apartment.

You should now be able to:
1. Talk about your house or apartment.
2. Negotiate with a potential landlord about a possible lease.

Paglalarawan ng Damdamin (Expressing One's Feelings)

 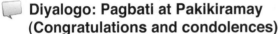 **Diyalogo: Pagbati at Pakikiramay (Congratulations and condolences)**

Read the dialogue below. After completing this chapter, practice this dialogue using your own information. Review life events studied earlier (birth, weddings, funerals). Note the idiomatic expressions introduced in this lesson.

CLARA : **Juan! Kumusta ka?**
Juan! How are you?

JUAN : **Mabuti naman. Masayang-masaya ako ngayon.**
Fine. I am very happy.

CLARA : **Balita ko ay natanggap ka raw sa law school.**
I heard that you got accepted into law school.

JUAN : **Oo nga. Nagbunga rin ang pagsusunog ko ng kilay.**
That's right. My studying hard bore fruit.

CLARA : **Binabati kita.**
Congratulations.

JUAN : **Salamat, Clara. May kasiyahan kami mamayang gabi. Puwede ka ba?**
Thank you, Clara. We have a party tonight. Can you make it?

CLARA : **Pasensiya ka na, pupunta ako sa lamay ng tiyahin ko.**
I am sorry, I will go to the wake of my aunt.

JUAN : **Ganoon ba? Nakikiramay ako. Kaya pala mukha kang Biyernes santo.**
Is that so? My condolences. That's why you look sad.

CLARA : **Salamat. Malapit ako sa kanya.**
Thank you. I was close to her.

JUAN : **Talaga?**
Really?

CLARA : **Oo, akala ng iba ay istrikta siya.**
Yes, other people thought she was strict.

JUAN : **Ganoon ba?**
Is that so?

CLARA : **Pero mabait siya. Matigas lang ang mukha.**
But she was kind. She just looked stern.

JUAN : **Ano ang ikinamatay niya?**
What did she die of?

CLARA : **Atake sa puso.**
A heart attack.

  ## Bokabolaryo

Study the following words. Some of them were used in the dialogue you just read and some of them will be useful when you make your own sentences for your dialogues.

Mga salitang nagpapahayag ng damdamin at mga idiomatikong ekspresyon (Words that express feelings and idiomatic expressions)	
Masayang-masaya	*Very happy*
Malungkot	*Sad*
Nagagalit	*Angry*
Nag-aalala	*Worried*
Natatakot	*Afraid*
Umiyak	*Cried*
Tumawa	*Laughed*
Ngumiti	*Smiled*
Nakangiti	*Smiling*
Kaya (accent on the second syllable)	*That is why/and so*
Pagsusunog ng kilay	*Working hard*
Mukhang Biyernes Santo	*"Looks like Good Friday during Lenten Season" (looks very sad)*
Malapit (diin sa ikatlong pantig) [emphasis on the third syllable]	*Close*
Matigas ang mukha	*Looks stern*
Magaling	*Good (referring to ability)*

Pagbabalik-Aral at Pagpapalawak (Review and Expansion)

Review the following words and phrases about life events that you have learned in an earlier chapter. Then, study the new words. Since these words were given using the completed aspect of the verb, practice conjugating these words in the contemplated aspect. These will be useful to you when you express feelings.

Ipinanganak	*Was born*
Nanganak	*Gave birth*
Bininyagan	*Baptized*
Nagtapos ng pag-aaral	*Graduated*
Natanggap sa trabaho	*Got accepted for a job*
Natanggal sa trabaho	*Got fired from a job*
Nawala	*Lost*
Tumanggap ng karangalan	*Received an award*
Ikinasal	*Got married*
Nabuntis/Nagdalang-tao	*Got pregnant*
Nagkasakit	*Got sick*
Namatay/Yumao	*Passed on*

Mga Halimbawang Pangungusap

Practice saying these sentences aloud, to get a feel for how this chapter's vocabulary and grammar work in Filipino.

1. **Masayang-masaya si Juan dahil natanggap siya sa law school.**
   Juan is very happy because he got accepted at law school.
2. **Malungkot si Clara dahil yumao ang tiyahin niya.**
   Clara is sad because her aunt passed on.
3. **Mabait pero mukhang strikta ang tiyahin ni Clara.**
   Clara's aunt is kind but looks strict.
4. **Mukhang strikta ang tiyahin ni Clara dahil matigas ang mukha nito.**
   Clara's aunt looks strict because her face looks stern.
5. **Napakasaya ni Belinda dahil nagdadalang-tao siya.**
   Belinda is very happy because she is pregnant.
6. **Napakalungkot ni Randy dahil natanggal siya sa trabaho.**
   Randy is very sad because he was fired from his job.
7. **Lagi siyang absent kaya natanggal siya sa trabaho**
   He is always absent, and so he was fired from his job.

  Pagsasanay

Study the following pictures and try to create a situation based on each. Then ask and answer questions about the picture. Also, write as many sentences as you can about the picture. These sentences can describe the people or the place, or narrate the situation.

Mga Halimbawang Tanong at Sagot

1. TANONG : **Bakit siya masaya?**
   SAGOT   : **Masaya siya dahil _____.**

2. TANONG : **Bakit siya malungkot?**
   SAGOT   : **Malungkot siya dahil _____.**

3. TANONG : **Bakit siya nagagalit?**
   SAGOT   : **Galit siya dahil _____.**

4. TANONG : **Ano ang ikinamatay ng asawa niya?**
   SAGOT   : **Kanser ang ikinamatay ng asawa niya.**

5. TANONG : **Bakit siya natanggap sa trabaho?**
   SAGOT   : **Natanggap siya sa trabaho dahil magaling siya.**

Mga Halimbawang Pangungusap

1. **Masaya si _____.**

2. **Nanalo siya sa song-writing contest.**

3. **Nanalo siya ng sampung libong piso.**

4. **Nawala ang pera niya.**

5. **Malungkot na malungkot si _____.**

Larawan Blg. 1

Mga Tanong at Sagot

1. TANONG : _____?
   SAGOT   : _____.

2. TANONG : _____?

   SAGOT   : _____.

3. TANONG : _____?

   SAGOT   : _____.

4. TANONG : _____?

   SAGOT   : _____.

5. TANONG : _____?

   SAGOT   : _____.

Mga Pangungusap

1. _____

2. _____

3. _____

4. _____

5. _____

Larawan Blg. 2

Mga Tanong at Sagot

1. TANONG : _____?

   SAGOT   : _____.

2. TANONG : _____?

   SAGOT   : _____.

3. TANONG : _____?
   SAGOT   : _____.

4. TANONG : _____?
   SAGOT   : _____.

5. TANONG : _____?
   SAGOT   : _____.

Mga Pangungusap

1. _____

2. _____

3. _____

Larawan Blg. 3

Mga Tanong at Sagot

1. TANONG : _____?
   SAGOT   : _____.

2. TANONG : _____?
   SAGOT   : _____.

3. TANONG : _____?
   SAGOT   : _____.

4. TANONG : _____?
   SAGOT   : _____.

5. TANONG : _____?
   SAGOT   : _____.

Mga Pangungusap

1. _____

2. _____

3. _____

 ★ **Gawain**

In an earlier lesson, you learned how to express congratulations and condolences. Review the expressions you have learned as well as the new ones introduced in this chapter through role-plays.

Pick one of the situations below. Then, classroom learners should go around the room asking others how they feel. Independent learners should write down dialogues.

Mga Posibleng Sitwasyon (Possible situations)

Estudyante 1: **Nanalo ka sa timpalak** (contest) **sa pagsulat ng sanaysay o essay.**
Estudyante 2: **Yumao ang lola mo.**
Estudyante 3: **Nakakuha ka ng scholarship.**
Estudyante 4: **Nasunog ang bahay mo.**
Estudyante 5: **Ikakasal ka.**
Estudyante 6: **Malubha ang sakit ng nanay mo.**

Mga Ekspresyong Puwedeng Gamitin sa Pagsasadula (Expressions you can use in the role-play)

Binabati kita!	*Congratulations to you!*
Kay sayang balita!	*What happy news!*
Ikinalulungkot ko ang balitang 'yan.	*That news makes me sad.*
Nakikiramay ako.	*My condolences.*
Tunay kang karapat-dapat!	*You are truly deserving.*
Napakalungkot ng balitang iyan.	*That news is so sad.*

Dagdag-Aral (Additional study): Iba Pang Idiomatikong Ekpresyon (Other idiomatic expressions)

Mababaw ang luha	*Cries easily*
Maitim ang budhi	*Bad or evil person*
Nagsunog ng kilay	*Studied hard*

Walang pagsidlan ng galak	*Very happy*
Hindi maipinta ang mukha	*Looks irritated and/or bothered and sad*

Mga Tala Sa Kultura

When translating or trying to understand idiomatic expressions, remember that these expressions are bound to the culture of the country. Let us look at a few examples.

One is the English expression "milking the cow." When we translate this into Filipino, we cannot say "**paggagatas sa baka**" (literally, milking the cow). A better translation would be "**palabigasan**" (getting rice from). Why? Because rice, being the staple food of the Philippines, is a truer image and because "**palabigasan**" is an indigenous idiomatic expression referring to a source of money.

Another English expression is "burning the midnight oil" which means working hard. This connotes an earlier time, before electricity—when one probably worked or studied using oil lamps. In Filipino, the equivalent is "**nagsunog ng kilay**," perhaps referring to a person reading so close to a gas lamp that his/her eyebrows are in danger of being burned.

Similarly, the English expression "siren song" refers to something that seduces and is said to have been derived from the Greek epic, the *Odyssey*. Should we translate this expression into Filipino, a more appropriate term would be "**awit ng adarna**." This refers to the seductive song of the **adarna** bird (discussed in Lesson 20) from a popular metrical romance.

Studying Tagalog/Filipino idioms will make it easier for you as a language learner to better understand what you read, and to better appreciate the culture of the Filipino people.

  Pagbabasa

Read the following nonfiction text, and then answer the questions that follow. Study the following words before reading the story. You have learned some of the words in earlier lessons; they are listed here for you to review.

Daan-daang libo	*Hundreds of thousands*
Sementeryo	*Cemetery*
Nakitang patay	*Found dead*
Nakatali	*Tied*
Pinahirapan	*Tortured; literally, given hardship*
Tagapangulo	*President*

Ang Libing

Daan-daang libong tao ang dumalo ng kanilang libing. Hindi mahulugang-karayom ang martsa. Labindalawang oras silang naglakad para ihatid sa sementeryo ang dalawang lalaking namatay, at makiramay sa kanilang mga pamilya. Malungkot na malungkot ang lahat at may mga umiiyak; mukhang Biyernes Santo ang mga mukha. Marami rin ang galit na galit dahil sa nangyari.

Ika-23 ng Nobyembre 1986. Nakitang patay sina Rolando Olalia at Leonor Alay-ay. Nakatali sila at may diyaryo sa bibig. Pinahirapan muna sila bago binaril. Hindi alam ng mga pulis kung sino ang pumatay kina Olalia at Alay-ay.

Si Rolando Olalia ang tagapangulo ng Kilusang Mayo Uno, ang organisasyon ng mga anakpawis. Drayber niya si Leonor.

1. Ilang tao ang pumunta sa libing?
2. Ilang oras silang nagmartsa?
3. Kailan pinatay sina Olalia at Alay-ay?
4. Sino si Rolando Olalia?
5. Sino si Leonor Alay-ay?

✏ Pagsusulat

In a paragraph, narrate a recent life event. Then express your feelings.

⚑ Paglalagom

In **Aralin 30**, you have:
1. Reviewed and learned new words and expressions about life events,
2. Learned how to talk about your feelings,
3. Reviewed and learned new idiomatic expressions.

You should now be able to:
1. Talk about important events in your life.
2. Express congratulations and condolences.
3. Use idiomatic expressions in Filipino.

Aralin
Lesson **31**

Pagsasalaysay ng Pangyayari
(Narrating an Incident)

 Diyalogo: Isang Aksidente (An accident)

Read the dialogue below. After completing this chapter, practice this dialogue using your own information.

MARIA : **Narinig mo ba ang balita?**
Have you heard of the accident?

PEDRO : **Ano ang nangyari?**
What happened?

MARIA : **Naaksidente si Juan.**
Juan met (with) an accident.

PEDRO : **Saan?**
Where?

MARIA : **Sa Katipunan Avenue. Nabangga ang kotse niya.**
At Katipunan Avenue. His car got hit.

PEDRO : **Kumusta na siya?**
How is he?

MARIA : **Nasa ospital siya.**
He is in the hospital.

PEDRO : **Kailan nangyari ang aksidente?**
When did the accident happen?

MARIA : **Kaninang bandang alas-diyes ng umaga.**
At around ten o'clock in the morning earlier.

PEDRO : **Kumusta ang isang drayber?**
How is the driver?

MARIA : **Sa kasamaang palad, nasawi ang isang drayber.**
Unfortunately, the driver passed on.

Bokabolaryo

Study the following words. Some of them were used in the dialogue you just read and some of them will be useful when you make your own sentences for your dialogues.

Balita	*News*
Aksidente	*Accident*
Naaksidente	*Met (with) an accident*
Insidente	*Incident*
Drayber/Tsuper	*Driver*
Bumbero	*Firefighter*
Sa kasamaang palad	*Unfortunately*
Nasawi	*Died*
Kinapanayam	*Interviewed*

Mga Halimbawang Pangungusap

Practice saying these sentences aloud, to get a feel for how this chapter's vocabulary and grammar work in Filipino.

1. **Naaksidente si Juan sa Katipunan Avenue.**
   Juan met (with) an accident at Katipunan Avenue.
2. **Nabangga ang kotse ni Juan bandang alas-diyes ng umaga.**
   Juan's car got hit at around ten o'clock in the morning.
3. **Nasa ospital si Juan.**
   Juan is in the hospital.
4. **Nasawi ang drayber ng isang kotse.**
   The driver of the other car passed on.
5. **Kinapanayam siya ng reporter.**
   The reporter interviewed him/her.

Dagdag Na Bokabolaryo

Study the following words. Some of them were used in the dialogue you just read and some of them will be useful when you make your own sentences for your dialogues.

Nabundol	*Got hit, person or vehicle, two or more vehicles*
Nasagasaan	*Person was run over by a vehicle*
Dinukot	*Was abducted*
Nasunog	*Burned*
Namatay	*Died*
Malubha	*Serious condition*
Nasugatan	*Got injured*
Naputol ang paa	*Foot got cut*

Pagsasanay

Read the following brief news items. Then ask and answer questions about the following incidents.

Balita 1

Nabundol ang isang bata ng isang trak kahapon nang alas-diyes ng gabi. Dinala ang bata sa ospital. Malubha ang bata.

Mga Tanong at Sagot

1. TANONG : _____?
   SAGOT   : _____.

2. TANONG : _____?
   SAGOT   : _____.

3. TANONG : _____?
   SAGOT   : _____.

4. TANONG : _____?
   SAGOT   : _____.

5. TANONG : _____?
   SAGOT   : _____.

Balita 2

Dinukot ang dalawang estudyante sa Bulacan noong Linggo. Hindi sila makita. Umiiyak ang mga nanay nila nang kinapanayam ng reporter.

Mga Tanong at Sagot

1. TANONG : _____?
   SAGOT   : _____.

2. TANONG : _____?
   SAGOT   : _____.

3. TANONG : _____?
   SAGOT   : _____.

4. TANONG : _____?
   SAGOT   : _____.

5. TANONG : _____?
   SAGOT   : _____.

Balita 3

Nagkaroon ng sunog sa U.P. Village kaninang alas-dos ng umaga. Dalawa ang nasawi. Dalawampung bahay ang nasunog dahil nahuli ang mga bumbero.

Mga Tanong at Sagot

1. TANONG : _____?
   SAGOT   : _____.

2. TANONG : _____?
   SAGOT   : _____.

3. TANONG : _____?
   SAGOT   : _____.

4. TANONG : _____?
   SAGOT   : _____.

5. TANONG : _____?
   SAGOT   : _____.

★ Gawain

Read the brief news items again. Then, create a dialogue narrating the incident. Classroom learners can work in pairs or groups while individual learners should write the dialogue.

Mga Tala Sa Kultura

Among the first newspapers published in the Philippines were *La Estrella* (founded October 14, 1896; became a daily on February 1, 1947), *Diario de Manila* (1848–1899), *El Catolico Filipino* (from February 1, 1862), *El Porvenir Filipino* (from 1865), *Libertas* (1899–1918), and *Diariong Tagalog* (from 1882). Most of these newspapers were published in Spanish, the language of the privileged class during this period. The clout of the Catholic Church is also reflected in the publication of two religious newspapers.

However, newspapers also became venues for writers to advocate for reform and revolution. In Spain, student patriots such as Marcelo H. del Pilar, Graciano Lopez Jaena, and Jose Rizal published the paper *La Solidaridad* (1899–1895). In Manila, other newspapers considered revolutionary were *La Independencia, La Republica Filipinas, La Revolucion, El Renacimiento, La Vanguardia,* and *Kalayaan* (Freedom), the newspaper of the revolutionary organization the Katipunan.

At the turn of the 20th century, with the colonization of the Philippines by the United States, two of these newspapers, *El Renacimiento* and *Muling Pagsilang*, featured editorials and essays, the most famous of which is "**Aves de Rapiña**" ("Birds of Prey"), opposing American imperialism. An interesting form also introduced during this period was the **dagli**, considered to be the forerunner of the short story. Some of the **dagli** published called for independence or criticized the increasing colonial way of thinking of the Filipinos.

Early English-language newspapers were the *Manila Times* (founded 1898), the *Manila Daily Bulletin* (founded 1900), and the *Philippines Herald* (formerly Cable-news American but renamed when acquired by Filipinos). Both the *Manila Times* and the *Bulletin* continue to be published today.

During Martial Law, a period of strict censorship, several fearless publishers dared to use print media to criticize the regime. Among the newspapers that people turned to for news were *Malaya* and *Mr. and Ms. Special Edition*. There were also underground newspapers such as *Ang Bayan* (The Country/People) and *Liberation*.

While English was the language primarily used by most newspapers and Filipino/Tagalog was considered to be the language of tabloids, two notable endeavors are *Diyaryo Filipino*, the first broadsheet in Filipino published in the 1990s with National Artist Virgilio Almario as its publisher, and, more recently, *Pinoy Weekly,* an online newspaper in Filipino, which not only publishes news articles, columns, and literature, but also features short videos.

  Pagbabasa

Read the following authentic news item from the online Filipino-language newspaper *Pinoy Weekly*, and then answer the questions that follow. Study the following words before reading the story. You have learned some of the words in earlier lessons; they are listed here for you to review. You can also refer to the glossary at the back of the book.

Pinaiimbistigahan	*Having investigated*
Militante	*Militant*
Umano	*Alleged*

Paglabag	*Violation*
Soberanya	*Sovereignty*
Inaahon	*Brought to the surface*
Erya	*Area*
Nananawagan	*Calling to*
Gumagala	*Roaming around*
Puwersang militar	*Military forces*
Binatikos	*Criticized*
Di-awtorisado	*Unauthorized*
Pahayag	*Statement*
Permiso	*Permission*
Ipinagtataka	*Surprised*
Ibasura	*Throw out to the garbage bin*

Banggaan ng Submarinong Tsino at Barko ng US Navy, pinaiimbestigahan

ni Ilang-ilang Quijano
Pinoy Weekly, *Ika-8 ng Hunyo 2009*

Pinaiimbestigahan ng isang militanteng grupo at isang senador ang banggaan kamakailan ng isang submarinong Instik at barko ng US sa territorial waters ng Pilipinas dahil sa umano'y paglabag ng mga dayuhan sa soberanya ng bansa.

Noong Hunyo 12, nagbanggaan ang USS John McCain at isang submarinong Instik malapit sa Subic Bay. Bumangga ang submarino sa underwater sonar array, kagamitan para sa underwater surveillance, na iniaahon ng destroyer na USS John McCain.

"Ano ang ginagawa ng US warship sa erya? Gayundin ang submarinong Instik? Nananawagan kami kay Pangulong Arroyo na ipatawag ang mga opisyal ng gobyerno US at Tsina para ipaliwanag kung bakit gumagala ang kanilang mga puwersang militar sa ating karagatan," sabi ni Antonio Tinio, tagapangulo ng Alliance of Concerned Teachers (ACT).

Binatikos ni Tinio ang pagiging tahimik ni Arroyo sa nasabing insidente na umano'y isang "paglabag sa soberanya ng bansa." Sa ilalim ng Konstitusyong 1987, ipinagbabawal ang di-awtorisadong presensiya ng mga dayuhang tropang militar.

Sa isang pahayag, sinabi ni Lt. Col. Edgar Arevalo, tagapagsalita ng Philippine Navy, na naganap ang banggaan sa international waters at hindi sa teritoryo ng bansa.

Pero ayon kay Tinio, "tangkang pagtatakip sa insidente" ang ganitong pahayag ni Arevalo.

Samantala, naniniwala si Sen. Rodolfo Biazon na kailangang imbestigahan kung may nilabag na batas ang mga dayuhan sa pagpasok sa bansa ng kanilang mga sasakyang pandigma.

"Kung lumahok ang USS John McCain sa Balikatan Exercises, at pumunta sa Subic para mag-refuel, kailangan nito ng permiso para makapasok at makalabas ng Philippine waters," sabi ng senador.

Ipinagtataka ni Biazon kung bakit hindi alam ng Philippine Navy na kalahok ang barkong pandigma sa Balikatan Exercises o ehersisyong militar sa pagitan ng mga tropang Pilipino at Amerikano.

Samantala, muli namang nanawagan ang ACT na ibasura ang Visiting Forces Agreement na pumapayag sa pagpasok ng mga tropang Amerikano sa bansa.

1. Ano-ano ang mga nagbanggaan?
2. Ano ang sinabi ni Antonio Tinio?
3. Sino ang tagapagsalita ng Philippine Navy?
4. Ano ang sinabi ng tagapagsalita ng Philippine Navy?
5. Ano ang pangalan ng ehersisyong militar sa Pilipinas?
6. Anong grupo ang nanawagan tungkol sa Visiting Forces Agreeement?

✏ Pagsusulat

Write a brief news item.

🚩 Paglalagom

In **Aralin 31**, you have:
1. Studied words and phrases that can help you in narrating an incident,
2. Practiced reading a news item.

You should now be able to:
1. Read news items in Filipino with the aid of a dictionary for more difficult words.
2. Narrate an incident.

Pangangatwiran (Reasoning)

  Diyalogo: Hindi Ako Papayag Diyan!
(I can't agree to that!)

Read the dialogue below. After completing this chapter, practice this dialogue using your own information.

ANAK   : **Nanay, puwede ho ba akong pumunta sa Davao?**
Mom, can I go to Davao?

NANAY : **Aba, hindi puwede. Delikado sa Mindanao.**
Of course not. Mindanao is dangerous.

ANAK   : **Hindi naman lahat ng lugar sa Mindanao ay delikado.**
But not all the places in Mindanao are dangerous.

NANAY : **Baka makidnap ka.**
You might get kidnapped.

ANAK   : **Mag-iingat ho ako.**
I will be careful.

NANAY : **Kahit na. May travel advisory na hindi dapat magbiyahe ang mga Amerikano sa Pilipinas.**
Even so. There is a travel advisory that Americans should not travel to the Philippines.

ANAK : **Pero mukha naman ho akong Pilipino.**
But I look like a Filipino.
NANAY : **Naku, wala ka namang gagawin sa Davao.**
But you will not be doing anything in Davao.
ANAK : **Gusto ko hong pumunta sa Pearl Farm.**
I want to go to Pearl Farm.
NANAY : **Sa Boracay ka na lang pumunta. Maganda rin ang dagat doon.**
Just go to Boracay. The beach is also beautiful there.

  ## Bokabolaryo

Study the following words. Some of them were used in the dialogue you just read and some of them will be useful when you make your own sentences for your dialogues.

Delikado	*Dangerous*
Makidnap	*To be kidnapped*
Mag-iingat	*Be careful*
Mukhang Pilipino	*Looks like a Filipino*

Mga Halimbawang Pangungusap

Practice saying these sentences aloud, to get a feel for how this chapter's vocabulary and grammar work in Filipino.

1. **Gustong pumunta ng anak sa Davao.**   *The son/daughter wants to go to Davao.*
2. **Ayaw ng nanay na pumunta ang**   *The mother does not want her son/*
   anak sa Davao.   *daughter to go to Davao.*
3. **Delikado sa Mindanao.**   *It is dangerous in Mindanao.*

★ Gawain 1

Study the dialogue you have just read. Practice using Filipino in giving and responding to arguments.

Outline the son/daughter's arguments.
1.
2.
3.
4.
5.

Outline the mother's arguments.

1.

2.

3.

4.

★ Gawain 2

Choose a situation. List your arguments. Engage a classmate in a role-play. Independent learners should write the dialogue of the argument.

Sitwasyon 1
Gusto ng anak na lumipat ng kurso mula Business Administration tungo sa Creative Writing.

Mga Argumento
1.

2.

3.

Sitwasyon 2
Gusto mong sumama ng rally laban sa giyera. Ayaw sumama ng iyong kaklase.

Mga Argumento
1.

2.

3.

Sitwasyon 3
Gusto mong huminto ng pag-aaral. Ayaw pumayag ng tatay mo.

Mga Tala Sa Kultura

Debate using poetry is a tradition in the Philippines. Especially popular during the American colonial period (1899–1945) was the **balagtasan**, or verbal joust. The **balagtasan** draws inspiration from the **duplo**, a traditional game played during funeral wakes. In the **duplo**, the "hari" (king) pretends to be looking for a lost bird, and blames a player (either a **belyako** or a **belyaka**), who in turn defends himself or in some cases, defends the woman (**belyaka**) accused.

At the height of its popularity, however, the **balagtasan** could be likened to an entertainment (similar to that of a stage play), and its participating poets were as popular as movie stars. The **balagtasan** was said to have been conceptualized on March 28, 1924 by a group called Kapulungang Balagtas to honor Francisco Balagtas (also known as Francisco Baltazar) in whose honor the verbal joust was named.

For several decades, the **balagtasan** continued to be popular, with topics mirroring the concerns of the time, such as independence, capitalism, tradition, and coalitions; or symbols which may be read as allegories (gold and metal; pen and sword; star and sun). It also inspired similar jousts in other languages in other parts of the country such as the **bukanegan** in Ilocos (honoring poet Pedro Bukaneg).

Although the popularity of the **balagtasan** has waned because of film, television, and other forms of entertainment, recently **balagtasan** has been used to articulate contemporary issues.

For further reading on the **balagtasan**, the best resource is Leo Zafra's book *Kasaysayan at Antolohiya ng Balagtasan* (History and Anthology of the Balagtasan) published by the Ateneo de Manila University Press in 1999. The above data on the history of the **balagtasan** comes from Zafra's book.

 ## Pagbabasa

Read the following opinion column. Then, answer the questions that follow. Study the following words before reading the essay. You have learned some of the words in earlier lessons; they are listed here for you to review. You can also refer to the glossary at the back of the book.

Kaliligo	*Just finished bathing*
Nanlalata	*Feeling weak*
Sinisisi	*Blaming*
Anti-bata	*Against children*
Isinasaad	*Implied*
Katawagan	*Name*
Pamaktol-maktol	*Exaggerated way of showing that one feels bad*
Paslit	*Child*
Pagsasaalang-alang	*Taking into consideration*
Bukana	*Front*
Pangkalahatan	*General*
Dumaranas	*Experiencing*
Salarin	*Murderer*
Imbis	*Instead*
Nakabatay	*Based on*
Pinapalutang	*Floating*
Pag-angkat	*Export*
Sinasaad	*Said*

Kaakibat	*Together*
Kawalan-kumpiyansa	*Lack of confidence*
Sagrado	*Sacred*
Sikreto	*Secret*
Nagpapaypay	*Fanning*
Nagpopolitisa	*Politicizing*

El Niño

ni Rolando Tolentino
Pinoy Weekly, *March 13, 2010*

Enero pa lang, tag-init na. Kaliligo pa lang, pinagpapawisan na. Iniisip pa lang kailangang bumiyahe sa labas, nanlalata na. Lahat ng ito ay sinisisi sa el niño. Na ipinagtataka ko dahil anti-bata ang isinasaad ng katawagan sa penomenon. Pamaktol-maktol daw kaya parang brat na lalakeng paslit.

Tulad ng pagsasaalang-alang sa paslit bilang esensyal na spoiled brat, kinakasangkapan din ang el nino bilang dahilan ng lahat ng kasalukuyang krisis. Madaling nakakita ng politikal na bukana si Gloria Arroyo.

Ang el niño ang salarin kung bakit may krisis sa enerhiya ang bansa, na parang ang pangkalahatang supply ng power ay nakabatay lamang sa hydro dam. At dahil may krisis sa bansa—sa partikular, sa Mindanao na dumaranas na ng anim na oras na blackout—muli na namang pinapalutang ang idea ng emergency power ni Arroyo.

Tulad ng nauna sa kanya, si Arroyo ay wala na namang masterplan para sa enerhiya, kasama ang paghahanap ng sustainable sources, tulad ng araw, hangin, at maging alon ng dagat. Imbis na ito ang tunguhin, ang direksyon ay pagsuporta sa planong coal plants, na ang panggagalingan ay mula sa pag-angkat ng batong uling sa Tsina, at ang muling pagbuhay sa nuclear, sa partikular ang Bataan nuclear power plant.

Ang el niño at ang pagsisimula ng power shortage sa Metro Manila at Luzon ay nagiging susi rin sa failure ng eleksyon sa Mayo 2010. Sa kauna-unahang pagkakataon, automated ang bilangan sa eleksyon. Ayon sa Comelec, mayroong battery life ang makinang bibilang na 16 na oras, at 11 oras lang ang laan sa pagboto.

Ang hindi sinasaad ay ang kulturang kaakibat ng blackouts, lalo na sa panahon, sa mismong araw, at matapos ang eleksyon. May pangkalahatang pakiwari ng agam-agam sa napakahalagang araw ng pagboto. At hindi nakakatulong ang kawalan-kumpiyansa ng mamamayan sa pagiging sagrado at sikreto ng kanilang balota at karapatang bumoto kung may malawakang blackout.

Ang epekto sa minimum, may resulta pero hindi lubos na katanggap-tanggap dahil sa konteksto ng pagkapanalo. Parating kabuntot ang katanungan at isyu hinggil sa pagmamaniobra at pandaraya. Sa maximum, ang "no el" (no elections) at maging failure of elections na scenarios.

No elections dahil hindi lubos na nakahanda ang infrastruktura at personnel para sa automated voting at counting. At wala rin namang malinaw na plano sa rekurso para sa balik manual na eleksyon. Failure of elections naman kapag aktwal na may pagbotong naganap, pero malawakan ang kondisyon para makwestiyon ang ehersisyo sa liberal na demokrasya.

Sa dalawang scenarios, si Arroyo lang naman ang makikinabang. Mas tiyak ang katig ng kanyang namamayaning burukrasya para sa mga scenario na maaring maganap. At ito ang rekurso ni Arroyo sa pagpolitisa sa phenomenon ng el nino: gawing lubhang mainit ang panahon at kondisyon ng eleksyon, pero gawin din, tulad ng el nino, na wala nang magagawa ang mga tao hinggil dito.

Sa kapaligiran ng U.P. at iba pang lugar, tuyot na ang damuhan. Matatamlay ang halaman. Ngayon ay may lamig pa sa umaga pero sa kalakhan ng araw, di lamang naglalaho ito, wala pang rekurso sa ibang maaliwalas na espasyo maliban sa malls at aircon na lugar. Naisip ko tuloy na ang disenyo ng mga gusali sa bansa ay talagang makakanluranin. Kailangan ng aircon para magkaroon ng katiwasayan sa mainit na temperatura.

Kapag nagbro-brownout, madilim at mainit ang loob. Walang klase, walang opisina. At kahit walang magagawa, hindi matiwasay ang pakiramdam. Tahimik na nakakaalarmang magbilang ng sandali. Madalas tumingin sa relo habang nagpapaypay kahit hindi naman mapapabilis ang pagtapos sa brownout.

Enero pa lang at mainit na. At ang tanging maagang nakikinabang sa el niño ay ang pangulong nagpopolitisa nito.

✏ Pagsusulat

Write an editorial on an issue that you care about.

🚩 Paglalagom

In **Aralin 32**, you have:
1. Learned words and phrases you can use in giving your opinions,
2. Practiced reading an editorial in Filipino.

You should now be able to:
1. Express your ideas and opinions.
2. Give arguments on a particular subject.

Speaking in Filipino: Notes on the Phonetic Features of the Language

How do we speak Filipino? To this, I respond with the most basic of responses: **"Ang bigkas ang siyang baybay, at ang baybay ang siyang bigkas."** Speak it the way it is spelled and spell it the way you speak it.

Here we'll go over some general notes about the phonetics of the language, based on the writings of P/Filipino linguists, then we'll explore guidelines from a popular expert, and finally, we'll review practical tips that I have used when guiding my students in the Filipino-language classroom.

General Notes[1]

Filipino is not a tonal language. However, a word may change its meaning because of the change in stress.

It is, however, a phonetic language.

To better understand the consonant phonemes, below is a useful chart from Schachter 1972:

	Labial	Labiodental	Dental	Alveolar	Palatal	Velar	Glottal
Stop: Voiceless	p		l			k	p
Stop: Voiced	b		d			g	
Nasal (Voiced)	m		n			n	h
Fricative (Voiceless)		(f)		s			
Affricate (Voiceless)				ts			
Lateral (Voiced)				l			

---

1. The discussion on phonemes comes from Cecilio Lopez's 1941 work *A Manual of the Philippine National Language* upon which his work *The Structure of Tagalog* (1980) was based; and from Schachter, 1972.

    Lopez lists 21 segmental phonemes and one-supra-segmental phonemic contract. Of these, there are fourteen consonants, five vowels, and two vowels.

    According to Schachter 1972, the five vowel phonemes are: the high-vowel phonemes /i/ and /u/; the mid-vowel phonemes /e/ and /o/ and one vowel phoneme with a range from mid to low /a/. From the point of view of tongue frontness, there are two front-vowel phonemes, /i/ and /e/ (characterized by spread lips), one central-vowel phoneme, /a/ (neutral lip position), and two back-vowel phonemes, /o/ and /u/ (rounded lips).

Tap or Trill (Voiced)				r			
Glide (Voiced)					y	w	

There are no aspirated sounds in Filipino.

There are five Tagalog diphthongs: **iw** (front); **ay, aw** (center); and **oy, uy** (back). Here are some examples of the diphthongs:

ay	**bahay**	*house*
aw	**galaw**	*move*
iw	**giliw**	*loved one*
oy	**tuloy**	*continue*
uy	**kasuy**	*cashew*

Stresses and Accents[2]

There are five principal stresses and three principal accents in Tagalog/Filipino. There are:

1. Penultimate stress or **diing malumay**. The stress is on the syllable before the last.
2. Penultimate stress and glottal or **diing malumi**. The stress is either on the penultimate syllable, or the first syllable in words with only two syllables. The vowel at the end is given a glottal sound, produced by the abrupt close of the throat. This is shown through a grave accent mark on the second vowel, for example, **awà** (pity), leading students (when reading old texts) to sometimes be confused, and think that the accent is on the last syllable.
3. Acute stress or **diing mabilis**. The stress is on the last syllable. In old texts, the acute or **pahilis** accent is used, for example, **labás** (outside).
4. Acute glottal or **diing maragsa**. The emphasis is on the last syllable with the glottal sound. In old texts, the circumflex or **pakupya** accent is used, for example, **tuyô** (dry).
5. Antepenultimate acute stress or **diing mariin**. This is a heavy stress given to a syllable before the penultimate syllable. The acute accent is used. Note that there may exist another stress in the word. An example is **lílima** (only five).

Aspillera 1980 also offers the following pronunciation reminders:
1. A difference in stress may cause a change in the meaning of the word;
2. With the addition of a ligature or suffix, the final glottal stop is lost;
3. Monosyllabic words take the stress of the preceding word;
4. To avoid mispronunciation, a glottal stop between a vowel and a consonant is represented by a hyphen.

---

2. The discussion on stresses and accents derives from Alejandro 1947 and Aspillera 1980.

Practical Notes

The following notes are from my experience in the language-learning classroom.

1. For native speakers in English, the first step is to forget about long vowel sounds. There are no long vowel sounds in Filipino.

2. There is also the tendency for some learners to end a sentence with a rising intonation. Be careful of this, as this sounds like you are asking a question. Unless you are asking a question, the intonation should fall—not rise—at the end of a sentence.

3. When you see two vowels together, bear in mind that they are not pronounced as one vowel. In English, when we see o and i together, as in "join," we know it is a one-syllable word, and we will create the sound "oi." In Filipino, if we see **baon**, **ao** will not create a sound similar to "aw." This word will have two syllables and will be pronounced as **ba-on**.

4. Do not be confused when you hear native speakers pronounce the word **lalaki** (man) as sometimes with an **i**, and sometimes with an **e** sounding like "**lalake**." In the ancient Tagalog script called **babayin**, the letters **i** and **e** shared only one symbol. Both pronunciations are acceptable.

5. Similarly, do not be confused when you hear native speakers shift when pronouncing **o** and **u**. An example is **puso**, which can sometimes be pronounced "**pusu**."

6. Do not extend the sound of the vowel. For example, when saying "**Kumusta ka?**" (How are you?), do not say "**Kumusta kaaaaaaa?**" A short **a** is a short **a**!

Finally, loosen up. Do not be afraid to speak Filipino. Unlike other languages where the exact and correct pronunciation is of paramount importance, no one will really mind if you make a few mistakes here and there. Obviously, there is a need to speak the language correctly. However, Filipinos will certainly appreciate you speaking the language even if you do make mistakes.

Thus, just speak it!

Works Cited:

Alejandro, Rufino. *A Handbook of Tagalog Grammar.* Manila: University Book Supply 1947.
Aspillera, Paraluman. *Basic Tagalog.* Manila: Rarebook Enterprises 1980.
Lopez, Cecilio. *Three Articles on Tagalog.* Quezon City: Archives of Philippine Languages and Dialects and the Philippine Linguistics Circle 1980.
Schachter, Paul and Fe Otanes. *Tagalog Reference Grammar.* Berkeley, Los Angeles, London: University of California Press 1972.

Why Filipino and Not Pilipino?
A Brief History of Making a Language the National Language

According to the 1987 constitution Article XIV, Section 6: "The national language of the Philippines is Filipino. As it evolves, it shall be further developed and enriched on the basis of existing Philippine and other languages."

The concept of an "evolving language" and consequently, an "evolving script," however, needs further explanation. The history of the Filipino language is strongly linked to the history of colonization, the assertion of independence and sovereignty, and the need to find a unifying language for the Philippines's around sixty ethnolinguistic groups.

The first constitution that provided for a national language was the 1935 constitution, which was promulgated during American colonial rule (1899–1945). Article XIV, Section 3 reads: "The Congress shall take steps toward the development and adoption of a common national language based on one of the existing native languages. Unless otherwise provided by law, English and Spanish shall continue as official languages."

Two years later, in 1937, the Surian ng Wikang Pambansa (Institute of National Language) was established. The Institute then decided to make Tagalog the basis of the national language on the following grounds:[1] first, Tagalog is widely spoken and is the language most understood in all the regions of the Philippines; second; it is not divided into smaller, separate languages as Visayan is; third, its literary tradition is the richest and the most developed and extensive; fourth, Tagalog has always been the language of Manila, and the political and economic capital of the Philippines under both Spanish and American rulers; and fifth, Tagalog is the language of the revolution and the Katipunan—two very important incidents in Philippine history. This then resulted in the standardization of the language, a new orthography, and guidelines for Tagalog grammar studied in schools. However, it was only in 1959 that a Department of Education Memorandum specified for the teaching of a national language called Pilipino.

The 1973 constitution was cognizant of both terms "Pilipino" and "Filipino." Article XV (General Provisions), Section 3, No. 1 states that: "The Constitution shall be officially promulgated in English and in Pilipino, and translated into each dialect spoken by over fifty thousand people, and into Spanish and Arabic." Section 3, no. 1 also uses the term "Pilipino": "Until otherwise provided by law, English and Pilipino shall be the official languages."

However, Section 3, No. 2 recognizes the future use of the term "Filipino." It says: "The National Assembly shall take steps towards the development and formal adoption of a common national language known as Filipino."

---

1. These reasons can be seen in Romualdez 1938 and Aspillera 1980.

This becomes reality through the 1987 constitution.[2] Article XIV: Education, Science and Technology, Arts, Culture, and Sports, Section 6, states as quoted earlier: "The national language of the Philippines is Filipino. As it evolves, it shall be further developed and enriched on the basis of existing Philippine and other languages."

What essentially were the changes brought about by the 1935, 1973 and 1987 constitutions? First, we should note that these constitutions were made following political change. In 1935, it signalled the establishment of the Commonwealth government. In 1973, the constitution "legitimized" Martial rule and paved way for the "New Society" and the authoritarian rule of President Ferdinand Marcos. In 1987, the constitution was again changed following the People Power revolt of 1986, the flight of Marcos to Hawaii, and the establishment of the revolutionary government of Corazon Aquino.

The rewriting of the constitutions paved the way for Filipino language experts and nationalists to lobby for a language that would be more accessible to the masses; for changes in the orthography; for legislation that would provide for institutes working in the interests of the national language; and for increased assertion of sovereignty. For example, it was important for many to make Pilipino (as it was then called) the "official language" because it was only then that this language could be used in court or in official documents. Otherwise, the bizarre system of having translators present in court (translating into English what a witness says in Filipino) would continue. Official documents pertaining to land ownership, for example, would continue to be written in English, thus disenfranchising those who knew only Tagalog/Pilipino/Filipino.

Similarly, in 1987 teachers, especially from the University of the Philippines, lobbied to introduce more letters to the Pilipino/Filipino alphabet because this would then signal the inclusion into Filipino of the letters of the Philippines' other languages.

Thus, the "history of the language" is also the history of a country and its people.

---

2. The 1973 Constitution is the constitution of Martial Law, proclaimed by President Ferdinand Marcos on September 21, 1972. The 1987 Constitution, on the other hand, is the constitution drafted by the constitutional commission created by the revolutionary government of Corazon Aquino. Aquino came to power in February 1986 after what is now known as the peaceful "Edsa revolt" that resulted in the exile of President Marcos. It is ironic that the "vision" of the constitution of the "dictatorship" was realized in the constitution of the revolt that toppled it.

A Culture through Its Words: Vocabulary Notes

As a "developing" language which seeks to integrate more words from other languages, Filipino vocabulary is constantly increasing. Two sourcebooks published by Sangfil or Samahang Filipino (Filipino Society) are therefore useful because of the publication of articles on the following: new vocabulary based on the experience of teachers from various disciplines (math, science, social studies) as they use Filipino as a medium of instruction; Filipino language planning; language policies; language and cultural institutions such as organizations and mass media; and language and issues such as globalization. The two sourcebooks published by Sangfil are *Ang Wikang Filipino sa Loob at Labas ng Akademya't Bansa* (The Filipino Language Within and Outside the Academe and the Nation) edited by Benilda Santos in 2003; and *Filipino at Pagpaplanong Pangwika* (Filipino and Language Planning), edited by Pamela Constantino in 2005.

Nuances in the Vocabulary
Here are some nuances in the vocabulary:
1. Lack of gendered pronouns.
   Pronouns are not gendered in Filipino. **Siya/niya/kanya** equivalent to his/her/him/ his/her/hers, can both be used to represent both the masculine and the feminine.

2. No inanimate third-person pronoun.
   Unless referring to pets, Filipino has no third-person pronoun.

3. The verb "to be."
   The Filipino word **ay** corresponds to the verb "to be" although it can be used for both singular and plural nouns. However, since the most common word order in Filipino is to put the predicate before the subject, the word **ay** is then skipped.

Common Terms and Concepts
Here are some common terms and concepts in Filipino that enable us to understand the language and the culture better.
1. The pronoun **kita**.
   The pronoun **kita**, as mentioned earlier, combines the meanings of a first-person-singular **ng** form and a second person singular **ang** form.
   EXAMPLE: **Pahihiramin kita ng libro.**
   I will lend you a book.
   (Literally, Will lend I you *marker* book.)

2. Words that refer to love.

    Filipino has many terms that refer to the verb "to love," including **minamahal**, **iniibig**, **sinisinta**, **tinatangi**, **pinipintuho**, **ginigiliw**, and **iniirog**. However, we should be careful especially with interchanging the words **minamahal** and **iniibig**. We use the term **minamahal** for parents, children, pets, work, etc. However, the term **iniibig** is used solely for the person/partner we love in a romantic way. Similarly, **sinisinta** and **iniirog** are also used in a romantic manner.

    EXAMPLES: **Mahal ko ang trabaho ko.**

    I love my work.

    (Literally, Love I *marker* work my.)

    Iniibig ko ang asawa ko.

    I love my husband.

    (Literally, Love I *marker* husband/wife my.)

    The only exception is love for country. We can say, **Iniibig ko ang Pilipinas.** (*I love the Philippines.*)

3. The difference between "thinking" and "expressing an opinion."

    The word "think," meaning "to ponder," corresponds to the Filipino word **iniisip**. To express an opinion, we use the Filipino words **sa akala ko**, or **tila**.

    EXAMPLES: **Iniisip ko ang mga programang pang-akademiko ng Kolehiyo.**

    I am thinking of the academic programs of the College.

    (Literally, Thinking I *marker plural marker* programs academic *marker* College.)

    Tila babagyo.

    I think it will rain.

    (Literally, I think will rain.)

4. Going, coming, and going home.

    In English, "to go" can be used both to mean, "to leave for a place or destination," and before a verb. In Filipino, the former is expressed with the word **punta**, while the latter is not used at all.

    EXAMPLES: **Pupunta siya sa unibersidad.**

    He/she will go to the university.

    (Literally, Will go he/she *marker* university.)

    Kakain ako mamaya.

    I am going to eat later.

    (Literally, Will eat I later.)

    Also, in Filipino, there is a specific word for going home, **uwi**: **Uuwi ako**. (*I am going home.*)

5. Culture-specific and "experience-specific" words

Some of the Filipino words are culture-specific and therefore have no equivalent in the English language. Moreover, there are words in English which have changed meaning, in their usage in Filipino. Here are some examples:

- **Pakikipag-kapwa-tao**, establishing and maintaining good personal relations with other people, by acts of kindness and service;
- **Ate** and **Kuya**, Elder sister and Elder brother; also, **Manang**, **Manong** (Elder sister/brother). There are many other words that connote relationships. For example, **Tiyo** and **Tiya** can mean not only one's uncle and aunt but also elderly people in the community;
- **Lambing**; **malambing**. A person described to be **malambing** is someone who shows his/her affection. However, one can describe the act of asking for a favor, or even occasional crankiness, as **paglalambing** (noun form).
- **Bayan**, a word that refers to all of the following: town, country, and people.
- **Sinalvage**, the word "salvage" used in the past form with the suffix **-in**, referring to a person summarily executed by the military.
- **Kasama** meaning "companion," used in the past few decades to mean "comrade," true especially for activist subculture.
- **Pagyao**. In Filipino, **yao** means both "to leave" and "to pass on," thus indicating an indigenous belief in the afterlife.

Improving Your Vocabulary

How can a learner improve his/her vocabulary? Here are a few helpful tips in improving your vocabulary:

1. Always try to know the root word. Remember that Filipino has a complex system of affixes. If you know for example the word **sayaw** (dance) you can guess that **sumasayaw** is a verb and that **sayawan** is a "dance" (an event of dancing).
2. It helps to know the Spanish and English influences in the language. For example, **awit** (song) is an indigenous term, but most people use **kanta** (from the Spanish word). Most technological devices and appliances retain their original word in English, and can also be spelled as such; for example, computer, refrigerator, microwave.
3. Remember to match words. For example, say **alas-singko** and **ika-lima ng hapon** (five o'clock). Do not say **alas-lima** or **ika-singko**.
4. Another common mistake is to say **dos piso** and **dalawang pesos**. When using the Spanish-derived word **dos** use **pesos**, and with the indigenous Tagalog word **dalawa** use **piso**.
5. Try to seek out and read authentic texts, even if your level is very elementary. Comic books, children's stories, and even online items can be good simple texts.
6. Group words together: for example, words related to the family, the house, the hospital.
7. Make writing a regular practice. This way you can accumulate a lot of "learner-need vocabulary."

Understanding "Margie": The Filipino Heritage Learner[1]

Who is the heritage learner (HL)? In my opinion, almost all heritage learners are "activists" in the broadest sense of the world.

Filipino American students see language learning as the first step towards understanding their roots, and according to Leny Strobel, as a step towards "decolonization." Thus, there are many different kinds of Filipino American activists—those involved in community issues such as veteran, health care, and labor rights; those who seek to learn about identity and are advocates of Filipino, Philippine and Filipino American studies; those who mentor Filipino American children and inspire them to go to college; those who are engaged in medical missions; those who participate in relief efforts when disaster strikes; those who participate in "projects" such as the building of houses through organizations like Gawad Kalinga and envision their work as charity; and finally, the activists involved in the national democratic movement in the Philippines.

Believing in the continuing neo-colonial relationship of the United States and the need for organized action, many of these Filipino American heritage learners go back to the Philippines to immerse themselves in urban and rural communities. Most of them learn Filipino precisely for this purpose—to better communicate with Filipinos who do not or hardly speak English, mainly peasants and workers in the Philippines.

What are their learning processes? What words are in their vocabulary as signified by their written and recorded texts? How is the learning process affected by their immersion in underprivileged communities in the Philippines? What are the dynamics between language acquisition and politics?

My research on language acquisition is informed by the study of Agnes He. Professsor He's paper "Heritage Language Across the Life Span" was presented in June 2009 at the Third Heritage Language Summer Institute. In her paper, she talks about Jason, a Chinese heritage learner. She presents several assumptions from a language socialization and a conversation analytic perspective:

The symbiosis of language and identity.
Language as a resource for shaping, maintaining and transforming identity.
HL acquisition and HL literacy acquisition processes as identity processes.
Ordinary, everyday interaction as the primary locus for language and cultural development.

---

1. This Appendix is excerpted from two larger projects: my study on Filipino American heritage learners, and on the intersections of language, literature, and diaspora nationalisms. For further information and insights on these topics, please refer to my complete essay "Understanding 'Margie': Notes on the 'Committed' Heritage Learner," available at the *Tagalog for Beginners* page at www.tuttlepublishing.com.

Professor He then traces Jason's experience as a CHL learner.

Here I attempt to trace a similar life span of learning—the language acquisition experience of the activist Filipino Heritage Learner (FHL).

Our first question: What do FHL learners know? Drawing from He's framework, I ask the below to ascertain a heritage learner's proficiency:

Phonology: Do they have Filipino pronunciation? How are they influenced by the other languages spoken at home?

Morphology: Do they understand how Filipino words are formed, especially the various affixes?

Syntax: Is grammar conscious to the FHL? Is their spoken speech different from their written texts?

Pragmatics: To what extent are they aware of different speech styles, genres, speech acts, speech events and their social distributions and functions?

For second-language learners, everything needs to be taught; however, it is more difficult to define the proficiency level of the FHL without a proficiency test.

Through observations, three in-depth interviews and a focused group discussion, I have come up with a composite character whom I will call Margarita Louella, with the nickname Margie. Why was she named Margarita Louella? Well, she was born in 1973, the year that Margarita Moran was crowned Miss Universe. Her mother's name is Lourdes and her father's name is Joel, thus the name Louella.

In our attempt to understand the activist FHL, let us turn to Margie Louella, our composite character based on my interviews with six FHL learners.

Margie was born in the U.S. She grew up in either a nuclear household with parents and siblings or in a single-parent household. Her mother speaks to her grandmother in Visayan, her parents speak to each other in Filipino, but they speak to Margie in English and the code-switching Taglish (or Tagalog English). There are three possible reasons for this use of Taglish: the neo-colonial relationship between the U.S. and the Philippines resulting in a colonial way of thinking among many Filipinos; the hegemony of the English language in the Philippines with language underlining disparities in class and status; and discrimination in the site of migration because of Filipino accents that mark the person's ethnic identity and otherness.

At four, Margie's mother would speak to her saying, "Let **ninang** make **subo** you." **Ninang** is the Filipino word for "godmother" and **subo**, the verb for "hand-feed," is made English by attaching the English verb "make." Her mother Lourdes code-switches because of the following: she is a product of bilingual education; as a child, she was fined for speaking Filipino in school; and in speech classes, she had to repeat over and over "This is an apple. This is an apple..." to get the perfect American accent.

In contrast, Margie's father struggled with the language because he attended a public school in Cagayan twelve hours from Manila. He can read and write, but hesitates when he speaks because he is afraid of pronouncing words incorrectly. When Margie was growing up, he took English classes. One time, he got angry at Margie's brother and said, "**Lintik kang bata ka...**" Years later, Margie would ask her Filipino teacher, "Why did my father call my brother a lighting?"

Margie grows up knowing the Filipino words for objects, a few body parts, and people: **kalamansi**, **adobo**, **lola**. She also knows that the prefix **mag-** when accompanied by a verb in English renders the verb Filipino—"**mag-toothbrush ka na**"—especially when commands are given. She knows basic greetings like "**Kumusta**" and "**Magandang umaga**" and "**salamat**." She watches a few Filipino movies but her household does not subscribe to the Filipino channel so she is not familiar with "Wowowee" (a Philippine variety show broadcast on ABS-CBN) nor addicted to any Filipino soap operas. Her mother tells her: "**Mahal Kita**."

It is in college that life changes for Margie Louella. To learn more about her identity, she enrolls in a Filipino/Tagalog class. She watches Filipino plays on identity by Teatro ng Tanan; one is entitled "**Tunggalian**" (Conflict); and the other is based on Freddie Aguilar's song "**Anak**." As she dances the **tinikling** at the Philippine Cultural Night (PCN) at her university, she also learns the favorite PCN word—**diwa** or "spirit." She becomes fascinated with the word **saing...sinaing** (cooked rice), **magsaing** (to cook rice)—ah, there is a Filipino word for cooking rice, and many words about rice. She tries to learn the **baybayin** and considers getting a tattoo of the word "**Malaya**" ("Free"). She becomes aware of student issues and joins the campaign for Filipino American Studies and Philippine Studies.

She learns about Filipino American history and the struggle of the farm workers. She becomes more involved in community organizing. At the Filipino community center, she greets the older Filipinos with "**Kumusta na po kayo?**"

Margie Louella joins a Filipino American political group. As her political consciousness grows, she learns the word "**hustisya**," and in political rallies can shout: "**Makibaka, Huwag Matakot**" (Struggle, Do Not Be Afraid!) and "**Ibagsak!**" (Down!). However, when one speaks to her in Filipino, her conversational ability is limited to five minutes.

Margie Louella travels to the Philippines three times:

First, to visit family, during the Christmas holiday season. She notices her relatives straining to speak to her in English.

Second, she returns for three weeks, spending half the time with her family and the other half volunteering with Karapatan (literally, "Rights"), a human rights organization.

However, when she attends a celebration hosted by the Amado V. Hernandez foundation (a non-government organization that gives writing workshops to workers and peasants) and listens to Filipino poetry, she realizes one thing—she does not know Filipino. She says to herself, "I do not want to end up like this...a person who does not know **Inang Wika** (Mother Language)."

On her third visit, she stays for five months, spending most of her time with peasant communities in the countryside. She learns more about the struggle of the Filipino people—and calls it "**paglalamay sa dilim**" ("to work in the darkness of night"). She now has a better word for "justice": the indigenous word "**katarungan**." She learns to sing songs such as "**Rosas ng Digma**" (The Rose of War). She is touched as she leaves the community when they give her a **despedida** for her **Maligayang Paglalakbay** (Happy Travels).

Back in the United States, she corresponds with people in the Philippines. Through numerous exchanges of letters and e-mails, she learns more about written Filipino.

The activist FHL thus is what I call an extremely motivated HL who needs the language as she becomes more politically involved. Filipino is her language because it is the language of the national democratic movement. Interestingly, this reason echoes the 1935 constitution, which shows that Tagalog was chosen as the basis of the national language, because it was the language of the Katipunan and the revolution.

I remember a photograph of the organization Anakbayan (Children of the People), a youth group in the Philippines with chapters in the U.S. The members are shown with their raised fists on Independence Day, with their costumes commemorating the 1896 revolution. We see the letter K on their hats, symbolizing the revolutionary group the Katipunan. K is a letter that in 1896 was not even in the Roman alphabet introduced by the Spaniards, but which was used to name the group, asserting the people's indigenous orthography. They hold a streamer with indigenous **baybayin** symbol K, a signifier that could be recognized by other activists as representing the underground Kabataang Makabayan.

The Filipino American activist's journey is not unlike that of the letter K—a story rooted in history, colonialism, and the struggle for sovereignty.

Grammar Index

Glossary

Aalis Leave
Abala Bother; busy
Abo Ash; gray
Abril April
Abugado Lawyer
Adobo Chicken or pork cooked in vinegar and spices
Agad At once
Agosto August
Ahas Snake
Akasya Acacia tree
Akin Mine
Aklat Book
Aklatan Library
Ako I
Aksidente Accident
Ala-una One o'clock
Alaga Pet
Alak Wine
Alam Know
Alamat Legend
Alas-diyes Ten o'clock
Alas-dos Two o'clock
Alas-dose Twelve o'clock
Alas-kuwatro Four o'clock
Alas-nuwebe Nine o'clock
Alas-onse Eleven o'clock
Alas-otso Eight o'clock
Alas-sais Six o'clock
Alas-singko Five o'clock
Alas-siyete Seven o'clock
Alas-tres Three o'clock
Alimango Crab
Alis Departure; leave
Almusal Breakfast
Ama Father
Amerikana Suit
Amin Ours (Plural Exclusive Pronoun)
Anak Son/daughter
Anibersaryo Anniversary
Anim Six
Animnapu Sixty
Ano What
Anti-bata Against children
Apat Four
Apatnapu Forty
Apo Grandchild
Apoy Fire
Araw Sun; day
Araw-araw Daily
Arkila Rent
Asawa Spouse
Aso Dog
Asukal Sugar
Asul Blue
At And
Atay Liver
Ate Elder sister

Atin Ours (Inclusive Pronoun)
Atis Sugar apple
Awa Pity
Awit Song
Ayaw Dislike; don't/doesn't want
Ayon According to
Ayusin Fix

Ba Used for "yes" and "no" questions
Baba Chin
Bababa Will get off
Babae Woman
Baboy Pork
Bago Before
Bago New
Bago ang Before (used for Indicating minutes)
Bagoong Fermented shrimp or anchovies
Bagyo Storm
Bahay House
Baka Beef
Bakuran Yard
Balakang Hips
Balat Outer covering; shell; skin
Balikat Shoulder
Balita News
Balkonahe Balcony
Balutin Wrap
Bandang Around
Bangka Small boat
Bangko Bank
Bansa Country
Banyo Bathroom
Barangay Smallest political unit
Baril Gun
Barko Large boat
Baro't saya Traditional blouse and skirt
Barong Tagalog Filipino national costume for men
Baryo Village
Baso Glass
Bataw Hyacinth bean
Bato Stone
Baul Chest
Bawal Forbidden
Bawang Garlic
Bawat Each
Bayabas Guava
Bayad Payment
Bayan Town/country/people
Baywang Waist
Berde Green
Beses Times

Bestida Dress
Bibig Mouth
Bibilhin Will buy
Bigas Uncooked rice
Bigla Suddenly
Bihag Prisoner
Bihira Rarely
Bilugan Round
Bilyon Billion
Binasa Read
Binatikos Criticized
Binayo Pounded
Binibini Miss
Bininyagan Baptized
Binuhos Throw (usually used for liquids)
Bisikleta Bicycle
Bisita Visitor
Bitamina Vitamins
Bituin Star
Biyahe Travel
Biyernes Friday
Biyulin Violin
Blusa Blouse
Bote Bottle
Botika Drugstore
Braso Arm
Bubong Ceiling; roof
Bughaw Blue
Buhok Hair
Bukana Front
Bukas Tomorrow
Buko Young coconut
Bulsa Pocket
Bumaba Went down
Bumaha Got flooded
Bumalik Go back
Bumbero Firefighter
Bumibili Buy
Bumibili Buying
Bumibisita Visits
Bundok Mountain
Buntis Pregnant
Burol Hill
Buwan Moon; month
Buwan-buwan Monthly

Daan Road; pass
Dadaan Will pass by (subject focus)
Dadaanan Will pass by (indirect object focus)
Dagat Ocean
Dagdagan Add
Dahan-dahan Slowly
Daigdig World
Dalampasigan Seashore
Dalawa Two
Dalawampu Twenty
Daliri Finger

Daliri sa paa Toes
Damit Dress/clothes
Dapat Should
Darating Will arrive
Dating Arrival
Daungan Pier
Deboto Devotee
Delikado Dangerous
Dentista Dentist
Deposito Deposit
Detenido Detainee
Di-awtorisado Unauthorized
Dibdib Chest, breast
Dila Tongue
Dilaw Yellow
Din/Rin Also
Dingding Walls
Dinismiss Got dismissed
Disenyo Design
Disyembre December
Dito/Rito Here
Diyan/Riyan There
Diyosa Goddess
Doktor Doctor
Doon/Roon Over there
Dormitoryo Dormitory
Drayber Driver
Dugo Blood
Dula Play
Dulo End
Dumadalo Attend
Dumalaw Visited
Dumaranas Experiencing
Dumi Manure
Dumiretso Go straight
Durian Durian (fruit)

Elementarya Elementary
  school
Enero January
Ensalada Salad
Ensayo Rehearsals
Ermitanyo Hermit
Eroplano Airplane
Erya Area
Eskinita Alley
Eskuwelahan School
Espanya Spain
Espesyal Special
Estados Unidos United States
Estasyon ng pulis Police
  station
Estasyon ng tren Train
  station
Estudyante Student

Gabí Evening
Gábi Yam
Gáling From
Gamot Medicine
Ganoon ba? Is that so?
Garahe Garage
Gatas Milk

Gawa sa Made of
Gilid Side
Ginang Mrs.
Ginisa Sauteed
Ginoong Mister
Gitara Guitar
Gitna Center; middle
Gradwadong pag-aaral
  Graduate study
Groseri Grocery
Grupo Group
Gubat Forest
Gulay Vegetables
Gumagala Roaming around
Gumaling Got well
Gumigising Wake up
Guro Teacher
Gusali Building
Gusto Like; want

Hagurin Massage
Halaan Clams
Halaman Plant
Halaman Plants
Haluin Mix
Hanggang To; until
Hapag-kainan Dining table
Hapón Japan
Hápon Afternoon
Hapunan Dinner
Harap Front
Hardin Garden
Hari King
Hatid Take someone to a
  place
Hatinggabi Midnight
Hayop Animal
Hilaga North
Hilaw Unripe
Hindi No
Hindi kailanman Never
Hindi maipinta ang mukha
  Looks irritated and/or
  bothered and sad
Hinog Ripe
Hinuli Caught
Hipon Shrimp
Hitsura Looks like
Hiwa Cut
Hiwain Cut
Hiwalay Separate
Hugis-puso Heart-shaped
Hukom Judge
Huli Last
Hulyo July
Humingi Asked
Huminto Stop
Humiram Borrowed
Hunyo June
Huwag Don't
Huwebes Thursday

Iba Different

Ibabaw Above
Ibabaw On
Ibasura Throw out/put in a
  garbage bin
Ibig Sabihin Meaning
Ibinigay Was given
Ibon Bird
Ihawin Broil
Ikalawa Second
Ikatlo Third
Ikaw You
Ikinalulungkot ko. I am sad
  about this.
Ikinasal Got married
Ikinukuwento Telling a story
Ilalagay Put
Ilalim Under
Ilan How many
Ilog River
Ilong Nose
Imbis Instead
Ina Mother
Inaahon Brought to the
  surface
Inalagaan Took care of
Inalok Offered
Inani Harvested
Inay Mother
Inempake Pack (a suitcase)
Inihanda Prepared
Inihaw Broiled
Iniipon Gathered
Iniresta Prescribed
Insidente Incident
Inumin Drink; to drink
Ipagulong Roll
Ipinagtataka Surprised
Ipinakita Showed
Ipinanganak Born
Iprito Fry
Isa One
Isasauli Will Return
Isda Fish
Isinasaad Implied; said
Isinuot Wore (completed
  aspect of Wear)
Iskedyul Schedule
Isla Island

Itaas On top
Itay Father
Itim Black
Itinanim Planted
Itinatag Established
Ito This
Iyan That (object is far from
  the speaker)
Iyon That (object is farther
  away)

Jeepney/dyip Vehicle made
  from surplus army jeep

Ka You
Ka-opisina Of the same office
Kaakibat Together
Kaarawan Birthday
Kaaway Enemy
Kababata Childhood friend
Kababayan Of the same town; of the same country
Kabundukan Mountain
Kadueto Duet partner
Kagabi Last night
Kagubatan Forest
Kahapon Yesterday
Kahel Orange
Kahoy Wood
Kaibigan Friend
Kailangan Need
Kakilala Acquaintance
Kaklase Classmate
Kalaban Adversary
Kalabasa Pumpkin
Kalagayan Condition
Kalahati Half
Kalamansi Philippine lemon
Kalan Stove
Kalaro Playmate
Kaliligo Just finished bathing
Kaliwa Left
Kalsada Road
Kalye Street
Kamag-anak Relative
Kamatis Tomato
Kamay Hand
Kami We (exclusive)
Kamias Tropical sour fruit
Kamukha Looks like
Kanan Right
Kanila Theirs
Kanin Rice
Kanina Earlier
Kanluran West
Kanser Cancer
Kanta Song
Kanto Corner
Kanya Hers
Kapatid Sibling
Kape Coffee
Kapitbahay Neighbor
Karagatan Ocean
Karangalan Award
Karatula Sign
Kare-kare Ox-tail stew in peanut sauce
Kasal Wedding
Kasama Included; companion; comrade
Kasambahay Person who lives in the same house
Kasayaw Dance partner
Kasi Because
Kasya Fits
Katamtaman Medium; just right

Katao Number of people
Katas Juice
Katawagan Name
Katimugan South
Katrabaho Coworker
Kaunti A few; a little
Kawalan-kumpiyansa Lack of confidence
Kawani Employee
Kay Marker to indicate ownership
Káya Can
Kayá That is why
Kayo You (plural)
Kayumanggi Brown
Kilay Eyebrow
Kina Plural marker to indicate ownership
Kinapanayam Interviewed
Kinuha ang larawan Took a picture
Klase Kind of; class
Klinika Clinic
Ko My, I
Kolehiyo College
Komedor Dining Room
Komunidad Community
Konduktor Conductor
Konsiyerto Concert
Kontinente Continent
Korona Crown
Kotse Car
Kubeta Toilet
Kulang Lacking
Kulay kape Brown
Kulay mais The color of corn; blonde
Kumakain Eat
Kumakanta Sing
Kumakaway Waving
Kumaliwa Turn Left
Kumanan Turn Right
Kumatok Knocked
Kumuha ng larawan Took pictures
Kundol Wax gourd
Kurbata Tie
Kusina Kitchen
Kutsara Spoon
Kutsarita Teaspoon
Kutsilyo Knife
Kuwaderno Notebook
Kuwadrado Square
Kuwarto Room/bedroom
Kuweba Cave
Kuya Elder brother

Labanos Radish
Labas Out/outside
Labi Lips
Labimpito Seventeen
Labindalawa Twelve
Labing-Anim Sixteen

Labing-Apat Fourteen
Labing-Isa Eleven
Labingwalo Eighteen
Labinlima Fifteen
Labinsiyam Nineteen
Labintatlo Thirteen
Lagda Signature
Lagdaan Sign your name
Lagnat Fever
Lagyan Put
Lalaki Man
Lalamunan Throat
Lalo na Especially
Lang Only
Langka Jackfruit
Lansones Lanzones (type of fruit)
Lapis Pencil
Larawan Picture
Laro Game
Lasa Taste
Leche flan Custard
Leeg Neck
Libre Free
Libro Book
Likod Back
Likod Back
Lila Violet/purple
Lilipat Move
Lima Five
Limampu Fifty
Linga Sesame seed
Linggo Sunday; week
Linggo-linggo Weekly
Litrato Photograph
Lola Grandmother
Lolo Grandfather
Loob In/inside
Lubid Rope
Luha Tears
Luma Old
Lumaban Fought
Lumalangoy Swimming
Lumampas Go past
Lumangoy Swam
Lumapag Landed
Lumilipad Fly
Lumipat Transfer
Lumpia Spring roll
Lunes Monday
Lungsod City
Luntian Green
Lupa Earth
Luya Ginger

Maaari May
Maaayos Will be fixed
Maalat Salty
Maanghang Spicy
Maaraw Sunny
Maasim Sour
Mababang paaralan Elementary school

Mababaw ang luha Cries easily
Mabait Kind/nice
Mabuti-buti Better
Madalas Often
Madaldal Talkative
Madaling-araw Dawn
Madumi/Marumi Dirty
Mag-check In To check in
Mag-Ingat To be careful
Mag-order To order
Maganda Beautiful
Magbasa To read
Maghanda Prepare
Magkahawak-kamay Holding hands
Magkaiba Different
Magkakakilala Know each other
Magkapareho Same
Magkita To meet
Maglalaro Will play (a game)
Magluluto Will cook
Magluto Cook
Magpapadala Send
Magpapalit Exchange
Magreserba To reserve
Magsasaka Farmer
Magsugat Be wounded
Magulang Parent
Magustuhan Will like
Mahaba Long
Mahal Expensive
Mahangin Windy
Mahihirap Poor
Mahúhuli Will be late
Mainit Hot
Maitim ang budhi Bad person
Makaligtaan Forget
Makalipas After
Makidnap To be kidnapped
Makikikain Will share someone's food
Makikiligo Will take a bath/ shower at someone's house
Makikiluto Will cook at someone's house
Makikipag-away Will fight with someone
Makikipag-usap Will talk to someone
Makikipagbati Will reconcile with someone
Makikipagkantahan Will sing with others
Makikipaglaro Will play with someone
Makikipagsayaw Will dance with someone
Makikipagtugtugan Will play (instruments) with others
Makikita Will see

Makita To see
Malaki Big
Malaman To know
Malamig Cold
Malápit Near
Malapít Near
Malayo Far
Maligaya Happy
Maliit Small
Malinis Clean
Malungkot Sad
Malungkutin Always sad
Masakitin Sickly
Maluwang Too wide
Mamaya Later
Mananayaw Dancer
Mang-aawit Singer
Mangga Mango
Manggagawa Worker
Mangingibig One who loves
Mani Peanut
Manibalang Between unripe and ripe
Manok Chicken
Mansanas Apple
Mantika Oil
Manunulat Writer
Mapait Bitter
Mapakla Acrid; tangy
Marami Many; a lot
Marso March
Martes Tuesday
Mas gusto Like better
Mas malaki Bigger
Masakit Painful
Masarap Delicious
Masaya Happy
Masayahin Always happy
Masayang-masaya Very happy
Masipag Industrious
Masungit Grouchy
Masyadong maalat Too salty
Mata Mata
Mataas na paaralan High school
Mataba Fat
Matalik na kaibigan Close friend
Matalino Intelligent
Matamis Sweet
Materyales Materials
Matigas ang mukha Looks stern
Matutuklaw Will be bitten; refers only to snake bites
Maulan Rainy
Maulap Cloudy
Maupo Please sit
May Have
Mayo May
Menos... Para Before (used for indicating minutes)

Meryenda Snack
Mesa Table
Metal Metal
Mga Used for the plural form
Militante Militant
Milyon Million
Minsan Once; sometimes
Minuto Minute
Miting Meeting
Miyerkules Wednesday
Mo Your
Mukhang Biyernes Santo Looks like Good Friday (Looks sad)
Mula From
Mula Noong Since
Mundo World
Munti Small
Mura Cheap
Musika Music
Mustasa Mustard

Na Already
Na Naman Again
Naaalala Remember
Naaksidente Met an accident
Nabali Got broken (for example, arm or leg)
Nabuhay Lived
Nabuntis Got pregnant
Nag-aalala Worried
Nag-aaral Study
Nag-abala ka pa. You shouldn't have bothered.
Nag-alok Offered
Nag-diyeta Dieted
Nag-eehersisyo Exercise
Nag-eensayo Rehearse
Nagagalit Angry
Nagba-brush Brush (hair)
Nagbabakasyon Go on vacation
Nagbabasa Read
Nagbakasyon Took a vacation
Nagbibihis Dress up
Nagbibisikleta Ride a bicycle
Nagdalang-tao Got pregnant
Naghahanap Looks for
Naghihilamos Wash (face)
Nag-i-scuba-diving Went scuba diving
Nag-i-isnowboarding Go snowboarding
Nag-i-skiing Went skiing
Nag-i-snorkeling Went snorkeling
Nag-iimbita Invites
Nagkasakit Got sick
Naglalakad Walk
Naglalaro Play (game)
Naglalaro ng soccer Play soccer

Nagluluto Cook
Nagmamahal Love
Nagmamaneho Drive
Nagpa-photocopy Have someone make copies for you
Nagpagamot Got treatment
Nagpagupit Have someone cut your hair
Nagpahinga Rest
Nagpaluto Have someone cook for you
Nagpamasahe Have someone give you a massage
Nagpapaypay Fanning
Nagpapraktis Practice (for example, martial arts)
Nagpatingin sa doktor Visited a doctor
Nagpatuwid Had (hair) straightened
Nagpipinta Paint
Nagpopolitisa Politicizing
Nagsa-shower Take a shower
Nagsa-skydiving Go skydiving
Nagsa-soccer Play soccer
Nagsauli Returned
Nagsesepilyo Brush (teeth)
Nagsi-skiing Go skiing
Nagsisimula Starts
Nagsunog ng kilay Studied hard
Nagsusuklay Comb
Nagsusulat Write
Nagtapos Graduated
Nagtatrabaho Work
Nagtatrabaho Working
Nagtitinda Selling
Nahahati Divide; split
Nahawa Got infected
Nahiwa Got cut
Nahulog Fell; dropped
Nais Would like
Naisip Thought
Naka-salamin Wears glasses
Naka-upo Sitting
Nakaaalala Can remember
Nakabatay Based on
Nakakahiya Shameful
Nakakainis Irritating
Nakakatanda Makes one look old
Nakalimutan Forgot
Nakangiti Smiling
Nakatali Tied
Nakatayo Standing
Nakatipid Saved money
Nakatira Live
Nakikinig Listens to (music, songs, radio)
Nakikiramay ako. My condolences.

Nakita Saw
Naliligo Take a bath/take a shower
Naman Also (used as an expression)
Namasyal Went sightseeing
Namatay Passed on; died
Nambubugbog Person who beats up another
Namili Went shopping
Namimitas Picking (for example, picking apples)
Namin Ours (exclusive)
Nanalo Won
Nananawagan Calling to
Nanay Mother
Nandito/Narito Here
Nandiyan/Nariyan There
Nandoon/Naroon Over there
Nang When; used as a relative pronoun
Nangangamba Afraid
Nanlalata Feeling weak
Nanonood Watches (television, movie, game)
Napagod Became tired
Napaka-alat Too salty
Napakahaba Too long
Napakaiksi Too short
Napakalaki Too big
Napakaliit Too small
Napakaluwang Too loose
Napakasikip Too tight
Napapalibutan Surrounded
Napaso Got slightly burned
Napatay Was killed
Naplano Planned
Naputol ang paa Foot got cut
Nars Nurse
Nasa Preposition indicating location
Nasawi Died
Nasugatan Got injured
Nasunog Got burned
Natalo Lost
Natanggal Got removed; got fired
Natanggap Got accepted
Natanggap Received
Natatakot Afraid
Natatapos Ends
Natayo Was built
Natin Ours (inclusive)
Natutulog Sleep
Naulanan Got rained on
Nawala Lost
Negosyante Business person
Ngayon Today
Ngayon Now (also means Today)
Ngipin Teeth
Ngumiti Smiled
Nila Their

Nilaga Boiled
Nilagang baka Boiled beef
Niya His/her
Niyayakap Hug
Niyebe Snow
Niyog Old coconut
Nobela Novel
Nobyembre November
Noo Forehead
Noong isang buwan Last month
Noong isang linggo Last week
Noong unang panahon Once upon a time

Oktubre October
Oo Yes
Opisina Office
Oras Time; hour
Orasan Clock
Ospital Hospital

Paa Feet
Paaakyatin To ask someone to go up
Paano How
Paborito Favorite
Pag-angkat Export
Pag-asa Hope
Pagbibiyahe Travelling
Pagdalaw Visit
Pagdikitin Seal
Pagdiriwang Celebration
Pagitan Between
Pagkatapos After; afterwards
Paglabag Violation
Paglalakbay Journey
Paglalayag Sail
Paglubog ng araw Sunset
Pagod Tired
Pagpasensiyahan mo na. I am sorry for this.
Pagsasaalang-alang Taking into consideration
Pagseselos Jealousy
Pagsinta Love
Pagsusunog ng kilay Working hard
Pagtigil To stay
Pahaba Lengthwise
Pahayag Statement
Pakibigyan Please give
Pakirehistro Please register
Pakuluin Boil
Palagi/Lagi Always
Palamigan Refrigerator
Palapag Floors/stories
Palaspas Dried fronds waved during Lent
Palasyo Palace
Palayan Ricefield
Palda Skirt
Paligid Surroundings

Paligid-ligid Around
Paliparan Airport
Palitan Exchange rate
Pamaktol-maktol Having a
tantrum
Pamangkin Niece/nephew
Pamasahe Fare
Pamaypay Fan
Pambura Eraser
Paminsan-minsan
Sometimes
Pampito Seventh
Pamumuno Led by
Panaderya Bakery
Pananalig Faith
Pandalawahan For two
Pang-anim Sixth
Pang-apat Fourth
Pangalan Name
Pangalawa Second
Pangatlo Third
Panghimagas Dessert
Panghuli Last
Pangit Ugly
Pangkalahatan General
Pangkat Group
Pangwalo Eighth
Panis Rotten/bad
Panlima Fifth
Pansampu Tenth
Pansiyam Ninth
Pantalon Pants
Panyo Handkerchief
Papasok sa klase Will go to
class
Papel Paper
Papuntang Going to
Paradahan Parking Lot
Paroroonan Destination
Pasahero Passenger
Pasalubong A present from
a trip
Pasaporte Passport
Pasensiya ka na. Sorry.
(Literally, Sorry you.)
Pasko Christmas
Paslit Child
Paso Burn
Pasukan Entrance
Pasyente Patient
Patani Lima bean
Patis Fish sauce
Patola Luffa
Paunang bayad Advanced
payment
Pauwi On the way home
Payapa Peaceful
Payat Thin
Payong Umbrella
Pebrero February
Pelikula Film
Pelikula Movie
Permiso Permission

Pilipinas Philippines
Pinabalik Asked to return
Pinadala Sent
Pinahirapan Tortured;
literally, given hardship
Pinaiimbistigahan Having
investigated
Pinaka-ayaw Like least
Pinakagusto Like best
Pinakamalaki Biggest
Pinakatuktok Highest point
Pinalitan Changed
Pinapalutang Floating
Pinaputok Fired
Pinasingaw Steamed
Pinisil Squeeze
Pinsan Cousin
Pintor Painter
Pintuan Door
Pinuno Leader
Pinya Pineapple
Pirma Signature
Pirmahan Sign your name
Pisara Blackboard
Pisngi Cheek
Piso Peso
Pito Seven
Pitumpu Seventy
Piyano Piano
Platito Small plate; saucer
Platito Saucer
Plato Plate
Po Honorific
Polo Shirt
Pransiya France
Pribado Private
Prito Fry
Probinsiya Province
Programa Program
Prutas Fruits
Pula Red
Pulang asukal Brown sugar
(literally, red sugar)
Pulis Police Officer
Pulitika Politics
Pulong Meeting
Pumanaw Passed on; died
Pumapasok sa klase Go to
class
Pumasok sa klase Attended
class
Pumunta Went
Pumupunta Go/Come
Pumupunta Going
Pumutok Fired
Punó Full
Puno Tree
Punta Come; go
Pupunta Will go
Pusa Cat
Pusit Squid
Puso Heart
Puti White

Puto Rice cake
Puwede Can
Puwede Can/May
Puwede May
Puwersang militar Military
forces
Puwet Buttocks

Radyo Radio
Rambutan Rambutan (fruit)
Rebelde Rebel
Rebolusyon Revolution
Regalo Gift
Relo Watch
Reseta Prescription
Restawran Restaurant
Rin Also
Rosas Pink

Sa In; on; at; marker to
indicate ownership
Sa kasamaang palad
Unfortunately
Sa pamamagitan Using
Sabado Saturday
Sabado De Gloria Holy
Saturday
Sabaw Broth
Saging Banana
Sagrado Sacred
Sahig Floor
Sala Living Room
Salamat Thank you
Salamin Glass; eyeglasses;
mirror
Salarin Murderer
Sampu Ten
Sana Hope
Sandaan A hundred
Sandalyas Sandals
Sanlibo A thousand
Sapatos Shoes
Sari-sari Various
Sarili Self
Sasakay Get on; ride
Sawsawan Dipping sauce
Sayang It's a pity
Sayaw Dance
Seda Silk
Segundo Second
Sementeryo Cemetery
Sentimos Centavos
Setyembre September
Sibuyas Onion
Sigarilyas Winged bean
Sigarilyo Cigarettes
Sige Okay/Sure
Sige na Please
Siko Elbow
Sikreto Secret
Sila They
Silangan East
Silid-kainan Dining room

Silid-tulugan Bedroom
Silya Chair
Simbahan Church
Simbolo Symbol
Sina Plural marker for names
Sinabi Said
Sinakop Occupied; colonized
Sinasaad Implied; said
Sine Film
Sine Movie
Sinehan Movie theater
Singkamas Turnip
Sinigang na baboy Pork in soured broth
Sinisisi Blaming
Sino Who
Sinulat Wrote
Sipon Cold
Sira Broken
Sisidlan Container
Sitaw String bean
Siya He/she
Siyam Nine
Siyamnapu Ninety
Siyempre. Of course
Siyensiya Science
Siyudad City
Soberanya Sovereignty
Sopas Soup
Sugat Wound
Suka Vinegar
Sukat Try on; size
Sukli Change
Sulok Corner
Sumakit Became painful
Sumali Join
Sumasakay Ride
Sumasayaw Dance
Sumbrero Hat
Sumisid Dived
Sumisigaw Shout
Sundalo Soldier
Sundo Pick up
Susi Key
Susunod Next

Tabi Beside
Tabletas Tablets
Tag-araw Summer
Tag-init Hot season/summer season
Tag-ulan Rainy season
Taga-saan From where
Tagapangasiwa Manager
Tagapangulo President
Taglagas Autumn/Fall
Taglamig Winter

Tagsibol Spring
Takot Afraid
Taksi Taxi
Tala Star
Talaga? Really?
Talon Waterfalls; also To jump
Talong Eggplant
Tambol Drum
Tanawin View
Tandaan Remember
Tanggalin Remove
Tanghali Noon
Tanghalian Lunch
Tanghaling tapat Exactly at noon
Taniman Plantation
Tao Person
Tao po! literally, Person here!
Taon Year
Taon-Taon Annually
Tapat Across
Tarangkahan Gate
Tasa Cup
Tatapusin Will finish
Tatay Father
Tatlo Three
Tatlumpu Thirty
Tawad Discount
Tayo We (inclusive)
Tela Cloth
Telebisyon Television
Telepono Telephone
Temperatura Temperature
Tenga Ear
Timog South
Tinapay Bread
Tindahan Store
Tindahan ng bulaklak Flower shop
Tindahan ng laruan Toy store
Tindahan ng prutas Fruit store
Tingnan Look
Tinidor Fork
Tinutusok Pierce
Tisa Chalk
Tita Aunt
Tito Uncle
Titser Teacher
Tiya Aunt
Tiyan Stomach
Tiyo Uncle
Tokador Dresser
Totoo Real
Toyo Soy sauce

Trak Truck
Traysikel Tricycle (motorcycle or bicycle with a sidecar)
Tren Train
Tsaa Tea
Tse! Expression of disgust
Tsina China
Tsuper Driver
Tubig Water
Tuhod Knee
Tulong Help
Tuloy ka Come in
Tumanggap Received
Tumawa Laughed
Tumayo Stand
Tumutugtog Play (an instrument)
Tunay Real
Tutugtog Will play
Tuwa Happiness
Tuyong-tuyo Very dry

Uban Gray/white hair
Ubo Cough
Ulam Anything eaten with rice
Ulan Rain
Ulat Report
Ulit Again
Ulo Head
Umaawit Sing
Umaga Morning
Umakyat Climb
Umano Alleged
Umikot Go round; go around
Umiyak Cried
Umupo Sit
Una First
Uniporme Uniform
Upo White squash
Upuan Chair
Uulitin Repeat

Wala Don't have
Walang anuman Welcome
Walang pagsidlan ng galak Very happy
Walo Eight
Walumpu Eighty

Y medya Half (used in telling time; thirty minutes)
Yari sa Made of
Yata Perhaps
Yumao Passed on; died